POINT OF NO RETURN

THE DEADLY STRUGGLE FOR MIDDLE EAST PEACE

GEOFFREY KEMP AND JEREMY PRESSMAN

CARNEGIE ENDOWMENT FOR INTERNATIONAL PEACE
in cooperation with
BROOKINGS INSTITUTION PRESS

© 1997 by the Carnegie Endowment for International Peace
1779 Massachusetts Avenue, N.W.
Washington, D.C. 20036
Tel.(202) 483-7600
Fax.(202) 483-1840
Internet: http://www.ceip.org

Point of No Return: The Deadly Struggle for Middle East Peace
may be ordered ($44.95, cloth; $18.95, paper) from Carnegie's distributor,
The Brookings Institution Press,
Department 029, Washington, D.C. 20042-0029, USA.
Tel. 1-800-275-1447 or 202-797-6258.
Fax 202 797-6004.

Edited by Rosemarie Philips.
Cover photo: David Rubinger/Black Star/PNI.
Design by Paddy McLaughlin Concepts & Design.
Printed by Automated Graphic Systems.

Library of Congress Cataloging-in-Publication Data

Kemp, Geoffrey, 1939-
Pressman, Jeremy, 1969-
Point of No Return: The Deadly Struggle for Middle East Peace / Geoffrey
Kemp and Jeremy Pressman.
p. cm.
Includes bibliographical references and index.
ISBN: 0-87003-020-5 (cloth)—ISBN 0-87003-021-3 (pbk)
1. Arab-Israeli conflict, 1993- 2. Middle East—Foreign relations. I. Pressman,
Jeremy, 1969- .II. Title.
DS119.76.K36 1997
327'.0956' 09049—DC21   97-29939
                                                                CIP

CONTENTS

PREFACE

Writing a book about the comprehensive Middle East peace process is a frustrating exercise—especially deciding when to conclude the narrative and go to press. A first draft of this study was completed in the fall of 1995. Then, on November 4th, the tragic assassination of Israeli Prime Minister Yitzhak Rabin plunged the region into turmoil. The subsequent events in Israel, concluding with the Palestinian suicide bombings in the spring of 1996 and the election of Likud leader Benjamin Netanyahu on May 29th, necessitated further revisions. A second draft was completed in the summer of 1996 only to be accompanied by the crisis over Jerusalem and the ensuing violence between Israeli and PLO forces. The Washington summit orchestrated by President Clinton in October 1996 and the subsequent agreement in January 1997 by Israel to withdraw from most of Hebron was another benchmark. This positive development however, was followed by a new crisis over the Israeli government's decision to begin construction of Jewish apartments at Har Homa (Jebel Abu Ghneim) in East Jerusalem—and more Palestinian suicide bombings. We concluded the text with minor modifications in September 1997.

No one can predict when the next crisis or breakthrough in the Middle East diplomacy will occur except that there will be one. We believe that the basic theme of this study—that the peace process has passed a point of no return—will hold no matter what happens in the months and years ahead.

Many people contributed to the completion of this book, including participants in several workshops organized in Italy, Austria, and Greece by the Carnegie Endowment's Middle East Arms Control project. We would specifically like to thank Morton Abramowitz, Paul Balaran, Michael O'Hare, and David Speedie for their support over the years. The study was made possible thanks to a generous grant from the Carnegie Corporation of New York. We also received support from the United States Institute of Peace for travel to the region.

Without the magnificent services provided by Jennifer Little, Kathleen Daly, and Chris Henley of the Carnegie library staff, we could not have completed the work. Several Carnegie Junior Fellows contributed to our work, including Caroline Drees, Elaine

Weiss, and Hala Tayarrah. We would also like to thank Chris Bicknell, who was our close colleague through the early days of this study. Maria Sherzad has been our inexhaustible, reliable, and supportive assistant since 1995. She has been responsible for much of the typing of the draft and has served as the vital link to both of us in the production process. Rosemarie Philips was a most professional and constructive editor; she contributed greatly to whatever lucidity and style this manuscript may have. Without the support, counsel, and expertise of Valeriana Kallab, the manuscript would still be incomplete; we thank her most sincerely. We also thank David Merrill, who prepared the maps, and Paddy McLaughlin for the cover design.

Many friends, colleagues, and officials provided insights and feedback on our work. Of those we can publicly acknowledge, we would especially like to thank Shahram Chubin, Zuhair Diab, Shai Feldman, Samuel Lewis, Hisham Melham, Fida Nasrallah, Robert Satloff, Roscoe Suddarth, Abdullah Toukan, and Thanos Veramis. Finally, we thank Audrey Sobel and Tamara Weisberg for their support, patience, and encouragement against the backdrop of revisions, delays, and frustration endemic to any study of the Middle East.

Geoffrey Kemp and Jeremy Pressman
September 1997

INTRODUCTION

Peace treaties alone do not assure peace; and peace, by itself, is no panacea for economic growth and prosperity. The most deadly wars of the past hundred years were fought between countries that enjoyed full diplomatic relations and extensive mutual trade and cultural contacts. However, in the Middle East, a peace process—accompanied by political stability—is the only rational route to follow if the region wishes to break free from an endless cycle of violence, crippling arms expenditures, stunted economic growth, and authoritarian, often cruel, regimes. The logical culmination of the peace process would be a resolution of the Arab-Israeli conflict and many other regional conflicts, including intra-Arab, Turkish-Arab, and Iranian-Arab disputes.

Until late 1995, there was considerable optimism that the first steps toward peace were making significant progress. Then, between November 1995 and March 1997, the Arab-Israeli peace process received a number of shocks that some believe will lead to its postponement or eventual collapse. The assassination of Israeli Prime Minister Yitzhak Rabin on November 4, 1995, by an Israeli-born Jewish extremist spurred national revulsion against Israel's far right and caused the electoral fortunes of the rightwing opposition leader, Likud challenger Benjamin Netanyahu, to plummet. If Shimon Peres, who replaced Rabin as prime minister, had called an election in the early days of 1996 soon after Rabin's assassination, he would almost certainly have won. Yet he delayed, partly in response to U.S. pressure to continue negotiations with Syria and partly because he felt early elections would appear unseemly and opportunistic. Then, in February and March 1996, four suicide bombings by Palestinian extremists killed close to sixty Israelis and spread fear on the streets of Tel Aviv and Jerusalem. Overnight, Peres's lead in the polls evaporated, and he was not able to convince enough voters in the May election that he could assure their personal security. His loss in the election to Benjamin Netanyahu was a stunning surprise to most outside observers, including the Clinton administration. Peres's chances of reelection were damaged not only by the suicide bombings but also by a strong anti-secularist ultra-orthodox vote for Netanyahu; anti-incumbent Russian immigrant votes; and a

1

weak, undisciplined Labor campaign in contrast with the focused, well-run Likud campaign.

Although the early days of the Netanyahu government were noticeably quiet, the violent eruptions that occurred between Israeli and Palestinian forces in September 1996 following the opening of a tourist tunnel in Jerusalem showed how much the peace process had deteriorated. After three months of tortuous negotiations, Netanyahu and Palestinian leader Yasser Arafat reached agreement in January 1997 to withdraw Israeli forces from most of the city of Hebron and set a new timetable for future Israeli withdrawals from the West Bank. The new accord was short-lived. In March 1997, a political crisis over Israel's decision to begin work on an apartment building at Har Homa in East Jerusalem led to further violence, including a Palestinian suicide attack on an Israeli cafe in Tel Aviv killing four people. This was followed by several months of tension culminating with another suicide attack in Jerusalem on July 30 that killed 16 Israelis and Arabs. The July attack prompted draconian Israeli measures against the Palestinian Authority and pessimism that the peace process could advance. It prompted U.S. Secretary of State Madeleine Albright to give her first major speech on the Middle East and a renewed American effort to break the deadlock.

A breakdown in Arab-Israeli negotiations would have severe repercussions throughout the Arab and Middle Eastern world. Radicals who have claimed from the beginning of the peace process that Arab moderates were caving in to Israeli and U.S. hegemony will find their position reinforced. Their supporters in countries like Saudi Arabia, Jordan, and Egypt will be strengthened. Since public opinion does count in these Arab countries, despite the general absence of formal democratic institutions, their leaders will have to be more cautious in their relationship with the United States and Israel. This will weaken the American presence. It will give heart to Iraq's President Saddam Hussein and to the conservative Iranian mullahs as they pursue their different, but equally destructive, policies of regional hegemony. It will strengthen the Muslim fundamentalists in Turkey who wish to move Turkey away from a secular pro-Western, pro-Israeli stance. It will, in short, encourage the very sort of instability that the United States has worked to avoid.

A reduced American deterrent will increase the prospects for new regional conflict that could culminate in a new Middle East war involving weapons of mass destruction. At best, it could lead to social and economic chaos, which would be destabilizing in its own way. Under these circumstances, hopes for grandiose investment schemes and a new era of prosperity will dwindle, and ultimately control of the huge energy resources of the region could fall into the hands of anti-Western powers. This will have highly negative consequences for the United States and the West, the moderate Arab states, the Palestinians, and Israel.

In fact, this dire outlook is itself a huge incentive not to allow it to happen. The benefits of the peace process have been considerable, especially for Israel. Hence the United States and the new Israeli government, together with moderate Arab leaders, have far too much to lose to allow it to collapse. The Arab-Israeli peace process is supported by most governments in the world. Within the Middle East, the majority of countries endorse its general goals and the progress made to date, albeit with different degrees of enthusiasm.

The initial successes of the peace process derive from several key events in recent history: the 1973 Arab-Israeli War, the 1978 Camp David Accords leading to the 1979 Egyptian-Israeli Peace Treaty, the 1982-85 Lebanon War, the Gorbachev revolution and the breakup of the Soviet Union, the Palestinian Intifada, the 1991 Gulf War, the Madrid Peace Talks, the new global market place, and the communications revolution. Subsequent agreements have added momentum to the process: the 1993 Israeli-Palestinian Declaration of Principles (DOP or Oslo I), the 1994 Israeli-Jordanian Peace Treaty, the 1995 Israeli-Palestinian agreement (Oslo II), and the 1997 Hebron agreement.

We believe the peace process has now passed a point of no return. We use this term in the context of its original aeronautical meaning: "a designation of that limit point before which any engine failure requires an immediate turn around and return to the point of departure, *and beyond which such return is no longer practical.*"[1] To be precise, we believe that while there is no guarantee that the current peace process will move forward and reach the goal of a comprehensive settlement, it cannot regress to the conditions that prevailed prior to the Declaration of Principles between Israel and the Palestine Liberation Organization (PLO) in 1993. Moreover, the peace process cannot be "frozen." Middle East dynamics virtually assure that any pause in the process will be paralleled by negative activities that will contribute to further erosion of confidence among the parties.

However, the many complicated issues left to be resolved make the successful continuation of the Arab-Israeli peace process very difficult. Negotiating and sustaining a final peace agreement among Israel, the Palestinians, Syria, and Lebanon is itself a major task. If such an agreement is reached it will be a notable achievement, worthy of several more Nobel Peace prizes. It will certainly herald the beginning of a new Middle East. But will such an agreement be sustainable and will it bring hope for stability and prosperity? In reality, the peace process is a necessary, but only a first, step toward the ultimate goal of a comprehensive Middle East peace that includes a regional security regime.

To get to the final goal of a comprehensive settlement, many more obstacles than those remaining in the Arab-Israeli negotiations will have to be overcome. It will require that regional players reach further agreements to resolve other multilateral Arab-Israeli differences, as well as equally, if not more, serious intra-Arab, Arab-Turkish, and Arab-Iranian conflicts. Asymmetric trends in the Middle East suggest a widening gap between rich and poor, industrial and less industrial countries, and between secular and religious politics; they also point to a military imbalance of power that can only contribute to further antagonism and insecurity unless restrained by mutual consent. Any realistic appraisal of the long-term prospects of a comprehensive Middle East peace must take into account the impact these longer-term trends are likely to have on the ability of the countries in the region to sustain cooperation and to generate increased prosperity for the majority of their citizens.

Part I of this study focuses on the Arab-Israeli peace process, the many incentives to sustain it, the major outstanding obstacles that must be addressed if the Arab-Israeli peace process is to succeed, and the many sources of opposition to the process. It discusses on a country-by-country basis the major political difficulties that must be overcome if the process is to succeed.

Part II examines some of the obstacles to comprehensive peace that go beyond the immediate political and diplomatic bottlenecks and minefields of the Arab-Israeli conflict and Gulf crisis. It examines other Middle East conflicts, including disputes that have nothing to do with Israel; it examines economic, demographic, cultural, and ideological differences that pose formidable issues for all future regimes in the region; and it examines the military imbalance that is the source of the region's insecurity. The lack of a balance of power and the trend toward development of weapons of mass destruction are formidable obstacles to stability in the region.

Part III outlines the urgency for continued peace efforts in the Middle East and sets out three preconditions for a comprehensive peace: a continuing U.S. role, a final Israeli-Palestinian peace agreement, and structural reform by the key countries in the region.

We have deliberately chosen to begin with a review of the progress made toward Middle East peace before discussing the difficulties that lie ahead. Unless one is constantly reminded of how much the political environment has changed for the better in the past six years, it is easy to become mesmerized by and overwhelmed with the real and formidable obstacles that lie ahead.

PART I
THE ARAB-ISRAELI
PEACE PROCESS

CHAPTER ONE

CAN THE ARAB-ISRAELI PEACE PROCESS SUCCEED?

T he peace process made great progress between 1991 and 1996 because of fundamental changes in the global balance of power including the break up of the Soviet Union, the end of the Cold War, and the defeat of Iraq in the Gulf War. However, the future of the peace process is in doubt in the wake of new terrorism and the change in government in Israel. Optimists believe there is no realistic or sane alternative to a peace process; most governments desire greater security and prosperity—the most powerful argument for peace. Pessimists argue either that the peace process is injust or that it is too difficult to implement at this time; they question the assumptions of many grandiose economic forecasts.

THE UNCERTAIN POLITICAL ENVIRONMENT

T he origins of the Arab-Israeli peace process lie in the 1973 Arab-Israeli War involving Egypt, Syria, and Israel. For Israelis, the heavy casualties sustained in that conflict served as a bitter reminder that the continued occupation of Arab territories captured in 1967 would come only with a high price. At the same time, the 1973 war convinced several Arab countries that while military operations could force Israel to the negotiating table, they could not destroy the Jewish state.[1] Israel was too powerful to be defeated on the battlefield, and the human and economic price Arabs had to pay with each new war was increasingly unacceptable.

The 1973 war paved the way for Israeli-Egyptian and Israeli-Syrian disengagement agreements brokered by U.S. Secretary of State Henry Kissinger, followed by Egyptian President Anwar Sadat's historic trip to Jerusalem in November 1977. This, in turn, led to the 1978 Camp David Accords and to the 1979 Egyptian-Israeli Peace Treaty brokered by President Jimmy Carter. In equally important ways, the Palestinian Intifada, or uprising, which began in December 1987, convinced many Israeli leaders that the occupation of the West Bank and Gaza was costly in terms of Israeli casualties, unacceptable to the world community, harmful to Israel's image and economy, and counterproductive to its close relations with the United States. Moreover, the much-vaunted Israeli Defense Forces (IDF) were reduced to crowd control and police actions at the expense of morale and training.

On the international scene, the ascendancy of Mikhail Gorbachev as leader of the Soviet Union led to a dramatic reappraisal of Soviet Middle East policy, including the decision to put limits on military assistance to Syria. Gorbachev further argued that the Arab-Israeli conflict could not be solved by force of arms. This, in turn, forced Syria's Hafez al-Asad to reassess his position vis-à-vis Egypt and the Arab world, and ultimately the United States and Israel. As the Cold War globalization of the conflict was reversed, Israeli leaders no longer feared a Soviet threat behind the Arab opposition.

The next landmark was the 1990-91 Gulf crisis and war. The Gulf War greatly enhanced the position of pro-Western states in the region—the so-called moderates—and administered a setback to the rejectionist front. The decisive defeat of Iraqi President Saddam Hussein was also a defeat for his supporters in Jordan, Libya, the Palestinian community, Yemen, and elsewhere. Many Palestinians had supported Hussein's call for linkage between the resolution of the Iraqi-Kuwaiti dispute and the Israeli-Palestinian conflict. After years of political and military battles and few tangible gains, Palestinians had hoped that Baghdad's strong leadership would force a re-alignment of political power and strengthen Palestinian bargaining power.

Jordan's failure to back the allied war effort in a forthright manner led to its international ostracism. In 1990, the majority of the population in Jordan was Palestinian and strongly favored the Iraqi position. The Jordanian economy relied heavily on transactions and financial dealings with Iraq; Aqaba was an important transit point for Iraqi goods. Before the war, Jordan received $185 million annually in cash grants from Iraq and Kuwait as well as concessionary oil supplies from Baghdad. The Jordanian finance minister estimated that in the first year after the Iraqi invasion of Kuwait, the Gulf War cost Jordan over $2.1 billion.[2] Though Jordan had generally strong ties with Western countries, the leadership in Amman was considered part of the pro-Iraqi camp. As a result, the allied coalition gave Jordan the cold shoulder. Jordan's rehabilitation took some time. The signing of the Israeli-Jordanian Peace Treaty in October 1994 was a milestone in Jordan's return to Western favor.

10

In contrast, the Arab states that joined the anti-Iraq coalition were rewarded financially, politically, and militarily. Access to U.S. military technology was only one of the fringe benefits for supporters. Egypt sent troops to the Gulf and saw $6.7 billion in debt forgiven.[3] Syria, formerly treated as a terrorist-sponsor and pariah state, participated in the coalition and gained some political respect from Western countries. Syria received $700 million in credits from Japan and European countries, and over $2 billion in cash or pledges from Saudi Arabia and the Gulf states.[4]

Syria participated in the allied war effort against Iraq in part to compensate for the loss of Soviet support. Soviet client states were particularly hard hit by the end of the Cold War. In the period 1985-89, Soviet arms deliveries to Syria averaged $1.2 billion per year. This dropped to $317 million per year in 1991-93, a 74 percent decrease. Arms deliveries from Warsaw Pact countries dropped 58 percent during the same period.[5] The decline of Soviet patronage (including credit for arms deliveries) was probably the single most important factor influencing Syrian President Hafez al-Asad to change his policy of confrontation with Israel and to seek better relations with the moderate Arab states and the United States. The decline in Soviet military support was accompanied by a drastic change in Soviet political and diplomatic positions, which later were largely adopted by the new Russian government. During the Cold War, Moscow was a staunch political supporter of the Arab states. At the United Nations, for instance, Arab leaders could almost always count on Soviet support against the U.S.-Israeli position on a given issue.

The removal of the Soviet Union from the regional equation changed strategic alliances and the military balance. It weakened the conventional military power of the radical states that no longer had access to unlimited arms at cut rate prices and strengthened both U.S. allies and extremist groups that rely on unconventional tactics, including terrorism, to influence regional policies.

For these reasons, the Gulf War created an opening for a renewed diplomatic push for Arab-Israeli peace, the U.S. goal for many years. The war changed the climate of opinion among many political leaders in the Arab world. Policies rejecting Israel's right to exist were far less attractive. Militant Arab regimes could place little faith in a military solution to the Arab-Israeli conflict.

In the immediate aftermath of the Gulf War, the United States appeared invincible and carried great weight in international political circles; Soviet cooperation during the Gulf crisis was a dramatic reminder of how times had changed. When U.S. Secretary of State James Baker and others began to lobby for a formal peace process, some former opponents of peace with Israel recognized that participating in the peace process would be a way to compensate for supporting the losing side in the Gulf War. Jordan and the PLO, in particular, were contrite and eager to show good faith by joining the peace process. The PLO had suffered not only a political defeat but also a financial setback as a result of the war. Saudi Arabia and Kuwait ended payments to the PLO. Before the Iraqi invasion, sources of PLO funding included Saudi Arabia ($72 million/year), Kuwait ($24 million/year), and Iraq ($48 million/year).[6]

On March 6, 1991, just after the conclusion of the allied attack against Iraq, former U.S. President George Bush left no doubt that the Arab-Israeli conflict was a U.S. diplomatic priority. In a speech to a joint session of Congress, Bush said, "We must do all that we can to close the gap between Israel and the Arab states—and between Israelis and Palestinians. . . . There can be no substitute for diplomacy."[7] The momentum for starting a process ultimately proved unstoppable, and the first meeting of the key parties to the conflict was convened in Madrid, Spain, on October 30, 1991.

After this historic gathering, negotiations commenced on two official tracks, one bilateral, the other multilateral. The bilateral track involved direct negotiations between Israel and Syria, Israel and Lebanon, and Israel and a joint Jordanian-Palestinian delegation. In the early stages of the process, Israel's negotiations with the Jordanian-Palestinian team served as an umbrella for discussions with Palestinian and Jordanian negotiators. These bilateral talks were subjected to heavy media coverage, and Israeli-Palestinian talks made little substantive progress. The Israeli government of Prime Minister-Yitzhak Shamir was not prepared to deal directly with the PLO, and Shamir later confessed that he had no intention of making major concessions to the Palestinians and that he was primarily interested in dragging out negotiations for as long as possible while intensifying Israeli settlement activity on the West Bank. Shamir and other officials in his Likud government rejected an independent Palestinian negotiating team because they believed it would set a precedent for Palestinian independence, an outcome they considered unacceptable.

The defeat of the Shamir government in June 1992 and the ascendancy of Labor Party leader Yitzhak Rabin as prime minister changed the equation significantly. In the official talks, the Palestinians and Israelis negotiated without cover from the Jordanians, and in 1993, secret Israeli-Palestinian negotiations at Oslo bypassed official diplomatic tracks and produced a stunning breakthrough with an agreement on the Declaration of Principles (DOP).

The DOP, also known as Oslo I, revolutionized the Israeli-Palestinian relationship.[8] The draft agreement was initialed by Israeli and Palestinian negotiators in August 1993. This was followed by an exchange of letters between Yasser Arafat and Yitzhak Rabin on September 9, 1993, that paved the way for the formal signing ceremony on the White House lawn on September 13, 1993. As leader of the PLO, Arafat's letter recognized Israel's right to exist, accepted United Nations Security Council (UNSC) resolutions 242 (1967) and 338 (1973), renounced the use of violence, and pledged to restrain all PLO elements. He also pledged to repeal the clauses in the PLO charter that called for Israel's destruction or advocated an armed struggle against Israel. Rabin's letter, in turn, accepted the PLO as the legitimate representative of the Palestinian people and as Israel's negotiating partner. At the signing ceremony, the two men spoke—after forty-five years of conflict—in strong, emotional language about "the beginning of the end of a chapter of pain and suffering," "an opportunity for all forms of cooperation," and "embark[ing] on a new era in the history of the Middle East." Rabin movingly stated, "Enough of blood and tears. Enough!"[9]

A new era of Israeli-Palestinian relations began to unfold. The DOP was a skeletal framework for the transition from Israeli occupation of the West Bank and Gaza Strip to some indeterminate form of Palestinian self-rule over a five-year interim period. It contained a number of provisions: negotiations over "final status" issues—including Jerusalem, refugees, and borders—to begin not later than the start of the third year of the interim phase; Palestinian elections for a Palestinian Council; Israeli withdrawal from Gaza and the West Bank city of Jericho; Palestinian assumption of responsibility for civil affairs in various stages (in part the so-called early empowerment under which civil affairs such as education and tourism in areas still under Israeli control would be turned over to Palestinians); and continued Israeli protection of Israeli settlements and control of border crossings. On many issues (e.g., the size of the Jericho area), exact details were to be worked out in later negotiations. As Palestinian critics were quick to point out, the DOP did not contain an explicit guarantee of the Palestinian right to self-determination.

As Israeli and Palestinian negotiators wrestled with countless details needed for implementation, Israel and Jordan moved quickly to consolidate the peace front. Progress was rapid, and by the summer of 1994, it appeared that a larger breakthrough would be possible. The Israeli-Jordanian Washington Declaration of July 25, 1994, contained the broad outline of peace, and both sides pledged to move quickly toward a final treaty. Israel and Jordan surprised many observers with the speed of their talks and their feelings of warmth for each other. The treaty was signed on October 26, 1994. Taken together, the Israeli-Jordanian treaty and the Israeli-Palestinian agreements generated a new euphoria and unrestrained optimism among participants and observers. The ensuing years witnessed several other notable milestones, including the signing of a second Israeli-Palestinian agreement in September 1995 (Oslo II); the elections of Arafat as *raes* (president/chairman) of the Palestinian Authority and of an eighty-eight member Palestinian Council in January 1996; and the revocation, in April 1996, by the old Palestine National Council of the clauses in the Palestine National Charter that called for the destruction of Israel through the armed liberation of Palestine.

While the bilateral Arab-Israeli negotiations have rightfully commanded the headlines since October 1991, multilateral efforts to build a brighter future in the Middle East were successful in bringing long-time enemies together and addressing major challenges facing the region in the years ahead. The five multilateral working groups launched in Moscow on January 28-29, 1992, formed the core of the multilateral negotiations but other steps and meetings have also contributed to the process. The five official working groups covered arms control and regional security, water resources, the environment, economic development, and refugees. The meetings involved tens of countries, including Canada, Egypt, the European Union, Israel, Japan, Jordan, Morocco, Oman, Qatar, Russia, Saudi Arabia, Tunisia, Turkey, and the United States. At the multilateral meetings, Israeli representatives and Arab officials from some countries met officially for the first time.

These multilateral talks—instead of narrowly focusing on ways to untangle bitter border disputes or military confrontations—looked for common ground on important economic and military issues. In this sense, they were to serve as confidence-building measures. Over many months, Arab and Israeli delegates participated in dozens of joint meetings where they networked, socialized, and exchanged ideas. They discussed proposals to develop a structural framework for enhancing trust and cooperation in the region. Eventually, the work of these representatives may very well lay the groundwork for new institutions and tangible gains for the participating countries.

In 1995-96, the events that culminated with the election of the Netanyahu government in Israel brought a new sense of uncertainty and a virtual end to the multilateral process. Yet from a historic perspective, the multilateral talks demonstrated the potential for problem solving and the enormous scope for regional cooperation if the political climate is favorable.

THE CASE FOR CONTINUED OPTIMISM

Both military and economic considerations provide strong arguments for continuation of the Arab-Israeli peace process. Much progress has been achieved since 1991, and no one wishes to return to conditions prior to the 1993 Declaration of Principles. From a military perspective, continued conflict and an escalating arms race are very costly; there can be no classical balance of power in the Middle East, and thus regional players have been forced to look for a non-military solution. At the same time, structural changes in the global environment and the global economy make it increasingly difficult for Middle East regimes to survive and prosper in isolation from their neighbors and the rest of the world. For a growing number of people in the Middle East, the desire for prosperity is pushing business and consumer concerns ahead of romantic nationalist notions of combat and victory. As an added benefit, success on the Arab-Israeli front will improve the chances for an eventual settlement of outstanding problems in the Persian Gulf region.

Optimists might draw solace from the experience of Western Europe, which witnessed the two most violent and destructive wars in human history in the span of thirty-one years. These wars were nurtured by centuries-old animosities, spurring the vitriolic nationalism that led to World War I and the vindictiveness of the victorious allies at Versailles, which in turn fed Germany's bitter resentment and the subsequent rise of totalitarianism. In May 1945, there was nothing preordained about the peace that subsequently settled over Europe. Between 1945 and 1948, postwar Europe tottered on the brink of chaos and collapse. It was the combined wisdom of George Marshall, Harry Truman, Jean Monnet, and others that saved Europe from catastrophe and communism and paved the way for the Atlantic alliance and European unity.

15

In the early 1950s, the unification of Europe was considered a pipe dream. By the late 1940s, the United States and Britain had both concluded that Germany could no longer be kept weak and that, ultimately, German rearmament would be necessary to meet the challenges of the growing Soviet menace. This, of course, was anathema to France. The delicate balance that permitted the reintegration of Germany into Europe while at the same time finding ways to use its strength without being threatened was the genius behind the military and economic alliances that were created, including the North Atlantic Treaty Organization (NATO) and the European Economic Community (EEC). But European cooperation came about because it was a practical way of achieving what all the democratic regimes in the region wanted: security and economic growth.

Although the conditions in the Middle East do not replicate those in Europe, there are similarities. Most important, the central players in the Arab-Israeli conflict have reached the conclusion that further wars will not solve the problems of the region and that the economic consequences of continued conflict grow more painful each year. Furthermore, they have acknowledged that U.S. involvement is essential if the process is to succeed. They realize that the U.S. commitment to the peace process is based on highly practical considerations. The United States has vital strategic interests in the Persian Gulf which will be enhanced if Israel and the Arab states forge a comprehensive agreement. This will erode and undermine the power and appeal of Muslim extremism in important pro-Western countries such as Egypt, Saudi Arabia, and Turkey and will isolate extremist regimes such as Iran, Iraq, Libya, and the Sudan.

From where has the push for regional peace come? Perhaps the most articulate example of the optimistic perspective with regard to Arab-Israeli relations is in the writings and speeches of former Israeli Prime Minister Shimon Peres. Peres's vision of the "New Middle East" (the title of his book on the subject) resembles Western Europe today. He has argued that "our ultimate goal is the creation of a regional community of nations, with a common market and elected centralized bodies, modeled on the European Community."[10] On economic issues, Peres has written that "the continued advance toward economic compatibility among the countries of the region will enable the ultimate establishment of a regional economic system aimed at growth, development, and prosperity."[11] He has discussed a wide range of possibilities, including new investment, tourism, water sharing, desertification, biotechnology, infrastructure, transportation, and communications. Many Arabs would agree that such developments are possible and desirable once Israel withdraws from the Golan Heights, dismantles all Israeli settlements in the occupied territories, and accepts East Jerusalem as the capital of a Palestinian state.

The euphoria exemplified by Peres's book reached a peak following the signing of the Declaration of Principles between Israel and the PLO in 1993. Although the DOP was only the first of many agreements needed to resolve the Israeli-Palestinian conflict, many view it as critical. Peres summed up this perspective: "The plan for Palestinian autonomy essentially severs the past from the present. This design for a new Middle East is a passageway to a new future for all."[12] The 1994 Israeli-Jordanian treaty calls for a Conference on Security and Cooperation in the Middle East in an effort to replicate the Organization for Security and Cooperation in Europe.

While this unbridled optimism created false expectations and high hopes, it did not prevent gradual progress on various negotiating tracks. Until Rabin's death, he and his Labor-led government were aware that by establishing as many concrete manifestations of Israeli-Palestinian agreements as possible before the 1996 Israeli elections (expected in the fall of 1996 before Rabin's assassination), the Labor government could raise the cost of a Likud-led change of course. More agreements and the implementation of existing provisions would strengthen the belief, both in Israel and abroad, that the Israeli-Palestinian process was irreversible. With each step, the costs to the new Likud government of a policy alteration would climb a little bit higher.

The Israeli-Palestinian agreement known as Oslo II, signed in Washington on September 28, 1995, was just such a step. Oslo II is an intricate plan for the gradual relinquishment of Israeli control of Palestinian life in the West Bank. The agreement divided the West Bank—not including any part of Jerusalem—into three zones. Over time, Palestinians were scheduled to take control of all Arab civil affairs. Zone A consisted of eight West Bank cities (including Jericho, which was already under Palestinian control); Palestinian authorities were supposed to assume responsibility for internal security and public order, with the exception of some areas in Hebron. Zone B consisted of Arab towns and villages in the West Bank, and Palestinian police were eventually to take responsibility for order within specified towns, though Israel retained overriding security authority. In Zone C, including Israeli settlements, unpopulated areas, and land Israel viewed as strategic, Israel retained

17

full security authority, something that might be dealt with in "final status" talks. Changes would begin in Zone A, to be followed several months later in Zone B, and then, lastly, at six-month intervals in Zone C. After the Israeli redeployment from the eight West Bank cities, further redeployments were mandated to take place on September 7, 1996; March 7, 1997; and September 7, 1997.[13] Other sections dealt with joint Israeli-Palestinian patrols and the construction of bypass roads for Israelis.

Oslo II also provided for the election of a *raes* (president/chairman) and eighty-two-member council (later increased to eighty-eight members) to lead the Palestinian Authority during the interim phase, a period originally scheduled to last into 1999. Israel feared that allowing East Jerusalem Palestinians to vote or stand for election would prejudice future Israeli-Palestinian negotiations on Jerusalem's status so the elections allowed Palestinians in Jerusalem to vote using envelopes (similar to American-style absentee voting). Palestinian candidates who lived in Jerusalem needed to use a second address elsewhere in the West Bank or Gaza in order to be eligible.

As the election of the Likud government in May 1996 demonstrated, the political problem for the Labor government was that incremental progress looks rather insignificant when measured against the yardstick of a new utopian Middle East. In addition, deadly bombings against Israelis, including several attacks inside the Green Line—the de facto border between Israel and the Jordanian-controlled West Bank from 1948 to 1967—contrasted sharply with the descriptions of an era of new relations.

The disparity between expectations and reality has helped fuel disappointment and resentment in Israel. It has also led to a growing schism within Netanyahu's own coalition. His decision to withdraw Israeli forces from 80 percent of the city of Hebron in 1997 was regarded by right-wing hard-liners as treachery, since it committed a Likud government to the principle of exchanging part of the land of Israel for peace with the Palestinians. The ideological consequences of this schism are likely to be far-reaching; it will intensify the bitterness of the right when the negotiations on further territorial withdrawals and final status issues, including the future of Jerusalem, settlements, refugees, and final borders, get under way. In March 1997, the crisis over the construction of apartments at Har Homa (Jebel Abu Ghneim) was indicative of this bitterness and the violent Palestinian response.

Supporters of the peace process believe that such ups and downs are a regrettable but inevitable part of the road to peace.

Violence and poisonous rhetoric are the last gasps of rejectionists (extremist Israelis and Palestinians opposed to the peace process) wedded to yesterday's relations. Ultimately such opposition will lose support as more and more Arabs and Israelis see the benefit of ending the conflict and hostility. Optimists accept the dangers that inevitably accompany a radical re-alignment of regional political forces but argue that no other alternative offers a realistic model of stability. Theoretically, a classical balance of power among the regional states might provide the conditions for preventing a new war, but the fundamental asymmetries among the parties make this unlikely. Relationships that are so basically uneven will eventually lead to an imbalance of power and a consequent drift toward instability and war. In a new Middle East war, biological, chemical, or nuclear weapons could be deployed or even used. At a minimum, a new war would involve use of the most modern conventional munitions and long-range missiles. The new munitions are so lethal that much of the infrastructure of the adversaries could be destroyed, with horrendous economic and social consequences.

Shortly before the DOP was signed, Yossi Beilin, a Labor government minister and protégé of Peres, warned that continued delay, stalemate, and opposition to the peace process concessions would bolster extremist elements:

> Time is against us. It is against us because if nothing happens, extremism will flourish: distress, frustration, poverty, and belief in solutions other than the peaceful one. . . . Everywhere around us, in Israel itself and in the territories, those groups, be they Hezbollah, Hamas, or the Muslim Brotherhood, are trying to fight against pragmatic regimes in the area. Peace means affluence, even if it is a partial one. Peace means hope for the people of the region. The other alternative means a continuation and a strengthening of those extremists in the region.[14]

When Beilin weighed all the factors, he concluded that "all those things are making me and my colleagues very optimistic about the possibility of making peace."

Now in a position where he must produce tangible results, PLO leader Yasser Arafat has become part of the effort to end Israeli-Palestinian tensions once and for all. Arafat believes he has made significant concessions to Israel on security matters in the interest of keeping enough of the Israeli public supportive of the process that they allow it to move forward. Despite some speeches articulating long-term goals that sound hostile to Israeli ears, Arafat's actions suggest that he is ready for a two-state solution to the conflict. His conciliatory speech in Hebron on January 19, 1997, stressing the need for "a just and comprehensive peace" was interpreted by many Israelis in a more positive light than most of his previous utterances on such occasions. However, Arafat's behavior during the spring and summer of 1997—when Israel claimed he used Palestinian street violence as a political weapon against the Netanyahu government—once more cast him into the role of duplicitous villain in the eyes of many Israelis.

Before the 1996-97 violence, according to mid-1995 polling data, a majority of Palestinians either supported making peace with Israel or were moving in that direction. Close to one-third were willing to completely forgo land lost in 1948 in exchange for a Palestinian state in the West Bank and Gaza Strip with Jerusalem as its capital. An unstated additional percentage of Palestinians might be supportive of that option if there was some sort of financial compensation for 1948 losses. Palestinians were evenly split on the legitimacy of the armed struggle against Israel under present political circumstances, but over half opposed suicide bombings (one-third supported such bombings).[15] In general, Gaza residents were more likely to view Palestinian rule as beneficial since the early measures had enhanced freedom and personal security in Gaza. These data suggest that as the Palestinian Authority takes control of more territory in the West Bank, support for extremist positions and solutions will continue to dwindle. Another poll of Palestinians in mid-1995 showed steady two-thirds support for the negotiations process with Israel.[16] Arafat's tumultuous reception in Hebron in January 1997 was a further indicator that Palestinian extremists—many of whom live in Hebron—have little to offer if Arafat keeps delivering more of the occupied territory to Palestinian control.

In neighboring Jordan, King Hussein, Crown Prince Hassan, and other leaders have embraced the vision of a cooperative Middle East. They recognize that the conflict must be put to rest for greater economic benefits to flow to the region. Former Prime Minister al-Sharif Zayd Bin-Shakir noted that security and stability are "a basic foundation to achieve economic progress for the countries of the region."[17] King Hussein reportedly told one American Jewish group that "peace with Israel was the crowning achievement of all the years of my service to the people of Jordan and the people of this region."[18] In contrast, the Jordanian people have been more cautious in their appraisal of the new state of relations with Israel, but the implementation of additional agreements and the development of further ties is continuing, although at a more measured pace than originally forecast.

On political matters, Jordan has been successful in balancing ongoing efforts to democratize and the effect of participation by potential radicals. After widespread civil unrest in Jordan in April 1989, King Hussein relaxed pressures on journalists and announced parliamentary elections. In November 1989, in the first full parliamentary elections since 1967, Islamists captured 34 of 80 seats, a very strong showing. Although all political parties had been banned since 1958, their activities were tolerated.[19]

Democratization continued in Jordan after the Gulf War. In 1992, King Hussein terminated the emergency laws in effect since the 1967 Arab-Israeli War, reinstated a multi-party system, and lifted additional press restrictions.[20] King Hussein and other pro-peace-process Jordanians strengthened their position in the November 1993 elections that marginalized the Islamic opposition. Islamists[21] currently form the nucleus of the opposition to the peace process in Jordan. Successful normalization of relations with Israel should ultimately aid the Jordanian move toward openness. King Hussein remains committed to democratization: "We in Jordan are committed to democracy. I believe this is the only way in the long run to bring [the Arab World] closer together."[22]

Other Arab states have taken steps toward reconciliation as relations between Israel and some of the front-line parties have improved. Not only Egyptian President Hosni Mubarak and Jordan's King Hussein, but also Prime Minister Abdel-latif Filali of Morocco, Palestinian Authority officials, and government ministers from Oman and Qatar attended Rabin's funeral in November 1995.[23] Officials from Oman, Qatar, Tunisia, and Morocco had all met previously with Israeli representatives. Rabin himself had traveled to Oman in December 1994 and the two countries exchanged representatives in May 1996. Israeli and Arab leaders met in historic economic summits in 1994, 1995, and 1996 to discuss the region's economic future. Various levels of diplomatic and economic ties have been forged. Such relations are part of the Arab-Israeli thaw that optimists see as the wave of the future.

The peace process has also greatly increased Israel's ties further afield. According to data from the Israeli Foreign Ministry, about 40 percent of Israel's diplomatic ties were established or renewed between October 1991 and May 1996. This includes relations with thirty-four countries between October 1991 and September 13,

1993, and another thirty-three countries between then and May 1996. The Soviet Union and Israel opened relations in October 1991; since that time, Israel has established relations with numerous countries in Africa (including Ghana, Nigeria, and Zimbabwe) and Asia (including China, India, and Vietnam).[24] Indeed, the slow down in Israel's relations with the Arab world and the distinct chilling of relations with the European Union following Netanyahu's early hardline posturing was further proof for the optimists' view that eventually the Israeli right will recognize the positive correlation between territorial compromise and Israel's acceptance by its neighbors and the rest of the world.

Optimists believe that further breakthroughs in the Arab-Israeli peace process will reduce the appeal of radicalism and herald a new era of economic growth and prosperity. The region would then become a magnet for foreign investment and trade and would eventually become more integrated with the giant economic groups in Europe, Asia, and North America. This, in turn, could spur additional growth and opportunity in Central Asia with its abundant resources. In sum, the resolution of the Arab-Israeli conflict could become the precursor for an economic renaissance throughout the region and parallel improvements in living standards and human rights. It would also make it easier for the United States to continue to play the role of balancer in the Persian Gulf and thereby assure the security of oil supplies.[25]

PEACE, SECURITY, AND PROSPERITY

If the peace process is to succeed, the relationship between peace, security, and prosperity must be positive. It is the insecurity of Israel—in theory the most powerful country in the Middle East—that remains a key problem for attaining regional peace. As the following paragraphs argue, strong military forces alone cannot assure long-term security. Israel's security can be considered at three levels: personal security threatened by terrorism and random violence; threats to the state of Israel from the armed forces of neighboring Arab states; and threats to Israel from radical states armed with weapons of mass destruction. Israel needs the cooperation of the Palestinian Authority to control and contain terrorism. Secure borders with neighboring Arab countries are best guaranteed by peace treaties and arms control agreements. For the most ominous threat of weapons of mass destruction from countries like Iran and Iraq, Israel needs the support and cooperation of Arab countries and, especially, the United States.

To assure Israel's continued prosperity and to improve the economic conditions of Palestinians, the Israeli economy must continue to grow and Israel's economic relations with the rest of the world must flourish. This will not happen if the peace process is seriously derailed. Foreign investors will shun the region and several key states in Asia will be wary of expanding trade with Israel if the Arab world is once more united and antagonistic toward Israel.[26]

SECURITY ISSUES AND PEACE

In theory, it can be argued that Israel can rely on its own military capabilities to deter all three levels of threats. However, the history of the past fifty years demonstrates that a traditional balance-of-power system has not assured long-term peace and stability in the Middle East. Rather, in both the Arab-Israeli and the Persian Gulf theaters, the ever-changing military relationships and the parallel arms race contributed to a highly insecure, dangerous region with frequent inter-state wars, low-level conflicts, and terrorism. Moreover, as the Gulf War demonstrated, these two theaters are now closely linked through the technology of long-range missiles and strike aircraft. Except for North Korea, the most serious nuclear proliferation problems exist in the Middle East and the adjacent Indian subcontinent.

The most glaring lesson of the 1990-91 Gulf crisis was that Iraqi President Saddam Hussein believed he could use naked military aggression against a weak neighbor, Kuwait, and get away with it. Saddam Hussein did not take seriously notions about the obsolescence of war in the post-Cold War era. Today, more than six years after the Gulf War, there is no evidence to suggest that any of the key Middle East states have rejected the importance of maintaining strong military forces. Neither have they discounted the possibilities of new wars.

Yet the actual record of the past fifty years must surely reinforce the argument that Middle East wars have done little to resolve conflict and much to promote chaos and disruption. The sorry history of the Arab-Israeli wars reflects this reality. The Arab states discovered after major military defeats in 1948, 1956, 1967, and 1973 that military force could not destroy Israel. Israel, in turn, discovered that its victories did not bring security or peace and, on occasion, led to dangerous and costly encounters such as the War of Attrition (1968-70)[27] and the Lebanon War (1982-85). Egypt's intervention in Yemen in the 1960s

23

was another disaster, as was Libya's futile war in Chad in 1973. In the Persian Gulf, the 1980-88 war between Iran and Iraq was a major failure for both sides, involving huge financial and human costs from which neither country has yet recovered. The 1990-91 Gulf crisis and war resulted in an ignominious defeat for Iraq, and the subsequent years have witnessed its steady decline from one of the most advanced, richest countries in the region to a pauper state. Against this dismal record, a major new Middle East war would be a catastrophe for the region and probably relegate it to a global backwater for many years, similar, perhaps, to the situation in sub-Saharan Africa.

The Gulf War highlighted the dangers associated with the proliferation of weapons of mass destruction (WMDs), including long-range delivery systems, to the Middle East. Two dangers are especially relevant. First, introducing WMDs into a highly unstable region with unresolved conflicts can only exacerbate existing tensions and lead to an escalating qualitative arms race. This is more likely to increase the possibility of preemptive war than to precipitate the evolution of a stable balance of power based on mutual deterrence, as was achieved in Europe between NATO and the Warsaw Pact. While a stable balance of terror in the Middle East is theoretically possible, particularly if the key antagonists achieved secure nuclear or advanced conventional weapons capability within the same timeframe, in fact, such a balance is unlikely. Israel already possesses a formidable nuclear force, while Syria and Iran possess significant chemical and missile capabilities. Since a continuing unchecked arms race is unlikely to lead to a situation of parity or even mutual equivalence in capabilities, the asymmetrical pace of the military buildup itself becomes a source of instability.

Second, because of the different cultural attitudes of the major contestants in the Middle East, the use of weapons of mass destruction might be contemplated more readily than in many other regions of the world. There is fear—expressed routinely in Arab countries—that as long as Israel is the sole possessor of nuclear weapons in the region, a maverick Israeli leader, such as Ariel Sharon, might be tempted to flaunt Israel's nuclear monopoly, perhaps to the point of threatening to use it. It is not unreasonable to believe that the late Iranian leader Ayatollah Khomeini or Libya's Muammar Qadaffi might, under certain circumstances, have been tempted to use nuclear weapons against either the West or Israel or, in the case of Khomeini, Iraq. One can only speculate about what would have happened if Saddam Hussein had had a nuclear weapon during the Gulf Crisis. Would this have deterred the Western forces from massive military intervention to rescue Kuwait, or alternatively, would he have been prepared to use a weapon against Israel or his Arab neighbors?

In virtually all Middle East countries, populations, including the leaders, are concentrated in one, or at the most two, highly vulnerable cities. Egypt, while a large country, has all its power structure in Cairo. Because of Israel's tiny size, one nuclear weapon on Tel Aviv would threaten the existence of the Jewish state. Syria, Iraq, Saudi Arabia, and Iran are also vulnerable to one or two nuclear strikes.

Of course weapons, including weapons of mass destruction, do not cause wars. What counts is the political-military environment into which advanced weapons are introduced. If the environment is unstable and adversaries have a predilection to resolve disputes by force, certain types of new weaponry will increase threat perceptions and could provide a catalyst for war. But if the political-military environment is stable and the climate is supportive of reconciliation and peaceful dialogue—or, alternatively, if the likely casualties resulting from a new war are believed to be unacceptable to both adversaries—the introduction of new weapons may actually reduce the likelihood of war and could even contribute to stability.

There may be circumstances under which the introduction of weapons of mass destruction would reinforce deterrence in the Middle East. Some would argue that Syria and Israel have refrained from provoking each other in recent years in part because Syria has a formidable chemical arsenal and Israel has both chemical and nuclear weapons. On the subcontinent, India and Pakistan did not go to war over the crisis in Kashmir in spring 1990; fear of each other's undeclared nuclear weapons has been suggested as a contributing factor. These examples support the argument that a state's possession of nuclear or chemical weapons may make it more cautious about using such weapons against a well-armed adversary. In such a case, weapons may either act as a deterrent to war or at least put constraints on their use during a war.

In contrast, Israel's attack against Iraqi nuclear facilities in 1981 and Iraqi threats to retaliate against Israel with chemical weapons in spring 1990 point to the highly destabilizing potential of weapons proliferation in the Arab-Israeli context. Few believe the Middle East will be more secure if nuclear weapons ever fall into the hands of radical or revanchist regimes. Although

Israel's monopoly on nuclear-weapons possession in the Middle East may be regarded as a deterrent to war, it is also an incentive for the Arab countries and Iran to seek ways to get access to the bomb. Once this becomes a serious possibility, the probability of Israeli preemptive action grows.

So long as there is no comprehensive peace and rearmament continues in most Middle East countries, the financial burden of the arms race will remain a primary challenge for all regimes. Most Middle East countries are highly vulnerable to attack by advanced conventional munitions. As the Gulf War demonstrated, it took very few so-called smart munitions to cripple many of Iraq's utility systems. Likewise, the Israeli economy was paralyzed by the Iraqi Scud attacks; businesses lost millions of dollars of orders because factories were closed while workers sat in basements wearing gas masks. If obsolete, inefficient Scud technology could cause such a disruption to a modern, sophisticated economy, advanced missiles or aircraft could cause untold economic damage to the region's vulnerable infrastructure. Imagine what damage F-117-type bombers could do to the oil fields of the Gulf Cooperation Council (GCC) countries if used by a hostile power? The entire infrastructure of the Gulf, particularly the oil production, oil loading/unloading facilities, and water supply systems, could be quickly destroyed in a confrontation with an adversary equipped with smart munitions. Indeed, the high costs of modern conventional forces may encourage some regimes to look for weapons of mass destruction as the only way to overcome the formidable conventional power of countries like the United States and Israel. One of the most tangible long-term benefits of a full-fledged regional peace would be the reduction of defense burdens.

In sum, there is little reason to have confidence that a balance of power based on military strength can prevail among the regional players and every reason to believe that new wars in the Middle East are likely to be more widespread and dangerous than in the past. If nuclear or advanced conventional weapons are used in any quantity, entire economies and societies could be wrecked. Avoiding a Middle East apocalypse has now become a high priority for those within and outside the region. This, as much as anything else, is a strong imperative to continue the peace process.

While weapons of mass destruction pose the most serious security problem to the region, terrorism is the most likely threat. The primary sources of terrorism are extremist groups in Israel as well as in the Muslim world. In the latter case, they are often supported by governments, including Iran, Iraq, Syria, and the Sudan.

The most effective way to combat terror is for the moderate Arab governments and Israel to cooperate on security issues. It is ironic that the new Israeli government has realized that close cooperation with Yasser Arafat is essential if Palestinian extremism is to be curbed. Thus the former foes are locked in an umbilical relationship necessary for their respective political survival. Nurturing the peace process has now become a necessary adjunct of anti-terrorism even though progress in the peace process may trigger further terrorist attacks.

PROSPERITY AND PEACE

A second strong motivation for a continued peace process is the perceived benefits it will confer on various economies in the region. That being said, the relationship between the peace process and regional economic development is controversial, and economic arguments have been used to support a variety of contrasting positions. Advocates of the peace process have used rosy economic forecasts as an incentive to build popular support or to win over recalcitrant governments. In Jordan, for instance, the presumed economic benefits of peace became a tool to generate public support for normalization with Israel. The Jordanian leadership offered a grandiose vision of the benefits, initially overlooking the potential backlash from over-hyped agreements and a weaker-than-promised economic performance. Nonetheless, Jordan's approach is a dramatic example of the argument that peace provides economic benefits on both the national and regional level.

Others highlight not just future developments but the role that economics already plays in creating a climate conducive to peace process advances. From this perspective, general economic gains, whether or not they are related to the political process, lessen support for conflict and confrontational policies. As the desire for a middle-class lifestyle and conflict fatigue become more prevalent in Israel, for example, the desire to put the wars and confrontations in the past becomes stronger out of economic self-interest. This motivation, however, is vulnerable to security issues. The suicide bombings in Israel in February and March 1996 made security, not economic prosperity, the dominant issue in the 1996 Israeli election.

While economic forces have been influenced by the peace process, they may be wholly unrelated and still affect the desire for successful negotiations. Business leaders on all sides of the Middle East conflict have recognized the indirect damage caused

27

by conflict and expressed a desire to focus on economic issues instead of military and strategic ones. As J.R. Abinader, president of the U.S.-Arab Chamber of Commerce, once said, "No one is going to put ten cents into that region until it stabilizes. There has to be a sense of security."[28] Most top industrialists and members of the Israeli Manufacturers' Association backed the Labor Party in the 1992 and 1996 Israeli elections despite Likud's traditional pro-business stance. They believed that Labor's greater commitment to the peace process was now the ultimate pro-business position.[29] According to Uri Savir, director general of the Israeli Ministry of Foreign Affairs in the last Labor government, "The business community, the most conservative sector in society, has become the most avant-garde. They're moving ahead."[30]

There is little disagreement that past conflict has contributed to lower levels of trade and foreign investment in the region. In our view, even if Middle East economies are not transformed overnight, the peace process will lead to at least some economic benefits.

Foreign investors have been wary of the Middle East, limiting both the potential for involvement in world markets and the level of foreign investment. In 1992, a European official told Israeli correspondents, "Your region is not interesting for European investors because it entails political risks. Thailand and East European countries seem far more attractive."[31] Much-needed capital, foreign subsidiaries, and other forms of outside investment could give a major boost to countries that are able to overcome the conflict-oriented policies of the past forty years.

What is the likelihood that an entirely new regional economic order will emerge, with extensive intra-regional trade and foreign investment? Some visionaries such as Shimon Peres have argued that, with the resolution of the Arab-Israeli conflict, defense spending will drop and a peace dividend will pave the way to a bright economic future. New economic relationships will be possible as boycotts end and political roadblocks are removed.

It is possible that such developments will happen, but the timeframe is likely to be a matter of decades. Furthermore, numerous economic impediments, including the absence of sufficient economic liberalization in most countries, will probably ensure that successful political negotiations alone will not catapult the region into a glorious economic era. The long-neglected Palestinian economy, already lacking adequate infrastructure and functioning free-market institutions, has been further hampered by the Israeli-imposed border closure and consequent trade and employment restraints.[32] Yet it is worth considering the possibilities, not only because economic improvements could come faster than expected, but also because the grandiose plans and forecasts highlight areas where incremental change could take place. Even if defense spending is not entirely redirected, some countries might shift their resources into more productive realms. A Middle East common market along the lines of the European Union may remain a pipe dream for some time, but multilateral (if not actually regional) economic agreements can be signed and implemented.[33]

High levels of defense spending have had negative impact on some aspects of economic growth, thus sparking interest in placing curbs on defense expenditures. The economic factors supporting the movement toward arms control in the Arab world have been exhaustively reviewed by Yahya Sadowski,[34] who argued in 1993 that a new military spending debate in the Arab states was triggered largely by their faltering economies. According to Sadowski, the overall weaknesses of the Arab economies are due to many factors, including lower oil prices, overpopulation, economic mismanagement, foreign policy adventurism, and the Gulf War. The last event destroyed the aid donations system between the rich and the poor countries and drastically changed labor migration patterns. Refugees flowed into the poorer countries, thus eliminating remittances from their work in wealthier countries. As a result of these changes and previous policies, the region faces a shortage of capital and a large debt burden, much of which has come from military spending.[35] In this climate, international economic incentives could encourage regional disarmament.

Continued regional conflict impedes the economic benefits that accrue from geographic proximity. "Peace dividends would flow in abundance from combining a patchwork of economically isolated states and territories into a common market," according to one economic observer.[36] Without progress toward peace, these dividends cannot be realized and the opportunity costs are high. By cutting transportation and other transfer costs and utilizing economies of scale, the central states of the Arab-Israeil conflict could gain substantially from bilateral trade. One study estimated that annual trade between Israel, Egypt, Jordan, and Lebanon could amount to one billion dollars, not including oil.[37] Indeed, Israel, the West Bank, and Gaza already demonstrated the benefits of border trade. Before the Intifada, annual Israeli exports to the West Bank and Gaza totaled $1.1 billion. During the Intifada, Israeli exports to these areas dropped 50 percent. With the proper reforms and peace, the West Bank, Gaza, and Israel could "mesh nicely," perhaps returning to the earlier level of trade.[38]

The organizers of the Madrid Conference recognized the need to address the economic problems in the region and included an economic track, known as REDWG (Regional Economic Development Working Group), in the multilateral talks. More media attention, however, has been focused on major economic summits in 1994, 1995, and 1996.

The first Middle East/North Africa economic summit was convened in Casablanca on October 30, 1994, three years to the day after the Madrid Conference. The meeting, organized by the Swiss-based World Economic Forum and the New York-based Council on Foreign Relations, brought together 10 heads of state, 60 ministers, over 300 other officials, and chief executives of over 1,100 companies from 60 countries. While delegates to the meeting at the Casablanca royal palace heard many familiar rhetorical speeches, the more important discussions took place on an informal level as political and business people mingled, negotiated, networked, and shared specific ideas for economic cooperation.[39] Officials were unable to agree on establishing a regional development bank, but they supported an economic community involving "the free flow of goods, capital, and labor throughout the region." They agreed to establish a regional tourist board and called for a second economic summit.[40] The Israeli delegation distributed suggestions for regional cooperation projects totaling $18-$27 billion.[41] More important than any agreements reached, however, was the powerful symbolism of a new era represented by Arabs and Israelis jointly discussing the region's economic future.

The second summit opened in Amman in October 1995, and participants claimed that they would try to get down to actual business rather than focus on rhetoric and speechmaking. According to the summit declaration, the "goals of the summit were to facilitate the expansion of private sector investments in the region, to cement the public-private partnership which will ensure that end, and to work to enhance regional cooperation and development."[42] Additional parties brought long lists of proposed development projects, including $6.3 billion worth of ideas from the Palestinian delegation and $3.5 billion from the Jordanians.[43]

Despite opposition from some European and Gulf countries, the summit approved the formation of the Bank for Economic Cooperation and Development in the Middle East and North Africa, to be set up in Cairo and capitalized at $5 billion.[44] It remains to be seen whether or not the bank can get off the ground if Kuwait, Saudi Arabia, and the United Arab Emirates refuse to contribute. The conference also approved a number of other new institutions, including a regional tourism board, a regional business council, an Economic Summit Executive Secretariat in Rabat, and a monitoring committee secretariat for REDWG, the multilateral working group on regional economic development.[45] Israel signed a memorandum of intent to buy natural gas from Qatar, via Enron, a U.S. energy company; in one of the largest regional commercial projects, Israel will buy at least $400 million worth of liquefied natural gas annually if all goes according to plan.[46]

A third summit was held in Cairo in late 1996. There were many informal contacts among members of the business community, but the entire conference took place in the shadow of strained relations between Israel, under Netanyahu, and the Arab world. A fourth summit was scheduled to be held in Doha in late 1997.

CRITICS AND SKEPTICS

Many take a more pessimistic approach to the peace process. These points of view—explored in considerable detail in later chapters—fall into two general categories; those who disapprove of the peace process and those who do not believe it can work. Since these arguments are mostly covered in the country-by-country chapters, as well as in the discussion of military issues in chapter 10, this section includes only a brief summary before delving into some specific economic counter-arguments.

At the far end of the spectrum are outright rejectionists who not only denounce the current process but insists that no peace is possible between Arabs and Israelis and that conservative, pro-Western regimes in the Arab states should be replaced. Some, such as Iran, Damascus-based Palestinian militants, and the Israeli far right, have not accepted that the peace process has passed the point of no return. They still seek a rollback. Next come those who reject the peace negotiations on the grounds that they are dangerous to the interests of specific groups, be they Palestinians, Jordanians, Israelis, or Egyptians.

Skeptics are less critical of the process, but believe that the Middle East is too ridden with conflict and asymmetries to give much hope for lasting peace. Thus many Arabs and Muslims believe Israel is essentially an appendage of the West and will come to dominate the region as a result of its superior military power, its economy, and its American benefactors. Many Israelis, on the other hand, argue that the undemocratic nature of most Arab governments rules out any parallels with Western Europe and makes peace treaties with Arab countries weak instruments to ensure the peace.

In addition, some reject the idea that economic growth and prosperity are related to the peace process. Arab critics, including officials from Syria and Lebanon, denounced the 1995 Amman economic summit as a cover for Israeli economic hegemony. Israel had intentionally brought a smaller delegation to the second economic summit in order to allay Arab, and especially Egyptian, fears that Israel was seeking economic hegemony as the military side of the Arab-Israeli conflict comes to a close.[47] One Syrian newspaper argued that the "results of the conference are intended to achieve complete Israeli economic, political, and military hegemony over the region."[48] The speaker of the Lebanese parliament, Nabih Birri, called the Amman summit the most dangerous development in the region since the Balfour Declaration, a key document issued by the British government in 1917 that recognized the Jewish right to a homeland in Palestine.[49] Even as Lebanon's leaders criticized the gathering, however, Lebanese entrepreneurs recognized a good business opportunity and were present at the summit under the cover of other nations. Even Hamas, an Islamist, militant Palestinian organization, apparently had some attendees.[50]

In addition to those who reject economic cooperation on political grounds, some critics believe that talk of a Middle East peace dividend is not based on reality.[51] They argue that even under peacetime conditions, the economies of the region will not become especially intertwined and that their economic strengths and weaknesses are not well-matched. For example, according to these economic critics, economies in the region are only partially complementary since they produce many competitive goods such as agricultural products, handicrafts, and oil. Low purchasing power in almost every state and weak competitive positions will restrict the emergence of economies of scale. Major economic disparities in terms of per capita income, level of industrialization, and integration of technology (examined in chapter 9) separate the high- and low-technology countries as well as, more broadly, the rich from the poor. It is unlikely that foreign investment will fuel an economic boom, since the current Middle East share of total world foreign investment is less than 3 percent.[52] Military spending will not fall, as other regional tensions persist. Moreover, the armed forces are a major employer and, in some cases, a key pillar of support for the regime and thus unlikely to succumb to significant cutbacks. Economic underdevelopment and internal instability, often related to demographic and educational issues or infrastructure shortcomings, greatly undermines any hopes of economic growth and improvement. The peace process cannot solve intra-state economic problems that stand in the way of increased economic opportunity.

According to the critics, the track record on these and other concerns provides little room for optimism. The regional players have repeatedly demonstrated an unwillingness to surrender sovereignty in the name of regional economic organizations. Talk of a Middle East common market is just that—talk. Even the Arab Common Market has not worked; regional parties regularly look outside the region for access to commodities and services. Not including oil, Arab regional trade is only 4 percent of their total international trade.[53]

In considering these many hurdles, critics suggest that Egyptian-Israeli relations since 1979 provide the best guide to the economics of peace. The so-called cold peace has resulted in relatively few economic benefits for both sides and should be considered instructive for future deals, since this empirical failure of the peace dividend says as much about future economic prospects as do the theoretical concerns.

CONCLUSION

As is often the case with two starkly different visions, there are elements of truth in both the hopeful and the critical view of potential gains from the peace process. Those whose primary focus is on security issues note the dangers that persist in the region and the costs of an uncontrolled arms race. The optimists use these dire warnings to make the case for peace; the pessimists argue that until the political institutions of the region change, conflict between incompatible systems is inevitable.

Those who focus on economic issues agree that economic progress will only come if the peace process is coupled with other steps, such as reform. Optimists believe this can happen; pessimists argue it cannot or will not happen. The openings and relationships created by advances in the peace process are only one part of the economic picture in the region. In most cases, economic liberalization and reforms have played crucial roles in economic gains or the lack thereof. Such reform often preceded the peace process. But the two really work in tandem. After noting the role of reduced conflict, Joan Spero, former U.S. Undersecretary for Economic, Business, and Agricultural Affairs, explained: "Without liberalization, the economic opportunities created by regional peace will not materialize. And without economic growth led by strong private sector activity, the prospects for long-term regional peace and stability are vastly diminished."[54] The peace process can create openings, but they mean little if an economy is thoroughly unprepared for relations with regional and international economic parties. At the same time, economic reform can spur an economy and help bring about financial changes, but if conflict continues to scare away potential economic partners—whether companies, governments, or investors—progress will be limited.

Interest groups will develop from those who on the micro level are economically affected by the peace process even if on the macro level the net economic change is neutral or a modest improvement. Military officers may fear a loss of power and prestige without the Arab-Israeli conflict. Syrian businesses in Lebanon that benefit from Syria's dominant role in that country will not be happy if Lebanon breaks free from Syrian reins. But that does not mean that Syria as a whole will not be helped economically by peace. The peace process will create economic winners and losers, even if the overall or net economic effect on the region is positive.

The economic and military case for a continued and successful peace process is a strong rebuttal to lingering doubts, political uncertainty, and extremist violence. The changes in the regional and international environment created an opening and the peace process has helped various parties in the region capitalize on this opportunity. We believe the peace process will continue, but difficult and varied obstacles must be overcome for lasting progress.

CHAPTER TWO

UNRESOLVED BILATERAL ISSUES: TERRITORIAL DISPUTES AND FINAL STATUS ISSUES

Although economic and military realities are pushing Israel and several Arab countries toward conflict resolution, complex issues remain to be resolved. Finding mutually satisfactory solutions to Arab-Israeli territorial disputes and Israeli-Palestinian final status issues are key obstacles and will prove difficult for even the most skilled politicians and diplomats.

BILATERAL TERRITORIAL DISPUTES BETWEEN ISRAEL AND THE FRONT-LINE ARAB STATES

Conflicts over the control of spatial areas—land, sea, and air—have been a primary cause of both civil and inter-state wars from time immemorial. Disputes over territory generally fall into four categories. First, the territory (including seaways and rivers) can have strategic importance to one or more sides. Whoever controls the area in question has a distinct military advantage over the country that has no control; this advantage can be either offensive or defensive. Historically, control of high ground, passes, rivers, and ports has been an essential component of military strategy. Even in the era of long-range missiles and aircraft, strategic territory remains an extremely important factor in an area's security.[1]

Second, territory can have economic value to one or more parties; it may contain arable land, valuable minerals, hydrocarbons, animals, fish, or freshwater. Traditionally, more wars of conquest have been fought to gain control over valuable resources than to occupy territory purely for strategic reasons.

Third, territory may be important to a particular country or group for ideological or religious reasons. Land and rivers have great religious or emotional appeal to different groups. This can set in motion powerful political forces to secure control or re-take control of the area in question. The Crusades, for example, were fought to liberate territory from an opposing religion; today's fighting over mosques, temples, and churches falls into the same category.

Fourth, countries may be involved in territorial disputes for legal or historic reasons. These disputes continue until legal judgment is made about ownership of the land or sea in question, but in general countries do not go to war over them.

If a particular area or territory has strategic, economic, and/or ideological importance, the dispute is more serious than if it is simply a legal disagreement. In the Middle East, especially the Arab-Israeli conflict, the most profound and bitter conflicts are over territory that falls into one or more of the first three categories (see Figure 1).

Although most territorial disputes are bilateral, they may have regional implications. The Arab-Israeli disputes, especially over Palestinian rights and Jerusalem, are of interest to the entire Arab and Muslim world. Countries that might otherwise take little interest in Israel have been heavily involved, at least on the rhetorical level, in the Arab-Israeli confrontation. It is yet another issue that bridges the gap between the Persian Gulf and the Levant, combining with other factors to create the need for regional negotiations and regional solutions.

The unresolved territorial disputes between Israel and the Palestinians, Syria, and Lebanon are at the heart of the Arab-Israeli conflict. Without a resolution of the Israeli-Palestinian conflict over the control of the West Bank, Gaza, and Jerusalem, there will be no settlement; without such a settlement there will be no comprehensive Arab-Israeli peace. Though resolution of the Palestinian dispute is the precursor to further peace, the key to a wider agreement embracing the rest of the Arab world, especially the Arab Gulf, is almost certainly the question of the Golan Heights. Until Syria reaches a satisfactory agreement on the disposition of the Golan, it will not make peace with Israel and it is unlikely the key Gulf states, especially Saudi Arabia, will do so before Syria. Lebanon cannot negotiate a separate peace with Israel as long as Syria exercises its veto power over Beirut decision making. If Israel were to unilaterally withdraw from southern Lebanon, the United States or others might put pressure on Syria to withdraw its forces from Lebanon, although this is unlikely to be successful. Israel's withdrawal might, however, weaken Iran's role in

Figure 1
MIDDLE EAST TERRITORIAL DISPUTES

Types	Definition	Examples
Strategic	Control of disputed territory has significant impact on the military balance between adversaries.	Golan Heights West Bank Shatt-al-Arab South Lebanon Abu Musa
Economic	Control of disputed territory provides one party with significant economic advantage at the expense of the other.	Kuwait Iraq Tigris/Euphrates West Bank Abu Musa Offshore oil or gas disputes in Persian Gulf
Ideological/ Religious	Territorial dispute has significant political/cultural importance for one or more parties.	Jerusalem West Bank
Legal only	Territory subject to legal disputes over access and ownership but few strategic economic or ideological attributes.	Taba (Egypt–Israel: resolved by arbitration in 1986)

support of Hizbollah and could pave the way for closer Israeli-Lebanese relations short of a full diplomatic exchange.

Unfortunately, the remaining Israeli-Palestinian, Israeli-Syrian, and Israeli-Lebanese disputes each involve multiple economic and strategic considerations and will be difficult to resolve (see map). All three contested areas serve as a military buffer for Israel. In the case of the West Bank, resolution is further complicated by the strong religious claims to the land made by some Israelis. This is in marked contrast to territorial disputes Israel has settled with Egypt and Jordan in the last twenty years. Egypt and Israel relied on the principle of asymmetric reciprocity, mutual but uneven measures or limitations. For instance, both sides accepted limited force zones, in which troops and military equipment are restricted, but only one of the four zones, Zone D, is on the Israeli side of the border. Zones A, B, and C are all in Egyptian ter-

Map of Arab-Israeli Territorial Disputes

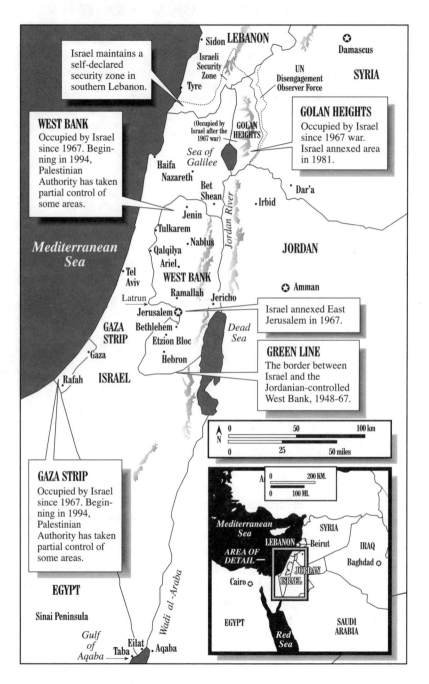

Israel maintains a self-declared security zone in southern Lebanon.

WEST BANK
Occupied by Israel since 1967. Beginning in 1994, Palestinian Authority has taken partial control of some areas.

GOLAN HEIGHTS
Occupied by Israel since 1967 war. Israel annexed area in 1981.

Israel annexed East Jerusalem in 1967.

GREEN LINE
The border between Israel and the Jordanian-controlled West Bank, 1948-67.

GAZA STRIP
Occupied by Israel since 1967. Beginning in 1994, Palestinian Authority has taken partial control of some areas.

ritory. But Egypt can point to the fact that it did not accept any security arrangements that were not also imposed upon Israel. Article IV of the peace treaty explains that, "In order to provide maximum security for both Parties on the basis of reciprocity, agreed security arrangements will be established including limited force zones in Egyptian and Israeli territory."[2] The 1994 Israeli-Jordanian treaty used novel methods of leasing land to overcome final differences on sovereignty and agricultural use; Jordanian sovereignty was acknowledged but the land was leased back to Israeli farmers.

ISRAEL-PALESTINIANS

The dispute over the West Bank involves all four categories of territorial dispute shown in Figure 1 and will therefore be one of the most difficult issues to resolve. In 1967, Israel captured the West Bank from Jordan and the Gaza Strip from Egypt. The pre-1967 borders of both territories posed great strategic risks for Israel. Today, these strategic risks are widely acknowledged in Israel, so even moderate Israelis have pushed for modification of the pre-1967 lines in order to enhance Israeli security under any final Israeli-Palestinian settlement.[3] Such adjustments are based on perceived security needs, ideological stands, existing road infrastructure and settlement patterns, and water supply concerns. Israel has long argued that the West Bank is a key strategic asset; the settler movement adds religious overtones with allusions to biblical Israel.

Gaza is less important to Israel. In the past, Israel made a strategic argument that control of Gaza was necessary to prevent Arab armies from driving up the coastline from the Sinai to Tel Aviv. Though there are a few thousand Israeli settlers in the Gaza Strip, some of whom live in settlements positioned to enhance the security of all of Israel, most Israelis, including right wingers, are not interested in retaining control over the overcrowded, poverty-stricken strip of land.

Starting in 1993, Israeli and Palestinian officials signed major interim agreements, including Oslo I and Oslo II, involving control of the West Bank and Gaza Strip. Israel is gradually turning over control of civilian powers and relinquishing its military presence in a patchwork of Arab cities and villages (see chapter 1). The process, which began in Jericho and much of Gaza in May 1994, was applied to the six largest West Bank urban centers in 1995, and extended to Hebron in January 1997. Permanent status talks, which are slated to decide the future of the Palestinian entity and its borders with Israel, opened in May 1996, but did not continue in the first year of the Netanyahu government. Agreements over the exact nature of borders on the West Bank and Gaza Strip are likely to involve Egypt and, especially, Jordan.

Water plays a central role in Israel's desire for control of the West Bank and adds an economic element to the issue. The West Bank mountain aquifer provides 177 billion gallons/year, of which Israel takes 80 percent.[4] The West Bank aquifer "provides a third of Israel's water consumption, 40 percent of its drinking water and 50 percent of its agricultural water."[5] Since 1967, Israel has prohibited the drilling of new Palestinian wells. Like all water distribution problems, the dispute over West Bank water involves both control of the land and who has legal rights to the water. Israel, for instance, might be willing to cede the land over most of the aquifer if water agreements guaranteed that Israel has the right to pump much of the aquifer's water.

ISRAEL-SYRIA

The Golan Heights dispute is primarily about strategic and economic issues. The relatively small but mountainous piece of real estate has great strategic value for both Israel and Syria. It is economically valuable for its agricultural land, including well-known wineries, and for the essential water supplied to the Sea of Galilee.

After World War I, France and England agreed to an international boundary between French-controlled Syria (and Lebanon) and British-controlled Palestine. The March 7, 1923, agreement set the international line that is still the focus of Israeli-Syrian talks. The original demarcation line took into account British concern for control of water sources and French interest in control of area roads.[6]

After the 1948 Arab-Israeli War, Israel and Syria did not fully resolve competing border claims. In postwar armistice negotiations, Israel pushed for a return to the international boundary, while Syrian representatives supported the ceasefire line that included some Syrian military gains west of the international boundary. While the two sides agreed that Syria withdraw from gains west of the international border and that a demilitarized zone (DMZ) would be established in the areas of Syrian withdrawal, they failed to determine sovereignty in the DMZ. The absence of an agreement on DMZ sovereignty left the door open for both sides to put forward different understandings of what had been agreed.

In May 1951, a serious confrontation led to de facto partition of the DMZ and new talks were held in 1952 and 1953 to divide the DMZ. By participating in such talks, Israel implicitly accepted that some part of the DMZ would go to Syria, even though the DMZ was west of the international border. These talks ended in 1953, again without coming to a final agreement. Border skirmishes continued until Israel captured the Golan in the 1967 war.

Israel has held the territory ever since. After reversing early Syrian thrusts, Israel made further gains in 1973. With the conclusion of the Israeli-Syrian Disengagement Agreement on May 31, 1974, Israel withdrew from territory gained in 1973. In 1981, Israel extended Israeli law to the Golan, a move many consider tantamount to annexation. In the peace negotiations that began in 1991, Syria has called for Israeli withdrawal to the June 4, 1967, lines, since this would include the return of territory Syria controlled west of the international boundary and bordering the Sea of Galilee, which is otherwise totally in Israeli territory. A final Israeli-Syrian border agreement must resolve the sovereignty of the pre-1967 DMZ in order to put Israeli-Syrian disagreements to rest.

Control of water sources is another critical issue to be negotiated. The Golan Heights provides 30 percent of Israel's drinking water.[7] The Jordan River is fed by four major sources in the north: the Dan River located completely within pre-1967 Israel (66-72 billion gallons/year), the Banias River on the Golan Heights (32-33 billion gallons/year), the Hasbani River in Lebanon about ten miles from the border with Israel (32-33 billion gallons/year), and run-off from precipitation and springs on the Golan Heights (28 billion gallons/year).[8] Israel's withdrawal from the Golan Heights and southern Lebanon would leave 55-60 percent of the northern sources of the Jordan River in the hands of other states. The Yarmuk River, which originates in Syria and runs along the Jordanian-Syrian border to Israel, provides an additional 26.4 billion gallons/year to the Jordan River just below Lake Tiberias. In 1974, Israeli Deputy Prime Minister Yigal Allon noted that Israeli control of the Golan is vital "in order to guarantee us a considerable portion of the water sources."[9] Though it can be questioned whether any Syrian government would deny these waters to Israel, since it would be a *casus belli*, Israel will likely insist on unilateral or international control of the water sources rather than return them to Syria.

Much of the discussion about the Golan is related to Israel's and Syria's strategic concerns. These are discussed in greater depth in subsequent chapters, but it is worth providing a brief review here. In the status quo, Damascus is only thirty-seven miles from the ceasefire line. The Israeli outpost on Mt. Hermon provides Israel with excellent eavesdropping and intelligence capabilities. If there were another war, Syria would be in a vulnerable position, since the loss of the Golan greatly reduced its defensive depth. Israel fears a similar loss of strategic depth if Syria again controls the mountainous plateau; this would increase Israeli vulnerability to a Syrian or Arab surprise attack. Israelis who live in the Hula Valley remember Syria shelling Israeli towns and fields and fear that tension in Israeli-Syrian relations could cause renewed shelling if Syria again possessed the Golan. As things currently stand, Israel's proximity to Damascus helps deter Syria, a benefit Israel would lose if it withdrew from the Golan.

ISRAEL-LEBANON

Israel has maintained a security zone in southern Lebanon since 1985, following the withdrawal of Israeli forces from most of Lebanon after the 1982 invasion. This has de facto moved the Israeli-Lebanon border a few miles north of the international line that has separated Israel and Lebanon since the 1948 Arab-Israeli War. The northern border of the security zone includes barbed wire fences, limited access, and observation posts. In many ways, the security zone is run by Israel and the Southern Lebanese Army as a separate entity from the rest of Lebanon.[10] All Israeli governments have declared that Israel has no territorial claims in Lebanon.[11]

Successful negotiations would likely lead to an Israeli withdrawal from the security zone and a restoration of the international border as the dividing line between Israel and Lebanon. Neither side rejects the existing international boundary. As mentioned above, water issues also are tied to Israeli control. Lebanese sources have made unsubstantiated claims that Israel takes water from the Litani River, a river entirely within Lebanon's borders that helps guarantee sufficient water supplies for all of Lebanon.

The Israeli zone has less strategic significance than the Golan Heights, where the control of territory has serious military implications for the security of both Israel and Syria. Losing the zone would make an equally wide strip of northern Israel vulnerable to rocket attacks and infiltration, but it would not create a strategic threat for the entire country. Similarly, the zone enables Israel to attack Lebanon from a more forward position but provides fewer strategic advantages than some other territories would provide; it does not, for example, add much to Israeli capabilities in large-scale conventional military engagements. However, Syrian military planners are concerned that Israel might use its presence in southern Lebanon to outflank the Syrian army and avoid a war on the Golan. Syria could do the same in reverse, i.e., it could outflank Israel in southern Lebanon to avoid war on the Golan; if the peace process breaks down and relations deteriorate, this would be an appealing option to Syria as long as Israel retains control of the Golan Heights.

ISRAELI-PALESTINIAN FINAL STATUS ISSUES

"Final status issues" refers to the negotiations, as detailed in the 1993 DOP, that must take place between Israel and the Palestinians before the two peoples can reach a lasting peace agreement. The central issues include the future of Jerusalem, the Palestinian diaspora and the right of return, the future of Israel's settlement activity, the configuration of final borders, and the status of the Palestinian Authority.

JERUSALEM

Any discussion about Jerusalem must begin with the competing definitions of the city; the definitions are indicative of the complexity of determining the future status of the city. Before 1948 and the creation of the state of Israel, the entire city was under British control. The 1947 United Nations partition plan called for the internationalization of the city, but during the 1948 war, Israel and Jordan each acquired control of part of the city. The dividing line between the two sides became a no-man's land, with Jordan controlling East Jerusalem and Israel holding West Jerusalem. The Old City, the ancient and most sacred part of Jerusalem, was held by Jordan but the boundary between Israel and Jordan ran along the Old City walls. In June 1967, Israel captured East Jerusalem and the West Bank from Jordan, and then in 1980 formally annexed East Jerusalem (as it had been defined by Jordanian authorities) and a larger area of adjacent land, together totaling almost twenty-eight square miles.[12] This new, larger, united Jerusalem under Israeli control is sometimes called Greater Jerusalem. Today, East Jerusalem includes the Old City, Arab East Jerusalem, and a ring of post-1967 Israeli Jewish neighborhoods.

43

Since 1967, successive Israeli governments have pledged that Jerusalem will never be divided again, as it was from 1948 to 1967. Israeli sovereignty claims clash with Palestinian calls for, at a minimum, the establishment of the Palestinian capital in East Jerusalem.[13] The city's status is further complicated by the rhetoric and claims of Jordan, Morocco, Saudi Arabia, Moslems in general, and a variety of Christian churches with a presence in the city. For all parties involved, most importantly Israelis and Palestinians, control of Jerusalem has become a central symbolic issue with tremendous political and religious significance.[14]

In addition to its symbolic and religious significance, Jerusalem is the center of Palestinian life in the West Bank.[15] East Jerusalem houses major hospitals, libraries, and educational institutions. Much of Palestinian commercial and financial life takes place in Jerusalem, and the city is the transport hub for the West Bank. With limited access to Jerusalem, as has been the case under prolonged Israeli closures, the West Bank is essentially divided in half, exacerbating problems already created by the geographic separation of Gaza and the West Bank. Israel is constantly on guard against Palestinian activities which Israel perceives as possibly setting a precedent in future negotiations for an official Palestinian presence in Jerusalem. Israel closely monitors Palestinian activities at the Orient House in East Jerusalem, activities that have aroused the ire of the Israeli right. Palestinian leaders would like to expand such activities and openly conduct governmental affairs from Jerusalem.[16]

Israel has maintained that a united Jerusalem shall forever remain as the Israeli capital under Israeli sovereignty.[17] In the minds of most Israelis, this leaves no room for an official Palestinian presence in Jerusalem even though Israelis rarely venture into most of Arab East Jerusalem. By 1995, 200,000 Israelis were living in East Jerusalem in new neighborhoods built in areas that Israel captured in 1967. Both Labor and Likud governments have presided over the continued expansion of Israeli neighborhoods in Israeli-annexed East Jerusalem. Israelis remember well the divided city that left the Old City of Jerusalem, including the holy Western Wall, out of reach from 1948 to 1967; the hazardous and sometimes deadly trip to Mt. Scopus—an island of land in East Jerusalem that was legally part of Israel from 1948; and the snipers along the Israeli-Jordanian border that cut through the city. Consequently, Israel argues that a united city is best for all parties and has assured Muslims and Christians access to holy sites since Jerusalem has been under Israeli control.

In view of the extreme complexity and large number of claimants, Jerusalem's future status will require delicate and far-reaching compromises. It remains to be seen whether Israelis, Palestinians, and others have enough foresight and imagination to agree upon a solution that simultaneously satisfies Israel's calls for an undivided capital city and Palestinian demands that the capital of Palestine be established in East Jerusalem. The crisis in early 1997 caused by the Har Homa (Jebel Abu Ghneim) construction suggests that Jerusalem is indeed a lightning rod for Palestinian and Israeli passions.

There is no shortage of proposals for sharing Jerusalem. In their groundbreaking collaborative attempt to find areas of Israeli-Palestinian agreement, Israeli Mark A. Heller and Palestinian Sari Nusseibeh note the possibility that rather than embodying inherent areas of disagreement, "Jerusalem is primarily a symbolic lodestone, on which all the emotions and sentiments of the conflict are focused."[18] They further state that very few people, Arab or Israeli, would like to see the city redivided by a physical wall. The long-term demographic and security implications of not compromising on Jerusalem's status may also bolster the exploration of other options. Many Israelis, already sensitive to Israel's demographic balance, are unlikely to look favorably upon absorbing the 150,000-200,000 Arab residents of East Jerusalem. Furthermore, Jerusalem could help to create stability in the Palestinian entity, which would function better with access to Jerusalem and the institutions and resources of Jerusalem's Arab community.

A number of creative proposals could be combined to develop a solution.[19] The Palestinian capital could formally be based in an outlying Jerusalem suburb such as Abu Dis or Al 'Ayzariyah; the Arabic name for Jerusalem, al-Quds, could be used in a creative fashion to seemingly rename part of Jerusalem (or suburban Jerusalem) to the benefit of the Palestinians. There could be a separate municipal council for Israel's Jerusalem and Palestine's Jerusalem, with neighborhoods divided by imaginary lines. A metropolitan municipality, elected by all the residents of Jerusalem, could sit on top of the two municipal councils. Intentional obfuscation may play a central role as would-be compromisers talk about a functional division of authority or internal autonomy. Sovereignty could be functional, single, split, joint, or shared.[20] Power and civic responsibilities could be divided among a variety of institutions and governmental bodies. In any case, the solution likely would require a "judicious combination of integration and separation."[21]

Secret talks held by Yossi Beilin, at the time an Israeli minister in the Labor government, and Mahmoud Abbas, a leading Palestinian negotiator, reached tentative agreements on such difficult issues as the future status of Jerusalem. Their agreement included many of these potential methods of compromise. In a presentation to the Washington Institute for Near East Policy in December 1996, Beilin summarized his views on Jerusalem:

> Palestinians would recognize West Jerusalem as sovereign Israeli territory and Israel's capital; this would bring world recognition of West Jerusalem as Israel's capital. For Palestinians, the geographic area of "al-Quds" is in fact much larger than the municipal boundaries of Israeli Jerusalem. Therefore, Israel would recognize a Palestinian capital in "al-Quds," which would actually be in an area like Abu Dis, currently a Jerusalem suburb. East Jerusalem would be designated by both parties as disputed territory with the *status quo* remaining in place for the indefinite future; Israel would still operate there as *de facto* sovereign but not recognized as such. The Palestinians would have extra-territorial status over the Haram al-Sharif (the Temple Mount), which essentially mirrors the current situation, in which the Islamic authorities control the site. The city of Jerusalem itself would be divided into boroughs, with each borough (e.g., Arab, ultra-orthodox Jewish Israeli, secular Israeli) enjoying a significant autonomy under a "roof municipality." Arab residents within Israeli borders could be citizens of the Palestinian state.[22]

THE PALESTINIAN DIASPORA AND THE RIGHT OF RETURN

Since 1948, the right of Palestinian refugees to return to their former homes in Israel has been a highly charged issue for both sides. While Palestinians have asserted an unconditional right to return, Israelis have maintained just as forcefully that such talk is wasted.

According to the U.N. Relief and Works Agency, there were about 2.7 million Palestinian refugees in Gaza, Jordan, Lebanon, Syria, and the West Bank in 1993. This includes refugees from the 1948 war and displaced persons (DPs) from the 1967 war. Some Israeli sources have suggested that the true total is closer to 2.3 million refugees.[23] The situation varies by country. In Jordan, approximately 700,000 Palestinian refugees (and DPs) have become Jordanian citizens and do not live in refugee camps. Lebanon, in contrast, has over 320,000 refugees who live in poor conditions and would greatly benefit from a resolution of the problem.

Palestinians stress that U.N. General Assembly (UNGA) resolution 194 calls for compensation or return for the 1948 Palestinian refugees. They would like to see "some symbolic recognition by Israel of the hurt that was done to the Palestinians made refugees in 1948."[24] They believe their right to return should be recognized in principle, and some refugees should be allowed to return to what is now Israel, even if it is a relatively small number. All others should receive financial compensation. In the Palestinian view, all Palestinians will be able to carry a Palestinian passport and return to a Palestinian state in the West Bank and Gaza, subject to the absorption limits of that state.

Israel views the Palestinian talk about the right of return as a security threat. Palestinian land and homes have now been used by Israelis for close to fifty years and the prospect of millions of Palestinians flooding into Israel is frightening in terms of the identity of the state and its economic well-being. Since the early 1950s, Israel has avoided any position on Palestinian refugees that admits culpability or responsibility for their plight. Many Israelis feel that a symbolically even exchange took place in the late 1940s when hundreds of thousands of Jews in Arab lands were forced to depart and were resettled in Israel. In contrast, Arab countries deliberately chose not to resettle the Palestinian refugees, and the Palestinians have paid the price. On a unilateral basis, Israel has conducted a small humanitarian program of family reunification. From June 1967 to June 1994, 22,179 of 70,000 Palestinian applications were approved, allowing Palestinians to return to their family and homes in the West Bank and Gaza.[25]

From the Israeli perspective, an equitable settlement must involve a total Palestinian renunciation of the right of return, in part so that irredentism is put to rest. Even if the family reunification program continues, no additional quota should be set for the symbolic return of Palestinians to Israel. Although Israel agrees that Palestinians should be able to move to the Palestinian entity, it is concerned about what effect a large influx of refugees would have on the stability of the Palestinian Authority. If the end result of the negotiations is Palestinian autonomy, Israel would regard even Palestinian immigration to the West Bank and Gaza as problematic. The June 1996 policy guidelines of the Netanyahu government rule out the Palestinian right of return to "any part of the Land of Israel west of the Jordan River."[26] Israel is willing to consider financial compensation if it is one of many contributors, but only in tandem with final renunciation of the right of return. At that time, the losses of Jews from Arab land should also be tallied.

A resolution of the refugee crisis will likely include variations of many of these items. As a general rule, financial compensation would be more prevalent than geographic relocation. Symbolic gestures, such as resettlement of a few thousand refugees inside pre-1967 Israel, should be considered if a substantial concession is unlikely. A broader, agreed-upon document could be very important; limited changes on the ground, such as the token return of a few refugees, could be coupled with statements that have few practical implications but carry significant emotional and psychological value, such as acceptance of partial responsibility by Israel or recognition by Palestinians that a compromise deal will be the final chapter in the Palestinian refugee problem. Lastly, a *modus vivendi* with Arab states might be found that allowed the absorption of many Palestinians who nevertheless retained some defined rights in the new Palestinian entity. In their secret talks, Beilin and Abbas agreed that no refugees would return to Israel, but there would be limits on immigration to the putative Palestinian state.[27]

ISRAELI SETTLEMENT ACTIVITY

Israeli governments, under both Likud and Labor leadership, have established a significant Israeli presence in the occupied territories through the building of settlements, outposts that remain one of the most daunting obstacles to Israeli-Palestinian peace. In 1993, Israel had 150 West Bank settlements, not including East Jerusalem, and another 16 in the Gaza Strip. In 1995, 147,000 Israelis lived in the West Bank and Gaza, amidst nearly two million Palestinians, again not including East Jerusalem.[28]

Over the years, Israel has justified the settlements in many ways. Some were built as security outposts to deter an Arab attack through Jordan. Israel wanted to establish a strong presence on strategic land in the Jordan Valley and on the hills of the West Bank. Massive building has solidified Israeli control of metropolitan Jerusalem, Ariel, and the Etzion bloc around Kfar Etzion (see map on p. 38). Some settlements were established to reclaim biblical Israel, such as the few hundred Israelis ensconced in the middle of Hebron. But most importantly, some Israelis—including former prime ministers Menachem Begin and Yitzhak Shamir—saw settlements as the best weapon in their battle to block a future withdrawal from the occupied territories. The larger the Israeli presence, the less land would have to be conceded. By intermingling the settlements with major Palestinian population centers, settlers made the establishment of a viable, territorially sound Palestinian entity almost impossible without dismantling the settlements. The settlements have turned into just the sort of obstacles to peace, albeit an imposed, dangerous peace in the eyes of settlers, that their founders intended. Thousands of settlers have vowed not to abandon their homes and settlements even if the government signs a paper agreement.

Many Israelis who live in settlements are not there for political or religious reasons. Financial incentives enticed many Israelis into bedroom communities of Tel Aviv and Jerusalem that happen to be in the West Bank. If financial compensation were offered to current settlers, at least one-third would probably accept a buy-out and move back to Israel.

Palestinians consider the settlements perhaps the most damaging effects of the oppressive Israeli occupation. The settlers have usurped land and resources; on average, they use far more water than Palestinians; and they regularly harass and attack Palestinians. Palestinians recognize that settler security has become an excuse for Israeli military activities and continued repression. Palestinians see no room for compromise: the settlements are illegal and cannot remain under Israeli control or sovereignty. To Palestinians, stolen Palestinian lands must be returned to their rightful owners.

Without attempting to present the details of a compromise solution, certain guidelines, not all of them compatible, might help create an agreement on dealing with Israeli settlements. Settlements and borders are intricately linked. The definition of the borders will help determine the status of each settlement; just as the location of the settlements will influence the delineation of the borders. In that sense, Israel's settlement policies of the last thirty years have achieved their desired objective. In terms of a deal, Israel might agree to dismantle isolated settlements, such as Netzarim in the Gaza Strip, while annexing large settlement blocs near Ariel, Kfar Etzion, and Maale Adumim (a Jerusalem suburb). In general, settlers could be offered financial compensation, an especially appealing option to the tens of thousands who came to the West Bank because of the excellent mortgages and other financial incentives. This might not lead to the closing of any one settlement, but it would lessen the severity of the overall problem.

Another issue is whether Israeli settlers could (or would want to) remain in settlements that are not contiguous to a post-treaty

Israel (pre-1967 Israel plus any annexed land). The options for such settlements are that they remain as isolated, extraterritorial Israeli islands; that they exist under Palestinian law; or that they have a status somewhere between these two poles, such as under a millet system with communal autonomy.[29] Beilin and Abbas agreed that most settlers live in territory that would be annexed to Israel. Other settlers would be offered compensation to move or they could live in the Palestinian state under special security arrangements.[30]

FINAL BORDERS

The Palestinian Authority's border objectives are well-known: the pre-1967 borders between Israel and Gaza and Israel and the West Bank. This would give the Palestinians total control of Gaza, the West Bank, and East Jerusalem, and this area would form the new Palestinian state. Minor border adjustments that benefit Israel may be possible, but these must be limited in scope and the Palestinians must be compensated with additional territory or some other advantage such as a firm transportation link between the West Bank and Gaza. In accepting only the West Bank and Gaza, many Palestinians believe they have already made a major compromise, since they feel that they are actually entitled to all of Palestine.

The Israeli viewpoint depends upon the government in power. Likud officials have called for Palestinian autonomy, in which case defining the borders is less important. If autonomy means that Israeli settlements remain in place and Israel retains control of the international borders, the lines under negotiation would only define the areas of Palestinian civilian control. The Palestinian areas would probably be spread throughout the West Bank and Gaza, with limited connections among the islands of Palestinian civilian control.[31] The lines drawn in Oslo II might represent such a scenario. If, however, Israel comes to accept a more concrete entity or Palestinian state, the borders would be more significant because they would divide two sovereign entities, an Israeli one and a Palestinian one. Former Prime Minister Rabin rejected the idea that Israel would go back to the pre-1967 boundaries. As discussed in chapter 3, he assumed Israel would annex East Jerusalem and the Etzion bloc, and Israel's security border would remain in the Jordan Valley. Even this leaves a larger area under Palestinian control than Likud has supported.

Countless plans and maps suggest border alternatives. They come almost exclusively from the Israeli side, since the Palestinian position relies on the well-known 1967 lines. From the Allon plan to the Sharon plan, Israeli leaders and analysts have suggested new ways of slicing up the West Bank.[32] Yigal Allon, a Labor party leader and Israel's minister of foreign affairs in the mid-1970s, called for "some minor tactical border alterations along the western section" of the green line (the pre-1967 Israel-West Bank boundary) and "absolute Israeli control" of the Jordan Valley except for a Palestinian corridor to Jordan near Jericho.[33] Ariel Sharon, a prominent hawk and minister in the Netanyahu government, put forward a proposal in 1981 that would have left most of the West Bank, including Bethlehem, Hebron, Jericho, and Ramallah, under Israeli control.

After considering three different scenarios, Joseph Alpher, an Israeli analyst, suggested in 1994 that Israel annex about 11 percent of East Jerusalem, Gaza, and the West Bank. For Israeli annexation, Alpher's "Moderate Territorial Compromise" plan included a three- to five-mile strip of land along the western section of the green line, the Latrun salient, Givat Zeev (north of Jerusalem), the Etzion bloc, Maale Adumim, and a small area south of Bet Shean (just south of the Sea of Galilee). Compared to pre-1967 Israel, the annexation would enhance Israel's security by thickening Israel's narrow, pre-1967 center or "waist" (by adding the strip along the green line), better protecting the Tel Aviv-Jerusalem highway (Latrun), and solidifying Israeli control of Jerusalem (Givat Zeev, Etzion, Maale Adumin). The remaining area, about 89 percent, would be turned over to the Palestinian entity. His plan includes Israeli early warning stations in the West Bank, two Israeli rapid intervention forces, and the removal of Israeli settlements in and around Hebron.[34] Alpher favored this plan over both total Israeli withdrawal and the establishment of a "special status region," an idea similar to many Likud proposals.

A final resolution would depend on the skill of the negotiators and the manner in which various areas or towns are traded between the two sides. In their secret talks, Beilin and Abbas developed an exchange of territories that would give Palestinians extra territory along the Gaza strip and give Israel some land in the West Bank in order to widen Israel's narrow waist.[35] Furthermore, much of the question of borders turns on yet another issue, the status and power of the Palestinian Authority.

THE FUTURE STATUS OF THE PALESTINIAN AUTHORITY

Though not explicitly mentioned in article five of the Declaration of Principles, the article that covers final status issues, Israeli and Palestinian negotiators ultimately must determine whether the Palestinian Authority serves as the head of an autonomous area (or an autonomous people), the government of an independent state of Palestine, or the junior partner in a confederation with Jordan.

For several months following the May 1996 election , the Netanyahu government and the Israeli right categorically rejected the possibility of a Palestinian state in the West Bank and Gaza. At best, Palestinians could hope for autonomy and possible links to the Jordanian regime, with Israeli participation. A Palestinian state would be a threat to Israel's existence that would serve as a springboard for future political and military attacks on Israel. On the Israeli left, some have come to accept the idea of a Palestinian state, and the Labor party deleted from its 1996 election platform an objection to Palestinian statehood. Though many Israelis remain strongly opposed to Palestinian sovereignty and independence on any land west of the Jordan River, even the Netanyahu government has moderated its views.[36]

From the Palestinian perspective, there will not be a solution to the Arab-Israeli conflict unless there is an independent Palestinian state in the West Bank and Gaza. Anything short of statehood is too great a denial of the Palestinian right to self-determination. Few Palestinians believe that autonomy or confederation can replace statehood as an answer to Palestinian national aspirations, though confederation could be considered at some point following statehood. Beilin and Abbas agreed upon a demilitarized Palestinian state with nearly all the attributes of sovereignty.[37]

While statehood seems to be an up or down proposition, the deliberate introduction of some ambiguity into the process might help bridge the gap and give some hope for a negotiated solution. First, the implementation of any plan may be gradual rather than completed overnight, allowing both sides slowly to get used to the new arrangement and win over domestic opponents. Second, linguistic terms may be employed in contrast with the reality on the ground in an effort to build support. In an earlier example, Yasser Arafat was elected "raes" of the Palestinian Authority in January 1996. Does this mean he is the chairman or the president of the Palestinian Authority? It depends whether one asks an Israeli or a Palestinian official. Further *intentional* linguistic ambiguity could help make future arrangements palatable to both parties. Third, the negotiators may avoid providing a direct answer on the question of statehood but instead deal with functional issues such as border control, Palestinian military and police units, and foreign relations. There would be no official decision on statehood (or not); rather, each individual would be free to assess the powers and responsibilities granted to the Palestinians and thereby make his or her own judgment. In a related sense, there may be room for mixed control that changes over time. All these techniques help create room for each side to appease its constituents while still making concessions and signing peace agreements.

Taken together, these unresolved Arab-Israeli issues provide a full plate for even the most skilled negotiators. Any one territorial or permanent status issue could obstruct the process and cause talks to break down. Because many of these issues have great symbolic, ideological, or religious symbolism for one or both sides, even finding practical compromises may not be enough.

CHAPTER THREE

ISRAEL, THE PALESTINIANS, AND THE PEACE PROCESS: INTERNAL DEBATES

The path from Madrid, via Oslo, to the Hebron agreement has been full of both euphoria and heartbreak for Israelis and Palestinians. Agreements, withdrawal, and hope have been matched by assassination, violence, and bitterness. Israel and the Palestinian Authority have yet to break the cycle of violence that has plagued their relations for so long. Opponents of the peace process are deeply entrenched in both the Israeli and the Palestinian community. While the important political strides should be acknowledged, understanding the perspective of the critics is central to assessing the viablity of the peace process in the coming years.

ISRAEL

To appreciate the difficulties in winning Israeli support for a negotiated peace settlement, it is necessary to understand the reasons and the thinking behind the schism in the Israeli body politique and Benjamin Netanyahu's narrow victory in the May 29, 1996, elections. While there remains no workable alternative to a negotiated, compromise solution to the Arab-Israeli conflict based in large part on principles established by the Labor party from 1992 to 1996, events in 1995-97 highlight the advantages and drawbacks for both major Israeli perspectives on the peace process. The death of Yitzhak Rabin and the brief rule of Shimon Peres demonstrated the shortcomings of unqualified support for the peace process; the first year of the Netanyahu administration brought into focus the potential problems with dramatically altering Israel's approach to Syria and the Palestinians.

The assassination of Israeli Prime Minister Yitzhak Rabin on November 4, 1995, served as a reminder of both the deep divisions in Israeli society over the Arab-Israeli peace process and the willingness of a militant minority to keep the West Bank and Golan Heights under Israeli control at any cost. The trauma of Rabin's death was followed by the resumption on February 25, 1996, of suicide bombings against Israelis. These actions created a second gaping wound in the fabric of Israeli society. Four bombings in just over a week left at least sixty dead and hundreds wounded, many critically. When the fourth bomber exploded himself among crowds of people in Dizengoff Center in Tel Aviv on March 4, the sense of anger, sadness, and helplessness reached new heights. The terrorists touched deep feelings of vulnerability among Israelis. Questions about the peace process were brought into sharp focus, presenting a stark counterpoint to hopeful visions of compromise and accommodation.

The Rabin assassination and the suicide bombings highlighted the ideological and strategic divisions in Israeli society. Rabin's death left the Labor-led government vulnerable to criticism on security grounds. Rabin's long and distinguished military career could no longer shield the Labor government from some of the security and strategic arguments of the opposition. Soon thereafter, Peres, as the the new prime minister, began a concerted effort to come to an agreement with Syria that would have involved a significant, if not total, Israeli withdrawal from the Golan Heights conditioned by elaborate security arrangements and a bilateral peace treaty. For many Israelis, this raised a central security concern—the loss of strategic depth on the Syrian front; it led a faction of the Labor Party, the Third Way, to break away, sapping Labor's strength at election time. Moreover, when Israel and Syria were unable to achieve an agreement, Peres was left having raised the issue with nothing substantive to show for it. Concern over the Israeli-Syrian negotiations and for their personal safety led many Israelis to believe that the cost of concessions was simply too high and a less conciliatory Israeli policy was appropriate even if it meant a longer occupation. Netanyahu exploited these concerns and pulled out a narrow victory of just under 1 percent of the vote.

As Israel's elected leader, Netanyahu is confronted with the same political and military problems but from the perspective of the Likud party and other Israelis who denounced Labor's rapprochement with the PLO and negotiations with Syria. Although they criticized Rabin's and Peres's approach, halting or significantly changing the direction of the process also has serious, and potentially harmful, implications. Totally rejecting Arafat and the Palestinian Authority could lead to Arafat's fall, chaos in the territories, and an even more hostile Palestinian leadership. Yet Likud has long been concerned that concessions to Arafat will only lead to greater and greater demands, a significant problem since Likud had envisioned at most limited autonomy for the Palestinians. Although Labor had been, according to Likud, too accommodating to Syria, Likud does not want to end negotiations with Syria for fear that it could lead to a military confrontation, either through Syrian proxies in Lebanon or, eventually, between Israeli and Syrian forces directly. Finally, even Likud economists concede that the economic boom would not have been of the same magnitude without the peace process.

An end to the peace process could bring Israelis unwelcome economic news from its trading partners in Europe or Asia, which would undermine Netanyahu's top priority of economic reform. Thus on Palestinian, Syrian, and economic issues, the Netanyahu government seemingly is caught between its ideological rhetoric and the practical implications of such moves. Though the Hebron agreement marked a new phase in Netanyahu's rule, it remains to be seen whether he is prepared to further compromise Likud ideology and risk the collapse of his coalition.

ISRAEL UNDER RABIN AND PERES

After their victory in the 1992 elections, Prime Minister Rabin and his government pursued peace agreements on all fronts. Dramatic secret talks in Oslo, Norway, led to an Israeli-Palestinian rapprochement in the form of the Declaration of Principles (DOP or Oslo I agreement) in September 1993; the Cairo agreement implementing the DOP and initial Israeli withdrawal from Gaza and Jericho in May 1994; and the Oslo II agreement in September 1995. After years of secret meetings, Israel and Jordan signed a peace treaty in October 1994; King Hussein and Prime Minister Rabin embraced each other warmly. However, these achievements came with a stiff price for Israelis in general and the Rabin government in particular. A rash of Palestinian suicide bombings in 1994-96 rapidly turned the high expectations of the 1993 Israeli-Palestinian White House ceremony into dashed hopes; the bombings also emboldened Israelis opposed to the deal with the Palestinians. The nature of the attacks and the high casualties greatly overshadowed the overall drop in the number of terrorist attacks against Israelis in the aftermath of Oslo I. Ironically, one of these Palestinian bombings saved Rabin from an earlier assassination attempt in January 1995. Rabin's confessed assassin, Yigal Amir, planned to make his first attempt on Rabin's life at an event which Rabin could not attend at the last minute due to the bombing at Beit Lid (in Israel) that killed approximately twenty Israeli soldiers.

57

The deadly bombings by Hamas and others had a great impact on the Israeli psyche. The issue of personal security came to dominate criticism of the Israeli-Palestinian agreements, and Rabin himself formulated Israel's negotiating position based on the need to strengthen Israelis' security, both in actuality and in the perceptions of the voting public.

This relentless concern with personal security in relation to Palestinian attacks contributed to the official ignorance of the threats from Israeli Jewish extremists. In the days after Rabin's death, it became clear that the Shin Bet and other Israeli security forces had never adjusted to the possibility of violence against the prime minister from the Jewish opposition. Amir waited for Rabin unmolested, a feat no Arab could have hoped to accomplish within sight of Israeli security.

Yet veteran observers of Israeli society had known for many years that violence against the Palestinians was a regular feature of extremist behavior. It should come as no surprise that Amir was known as especially brutal and unjust in his treatment of Palestinians during his army service or that an underground biography of Baruch Goldstein, the mass murderer who killed at least twenty-nine Palestinians in Hebron in February 1994, was found in his possession. The unpleasant truth is that, for years, Israel has treated right-wing militants with kid gloves as long as their violence was directed against Arabs. Even after the Hebron massacre, the government's crackdown on the radical right was conducted in a half-hearted manner; Jewish extremists supposedly wanted by the government mocked the official policy by repeatedly scheduling clandestine rendezvous with electronic and print media in Israel. The few Jewish settlers convicted of killing Palestinians in the West Bank were given only a few months in jail, if any. For a militant minority, violence was one tool in their battle to preserve Israeli control of the West Bank and block Palestinian aspirations for statehood.[1]

Thus when the far right came to think that Rabin was as threatening as the Palestinians, he became eligible for similar treatment. The violence that Jewish extremists had directed at Palestinians could now be turned against a Jewish leader. Amir and his alleged co-conspirators twisted Jewish law to justify the killing on the grounds that Rabin was a traitor who was going to relinquish Judea and Samaria (the biblical names used by many Israelis for the West Bank) and set the stage for Arab armies to destroy the rest of the Jewish state.

After Rabin's death, Peres's first four months went smoothly and his popularity remained high until the rash of bombings in

58

February and March 1996. Implementation of the Oslo II agreement had proceeded as planned and Palestinian elections in January 1996 solidified Arafat's standing. But the unprecedented pace and human toll of the bombings on February 25, March 3, and March 4, left Peres on the defensive and dashed the hopes of many peace process supporters. The long-term trends that continue to favor the general Labor approach understandably provided little short-term comfort to a grieving and angry Israeli populace.

Extremist violence by both Arabs and Israeli Jews demonstrates the depths of the feelings on both sides and the extent to which opponents are willing to go in order to block the peace process and prevent their own marginalization. It is ironic that the virulent opposition to the peace process coincided with an unprecedented boom in the Israeli economy.

THE ISRAELI ECONOMY

In 1994, Israel had the highest annual economic growth rate (6.5 percent) of any industrialized country, according to the International Monetary Fund.[2] Such positive economic developments as large-scale foreign investment, entry by previously wary multinational companies into the Israeli market, and booming trade with South and East Asia can be attributed to the peace process and the image of growing political stability, aided by a large influx of highly educated Russian immigrants and changes in the international arena.[3] Failure to continue peace negotiations could jeopardize these economic gains, even if Netanyahu hopes to provide a new economic push through substantial economic reform. Foreign investors have made clear that they closely monitor the peace process.[4]

Israel's foreign trade has increased tremendously in the last few years, and trade with East and South Asia has been a significant component. From 1990 to 1994, total Israeli imports and exports increased from $28.8 billion to $41.7 billion, an increase of 45 percent.[5] During the same period, trade with Asia rose from $3.0 billion to $5.3 billion, an increase of 78 percent. Japan is now a major trading partner, with $1 billion in Israeli exports in 1994; only the United States and the European Union import more. Israel's exports to Asia include precious stones and metals, machinery and electrical equipment, and chemical products; these exports reach many countries, including India, China, Pakistan, Indonesia, and South Korea.[6] Israeli business leaders are well aware of the role that peace has played in expanding Israel's trade; as one trade expert explains, "By signing peace treaties with the Palestinians and with Jordan, we have been allowed entrance into China. The real peace dividend for Israel is that the barriers are now down in the fastest-growing markets in the world, which are in the Far East, not the Middle East."[7]

In 1993, the European Community received 30 percent of Israel's exports and provided 49 percent of its imports.[8] Because Israeli policymakers believed that the 1975 trade agreement between Israel and the European Community did not protect Israel's economic interests in post-1992 Europe, a new agreement was signed in 1995 after several years of negotiations.[9] For Israel, the new agreement helps ensure continued prosperous economic relations with Europe.[10] Israel also has a special trade agreement with the United States. To many Israelis, modern consumerism and integration into the world economy symbolize the attainment of a measure of normalcy and international acceptance for a country long treated as a pariah state. In addition, Israeli defense expenditures have fallen from 34 percent of gross domestic product in 1975 to 14 percent in 1990.[11]

Between 1991 and 1995, total foreign investment increased sixfold[12] (see Figures 2 and 3). Big name companies such as AT&T, Motorola, Nestle, Volvo, Volkswagen, and Pepsico have all opened or expanded ties to Israel,[13] and Intel is planning to build a $1.6 billion semiconductor facility. Israel's generous and costly incentives help woo multinationals.

Until 1994, the six Arab countries that make up the Gulf Cooperation Council (Bahrain, Kuwait, Oman, Qatar, Saudi Arabia, and the United Arab Emirates) blacklisted foreign companies that trade with Israel. The Federation of Israeli Chambers of Commerce estimates that at the height of the Arab boycott, the boycott reduced Israel's annual exports and foreign investment by 10 percent each.[14]

Despite its growing economic power and the boom years of the early and mid-1990s, Israel faces significant economic challenges, including rising inflation, high interest rates, a large trade deficit, and a government budget deficit.[15] Upon taking office, Prime Minister Netanyahu pledged to push for economic liberalization and privatization. In Netanyahu's first month in office, the Israeli cabinet approved approximately $1.5 billion in fee hikes and cuts in government programs and subsidies.[16] Privatization may not be sufficient to ensure economic progress in areas such as public transport where public ownership is coupled with monopoly status. Internally, economic reform will pit the Netanyahu gov-

Figure 2
BUSINESS INVESTMENT IN ISRAEL (FOREIGN)
(billions of dollars)

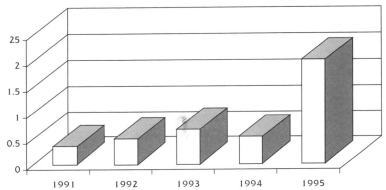

Source: Manufacturers Association of Israel in the *Washington Post*, June 25, 1996.

Figure 3
STOCK MARKET INVESTMENT IN ISRAEL (FOREIGN)
(billions of dollars)

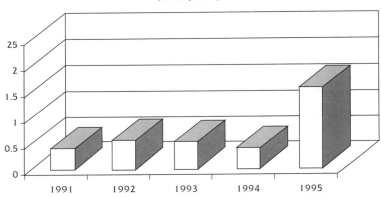

Source: Manufacturers Association of Israel in the *Washington Post*, June 25, 1996.

ernment against Israel's powerful trade unions. In addition, Israel needs to attract significant levels of additional foreign capital.[17] The first few months of Likud rule saw a pronounced drop in the Israeli stock market. Much of the Likud fiscal program will depend upon how foreign investors perceive Netanyahu's peace program and the reaction of the Arab parties. By mid-1997, Israel was in the midst of an economic slowdown, including rising inflation and unemployment and an annual GDP growth rate of only 2 percent (based on the first half of 1997).[18]

61

THE IDEOLOGICAL DIVIDE

The opposition of Israel's far right to the peace process and improved relations with the Arabs is driven in large measure by ideology. For many opponents of the Arab-Israeli agreements, religious influences provide an absolutist answer and justify complete rejection of calls for compromise, territorial exchanges, and new regional relations.

Often based on religious considerations, Israelis on the far right look at the world differently and emphasize their own agenda for the state of Israel. While the Labor-led government sought to fully integrate Israel into the world community and the Arab world, some opponents denounced these attempts, based on alleged Arab insincerity and duplicity and on internal callings of Judaism and their understanding of the religious process of redemption. Furthermore, no objective, let alone objectives espoused by the Peres government, is cause for relinquishing parts of the Land of Israel. The sacred territory is linked to the Jewish people through history and religion, a bond that has been developed and strengthened since 1967. A review of key events over the last thirty years reveals how the attachment to the occupied territories has grown stronger as Israeli settlers and far-rightists realized that they would have to make a last stand to stop the misguided policies of Israel's mainstream politicians. The strategic arguments mentioned below only serve to bolster the ideological opposition to compromise.

In suggesting that the far right is heavily influenced by ideological arguments, we do not mean to exclude the mainstream Israeli right from supporting many of these same beliefs. In fact, a large number of Israelis share many of these ideas, as well as strategic concerns. Moreover, there is no easy dividing line between the mainstream and the far right (except perhaps for extremely violent elements). But there clearly is broad disagreement over methodology, and most right-of-center Israelis reject militancy on these issues. More importantly, much of the mainstream right has come to recognize the irreversibility of the Oslo process to date.[19] The mainstream right recognizes existing political realities and eschews the absolutism of the fringe.

The Debate about "Normalcy." Not all Israelis want Israel to be considered a "normal" country, i.e., integrated into the regional and international communities. Even those who hold this aspiration recognize that it may be difficult to achieve. Nationalist elements take what they see as a more pragmatic position in arguing that Israel is fated to be alone (and therefore abnormal) on the international stage. Ultra-nationalists not only accept Israel's isolation, but celebrate it as proof of Israel's providential chosenness, making Israel's political fate a powerful religious tool.[20] As Israel's economy has taken off and international economic and diplomatic integration have proceeded in the mid-1990s, the very quest for normalcy that is driving many Israelis to support the peace process is at odds both with the predictions of nationalists who doubt the possibility of Israeli acceptance and with religious views that value Israeli isolation.

More extreme pessimism about the peace process is derived from long-held beliefs that the non-Jewish world remains inherently hostile to Jews and the state of Israel. This view holds that not even the United States can be trusted. The Jews of Israel must rely on themselves for survival and this means rejecting any agreement with Arabs that compromises security in exchange for transient agreements and empty promises of peace. Although this outlook virtually assures continued violence, Israel's physical survival will continue as long as Israel has strong military forces and retains control over the Golan, Judea, and Samaria. Bombings and other terrorist attacks may continue, but these acts will only strengthen Israel's determination not to compromise on the key territorial issues. If this approach involves a political confrontation with the United States and the end of American economic aid, it is the price Israel must pay to remain a secure, viable state.

This worldview derives from a long history of persecution and assaults by the outside world on Jews, of which the Holocaust was the most recent. The Muslim world is not truly accepting of a Jewish state. Given the opportunity, the Arabs, including so-called moderates in Jordan and Egypt, would indeed push the Jews into the sea. What has stopped them so far is superior Israeli military power. The Arabs and other Muslims have not forgotten—nor will they forget—the humiliations imposed on them by the colonial powers, the United States, and Israel. Sooner or later another leader like the late Egyptian President Gamal Abdel Nasser or Saddam Hussein will emerge quite prepared to carry the Arab/Muslim banner against the foreigners, the outsiders, and the interlopers. To believe, as Shimon Peres does, that the Middle East can evolve into a West European model of cooperative security is at best naive and at worst highly dangerous nonsense.

While these views are often expressed by Israeli pessimists, Israeli politicians who may believe them are usually more circumspect since they know full well the international costs of pursuing such hardline views. Instead they make the argument that the West, including Israel, is threatened by Muslim extremism and that Israel and the West must stand together to fight the radicals. This is the essence of the argument advanced by Prime Minister Netanyahu in his 1995 book, *Fighting Terrorism*.[21] Netanyahu, who knows that the United States is the key to Israel's survival, wants the two countries to be close to reduce the likelihood that the United States will abandon Israel in time of crisis.

Rabin explicitly rejected the anti-normalization currents in Israel in his inaugural address in 1992, when he told the Knesset:

> It is our duty, both to ourselves and to our children, to see the new world as it is today, to examine the risks and explore the chances, and to do everything so that the State of Israel becomes part of the changing world. We are no longer an isolated nation, and it is no longer true that the entire world is against us. We must rid ourselves of the feeling of isolation that has afflicted us for almost 50 years.[22]

In subsequent years, the Rabin government established diplomatic ties or semi-official relations with many countries, including a number in the Arab world.

The "Land of Israel." There is no single definition of the phrase the Land of Israel (*Eretz Yisrael*) and the term is used by both secular and religious Israelis to encompass many different geographic areas. Over the years, secular political figures have used the term to describe everything from the land between the Nile and Euphrates rivers to Israel (including the Golan, Gaza, West Bank, and Sinai) plus the Hashemite Kingdom of Jordan. Rabbi Yehuda Elitzur, associated with the settler movement *Gush Emmunim*, has emphasized the biblical origin of *Eretz Yisrael* and has argued that no part of the Middle East should be ruled out: The "borders as reflected in the lands conquered by the [biblical] 'generation that left Egypt'—including northeastern Sinai, Lebanon and western Syria, the Golan Heights, and much of Transjordan—are the lands Israel is required eventually to conquer and settle."[23] The religious right generally regards the western Land of Israel— Judea and Samaria (roughly the West Bank), Gaza, the Golan, and pre-1967 Israel—as the "irreducible minimum." Jews should remember their claims to the Sinai, Lebanon, and parts of the East Bank (Jordan) and take advantage of future opportunities to re-settle these lands; in the meantime, they should concentrate on consolidating Israeli/Jewish control over the land between the Jordan River and the Mediterranean Sea. According to this view, Jewish claims are rooted in the biblical promises made by God to the Jewish people.[24]

In practice, Elitzur's conclusion that settlement guarantees rights to the land is more important than differences in opinion about precisely which land should belong to Israel. He claims that "public settlement of Jews devoted to inheriting the land, in any part of the territory ever conquered by or promised to the ancient Israelites, is sufficient to transform that territory into a part of the 'holy Land of Israel.'"[25] Once Jewish settlers have set up camp, Israel must retain control of the land and the principle of land-for-peace is inapplicable. This expansive definition leaves no room for relinquishing territory and has obvious implications in post-1967 Israel, as demonstrated by the Land of Israel movement discussed below.[26]

Developments on the Israeli Far Right since 1967. In recent history, the turning point for the Israeli right was the quick Israeli victory in the June 1967 war that resulted in the capture of East Jerusalem, the West Bank, the Gaza Strip, Sinai, and the Golan Heights. This seemingly miraculous turn of events invigorated not only the mainstream right but also the religious messianism and nationalist Judaism on the far right. The dream of Greater Israel was rekindled for many secular and religious Israelis. Israelis could dream about the possibility of the Jewish state assuming biblical proportions. Both the particular territories captured (especially the West Bank) and the speed of the war led many to believe that there was a larger explanation than Israel's superior military capabilities and performance.

In September 1967, the Land of Israel movement issued a platform that claimed no Israeli government had the right to compromise any part of *Eretz Yisrael* occupied during the 1967 war. By 1968, the first Jewish settlers illegally moved into the West Bank. The Labor-led government made little effort to dislodge them and ultimately accepted the presence of settlers. From 1967 to 1977, Labor-led governments participated in the buildup of Israeli settlers and settlements, operating on the principle of establishing security outposts, but also allowing the growth of settlements based on religious and/or nationalist convictions. After 1977, Likud governments speeded up the pace and scope of the settlements.

During the post-1967 period, religious messianism resurfaced, often based on the thinking of Rabbi Avraham Itzhak HaCohen Kook, and control over territory became central in this

65

version of modern Judaism. To some religious Israeli Jews, the territorial gains of the 1967 war were another sign that Israel represents redemption for the Jewish people. To fundamentalists, *Eretz Yisrael,* including the newly captured West Bank, could not be relinquished because God promised it to Abraham; this was more important than any political or security arguments that may support the same conclusion. Withdrawal, then, was tantamount to forfeiting redemption. Complete national salvation could only take place in the context of the maximum possible Jewish control of the Land of Israel. Israeli leaders might be able to sway the political- and security-oriented public, but for these religious Zionists, the future of that land was not open to question.

This nationalization of Judaism, where the sanctity and centrality of the Land of Israel became the primary religious obligation, brought supportive religious adherents into direct conflict with Israel's democratic character. If Israel was a moral state with a special purpose as a Jewish state, that could not be changed by government action or majority vote. As part of its mission, Israel must bring Jews to the Land of Israel. Thus giving up the West Bank contradicts the purpose of the state. Secular Zionist elements on the right faced a similar confrontation between Zionism and democracy, but the more pronounced battle lines were drawn between the post-1967 religious messianism and the democratic legacy of the state. The revived religious angle downplayed the civil character of the state, and its religious identity became more important. In addition, the far right accepted non-Jews only on an unequal footing, thus rejecting humanism, universal morality, and equality for Arabs. The late Rabbi Meir Kahane, one of the fiercest leaders of the radical right, succinctly explained the contradiction:

> The liberal west speaks about the rule of democracy, of the authority of the majority, while Judaism speaks of the Divine truth that is immutable and not subject to the ballot box or to majority error. The liberal west speaks about the absolute equality of all people while Judaism speaks of spiritual status, of the choseness of the Jew from above all other people, of the special and exclusive relationship between God and Israel.[27]

Israeli democracy and the Land of Israel movement seemed destined to conflict.

The next major development came with the Camp David Accords and the 1979 Egyptian-Israeli Peace Treaty. Israeli Prime

Minister Menachem Begin, long schooled in Revisionist Zionism and leader of Likud and the Israeli right, agreed to return the entire Sinai peninsula to Egypt. Revisionist Zionism, a largely secular movement led in the pre-state years by Vladimir Jabotinsky, focused on the historic destiny of the Jews to regain control of *Eretz Yisrael.* The far right was shocked—both because of the loss of a part of the Land of Israel (according to some definitions) and because they feared that the Sinai withdrawal would serve as a precedent for resolving the controversy over the West Bank. Begin was no dove. The Israeli right had been betrayed by one of their own.

In the past, the more radical elements had been restrained by Likud's ties to mainstream Israeli politics; after Camp David and Begin's betrayal, numerous leaders and organizations stepped in to chart a new course. *Gush Emmunim*, the settler movement, became a significant extra-parliamentary force. Techiya was formed as a new, small, right-wing party in order to counter Likud's shift. In the early 1980s, Israeli security forces uncovered a Jewish terrorist organization that had bombed West Bank mayors and had plans to destroy the al-Aksa mosque in Jerusalem, an act that might have plunged the region into a new Arab-Israeli war. The shock of Begin's (and Likud's) change of course was soon replaced by new activity and new or invigorated movements on the far right.[28]

Throughout the 1980s, the Likud party was in the government, though it shared power with Labor from 1984 to 1990 in so-called national unity governments. After the return of Sinai to Egypt, Likud was unwilling to exchange other occupied lands in exchange for peace treaties. The costs of continued occupation and continued political stalemate with the Arab parties on the Palestinian question seemed manageable, except for PLO terrorism from Lebanon. Israel's large-scale invasion of Lebanon in 1982 succeeded in expelling the PLO but helped to create a more dangerous enemy—radical Islamists who used suicide tactics to kill Israelis. By 1985, Israeli troops had withdrawn from most of Lebanon.

The Palestinian Intifada began in December 1987 and shattered the manageable status quo in Gaza and the West Bank. It was yet another shock for the Israeli public and posed a new challenge for settlers, religious messianists, and other supporters of greater Israel. Public opinion was shifting in favor of compromise on the issue of the occupied territories. The Intifada strengthened the hand of Israelis who wanted to part with much of these territories and to reduce or eliminate Israeli control of hostile Palestinian populations. Israeli society began to tally in human, financial, and psychological terms the costs of holding on to the occupied territories. The Israeli military watched as service in the West Bank and Gaza reduced training time and lowered military preparedness for a larger military battle with the Arab states.

Those on the right who sought a modus vivendi with the Palestinians envisioned no more than Palestinian autonomy, as Begin agreed to at Camp David.[29] They now fear that the Oslo process will go much further. To the supporters of greater Israel, Oslo I, signed in September 1993, opened the door to Israeli land concessions on the West Bank to the Palestinians. The 1997 Hebron agreement, in which a right-wing Israeli government accepted the Oslo process, was a powerful blow to greater Israel adherents.

THE STRATEGIC DIVIDE

The second major aspect of the debate in Israel over the peace process revolves around strategic issues, which many Israelis see as intertwined with ideological arguments. After so many years of nearly universal military service, there is no shortage of military experts in Israel, both inside the Knesset and among the public at large. Thus it is natural that the strategic aspect of Arab-Israeli negotiations is a key element of the political debate. In fact, for many Israelis on both the left and the right, it has been the decisive factor. In a country that has feared for its existence for so many years—and especially before 1967—the impact that concessions on the West Bank and Golan Heights may have on the security of the state is a vital consideration.

Opponents of relinquishing the West Bank and Golan Heights claim that the loss of strategic depth will be a major blow to Israel's security position. The extra territory, they say, makes it easier for Israel to both absorb and launch military attacks and ensures that there is more time available for an Israeli response to an Arab surprise attack. Control of the land also provides more room for military training.

These opponents argue that a Palestinian state would be a base for Palestinian terrorism and could serve as a launching pad for a coordinated Arab attack against Israel. The suicide bombing campaigns prove that Palestinian control leads directly to Israeli deaths through terrorism. Arab control of the West Bank would allow an Arab coalition to cut Israel in half and destroy the Jewish state. When he was Likud opposition leader, Prime Minister Netanyahu often argued that Arafat is simply implementing the PLO's plan to first regain control of the West Bank and Gaza and then push onward to recapture the rest of Palestine, meaning pre-1967 Israel. The establishment of a Palestinian state offers a transit point for Iraqi, Libyan, Syrian, or even Iranian forces bent on destroying Israel. Palestinian irredentism, embodied in the right of return, is a more subtle but equally dangerous threat. A Palestinian state would be the first step in long-running Palestinian attempts to return hundreds of thousands, if not millions, of Palestinian refugees to pre-1967 Israel. Such efforts would destroy the Jewish character of the state, create demographic havoc, and possibly lead to a military confrontation. Israel cannot accept the return of these refugees and should not allow a Palestinian state, since it would only strengthen such schemes.

Loss of the West Bank will not only make Israel's coastal plain—with a majority of the population and industry—more vulnerable, it will also inhibit the proper functioning of the Israeli Defense Forces, according to this view. Israel, greatly outnumbered by the Arab armies, relies heavily on a mobilization of reserves in the first seventy-two hours of a war. Without the West Bank, Israel will have less warning of an Arab attack and military mobilization sites will be that much more vulnerable. This will force Israel to adopt a "trip wire preemptive strike posture," meaning that the slightest hint of Arab mobilization or attack will start a new war.[30] This approach forfeits any alleged peace and security gains that withdrawing from the West Bank gives Israel.

Critics of the peace process further argue that these principles also apply to the Golan Heights. By withdrawing from the Golan, Israel would hand Syria a commanding view of northern Israel. As it has in the past, Syria could use this topographical advantage to shell the Hula Valley or to launch a wider attack on northern Israel. Why should Israel turn over the high ground to Syria when there is no strategic advantage? At present, Israel's proximity to Damascus provides a greater deterrent to Syrian attack. If the Golan were not in Israeli hands, Syria would feel less threatened and therefore more willing to take military risks in the ongoing battle with Israel. In the face of such strategic temptations, Syrians and Palestinians are unlikely to allow a few pieces of paper and a commitment to non-belligerency to stand in the way of their catastrophic plans for the Jewish state.

Strategic analysts who support the peace process, including the late Prime Minister Rabin, reject these arguments. They question the one-dimensional interpretation of strategic depth, noting that it is only one of several important variables. Moreover, strategic depth is of little help against the emerging threat to Israel from weapons of mass destruction. The prospect of missiles, chemical and biological weapons (CBWs), and perhaps even nuclear weapons in the hands of several hostile states makes it necessary to remove the motive for attacking Israel, not just to prepare for a military confrontation that could result in massive losses for both sides.

Rabin often repeated that even if there is a Palestinian entity, the Jordan Valley will remain Israel's security border. He also rejected the argument that the only options were the status quo and Israel's less defensible borders of June 4, 1967. In defending the Oslo II agreement before the Knesset in 1995, Rabin outlined a number of border modifications:

> The borders of the State of Israel, during the permanent solution, will be beyond the lines which existed before the Six-Day War. We will not return to the June 4, 1967, lines. And these are the main changes, not all of them, which we envision and want in the permanent solution: First and foremost, united Jerusalem, which will include both Ma'ale Adumim and Givat Ze'ev. . .The security border of the State of Israel will be located in the Jordan Valley, in the broadest meaning of that term. Changes will include the addition of Gush Etzion, Efrat, Betar and other communities, most of which are in the area east of what was the "Green Line" . . . The establishment of blocs of settlements in Judea and Samaria, like the one in Gush Katif. . . . [31]

Rabin's inclusion of additional territory both refutes the image of a weak Israel confined to the pre-1967 lines and accepts that a total withdrawal to June 4, 1967, lines may have negative security implications for Israel. Israel also expects other provisions that protect Israel's security interests to emerge from the negotiations, including a demilitarized Palestinian entity, early warning stations, and a forward Israeli military presence at key points in the West Bank. In addition, the Israeli Defense Forces will benefit greatly from ending their role as day-to-day police officers for Palestinian society. Removal from that role will lift morale and, more importantly, allow the IDF to increase training time and military readiness for their true mission, defending Israel against a traditional military attack. The IDF was not founded to confront rocks and Molotov cocktails.

For proponents and opponents of the peace process, especially given Rabin's emphasis on the Jordan Valley as Israel's security border, the stability of the Jordanian government is crucial. For Labor, the treaty and warm relationship with Jordan greatly reduce the threat of an Arab coalition attack from the east. As long as Jordan is allied with Israel and the United States, the Hashemite Kingdom serves as a buffer against renewed Arab-Israeli hostilities. But this reliance on Jordan concerns at least some Likud strategists. The resulting security gains could be threatened as soon as a destabilizing factor, such as the establishment of a Palestinian state in the West Bank and Gaza, undermines King Hussein and topples the Jordanian government; it could even be threatened by a change in course by the current Jordanian government. According to these Likud thinkers, while peace with Jordan enhances Israel's security, these advantages would be forfeited if Israel allows the formation of a Palestinian state.

The strategic debate is also over political motives, as Rabin was well aware. In the long run, the peace process will lessen and then remove the motives for terrorism against Israelis and even for a coordinated Arab attack against Israel. Compromise agreements are the only way to settle the conventional military threat to Israel from neighboring Arab countries. Treaties are worth something, as over fifteen years of peace with Egypt have demonstrated; the warm relations with Jordan are a more recent example. The Palestinian refugee question remains a difficult issue, but it is explicitly part of final status talks, and supporters of the peace process hope that it can be resolved.

The peace process is also the best tool available to protect Israel against the rising WMD threat from rejectionist states such as Iraq, Iran, and Libya. Missiles and CBWs are already widespread among Israel's adversaries. While Israel bombed suspected Iraqi nuclear facilities in 1981, it failed to stop the Iraqi program. It is not effective, feasible, or politically palatable for Israel to bomb every suspected proliferant in the region. A better solution to nuclear proliferation involves a combination of a strategic deterrent (which Israel's clandestine nuclear program provides); removal of the differences that foster WMD threats and the possibility of WMD use in battle; and, probably most important, close strategic ties with the United States.

In the weeks preceding the 1992 Israeli elections, past and present members of the Israeli military publicly aired feelings of uncertainty and concern about the Middle East arms race and the possibility that the Arab states may acquire nuclear weapons of mass destruction. On June 15, 1992, then commander of the Israeli Air Force, Major General Herzl Bodinger, explained that "if countries in the region—like Iran, Libya, and other countries—will have nuclear weapons, this can endanger the whole area." Earlier on June 8, then chief of Military Intelligence, General Uri Sagi, said that Iran's nuclear project "might cause us to be concerned about our existence and basic security." In his opening speech to the Knesset as prime minister, Rabin said that "this [new, nuclear] reality requires us to give additional thought to the urgent need to terminate the Arab-Israeli conflict and to attain peace with our neighbors."[32] Both Likud and Labor officials think that the WMD threat is growing.[33] Proponents of the peace process argue Israel's best hope lies in reducing the adversarial aspects of its relations with such states.

Similarly, withdrawal from the Golan Heights can improve political and therefore security relations with Syria. Under Labor, Israel discussed the need for early warning stations and an array of security arrangements as part of any deal. Rather than being a secondary concern or supporting factor, such security arrangements are as important as the negotiations over withdrawal and normalization. Syria is the key remaining bastion of the rejectionist front, giving a foothold for Iran, Damascus-based Palestinian groups, and Lebanese hostility. A political agreement with Syria, even if it involves withdrawal from the Golan, will also cut off these other hostile forces, greatly improving Israel's security stance and removing the likelihood of attacks from Lebanon on Israel's north.[34]

It would be naive to minimize the many threats to Israel in the Middle East. But Israel is also a formidable military force with a large-scale nuclear deterrent. It has survived terrorism, seemingly overwhelming military odds, and surprise attack. As strategic supporters of the peace process see it, Israel can afford to relinquish territory if that brings political agreements, mollifies Arab hostility and the Arab motives for attack, and allows for significant security arrangements.

ISRAEL'S FUTURE IDENTITY

The nature of the debate about the peace process says much about the direction of Israeli society. What is the proper balance between the state's Jewish and democratic characters? How far will opponents go to prevent Israel from relinquishing the West Bank? What conclusions should be drawn from the terror bombings? In an interview shortly after Rabin's assassination, Ehud Olmert, the Likud mayor of Jerusalem, stated that democracy is and must remain a higher value to Israeli society than any given piece of land. If his perspective holds, the parameters of the peace process debate will be defined in a manner that allows legitimate dissent but prevents extremist excess. Yossi Klein Halevi raised another such balance: the tension between the unity of the Jewish people and the unity of the Land of Israel.[35] If the land is more important, further Jew-on-Jew violence and bloodshed is virtually guaranteed. One other commentator wrote that the leaders of Likud must tell their supporters "that God is not engaged in Israel's internal debate about its future borders, nor has He appointed the Palestinians as His, or Israel's, eternal enemies."[36] The interaction of democracy, Judaism, and land is bound to remain at the heart of the Israeli interpretation of decision making process.

The fundamentalist nature of Israel's radical right and its interpretation of Jewish law so as to justify terrorism and anti-democratic behavior suggest that this part of Israeli society has more in common with other Middle East fundamentalists than with mainstream Israeli supporters and opponents of the peace process. For the far right, the loss of the West Bank would be a stunning blow to their messianism and religious understanding of Israel's path since the 1967 war. For extreme Israeli nationalists, both religious and secular, Israeli policy of trading land for peace must be stopped. For a militant few, it must be stopped at any cost.

The Rabin/Peres government made significant progress on the peace process. Relations with Jordan and the Palestinians in spring 1996 were at a totally different point than just three years before. Israel's economy was booming and its international standing had reached new heights. For six months, Shimon Peres tried to carry forth the policies of Yitzhak Rabin—no easy task for any Israeli leader. Rabin, too, would have had a difficult time with the final status negotiations and the internal Israeli debate on borders, refugees, Jerusalem, and Palestinian statehood. The bombing campaign greatly complicated the situation, although bombings are likely to continue, even if the peace process stops. Peres took a risk with a renewed push for an Israeli-Syrian agreement.

Netanyahu saw the political opening created by the turmoil over the peace process and took full advantage of it. He is unlikely to either wholly embrace or wholly disregard Labor's approach. His decision to go ahead with the Hebron withdrawal and agree to a timetable for further withdrawals from the West Bank has created a rift within his party similar to that which occurred when Begin agreed to evacuate Sinai. In the last resort, he had to balance his own party's preference against the need to avoid creating a regional and international backlash against any intransigence or delay. Any Israeli government must weigh the costs of challenging the peace process. In May 1996, a slight majority of Israelis considered the price of territorial concessions too high. By the end of the year, the price of continued occupation and an uncompromising approach also seemed too high. However, the preferred solution cannot be developed by Israel alone, and thus far, we have seen only half the picture.

THE PALESTINIANS

Like Israeli society, Palestinians in the occupied territories are divided on the terms for making peace with Israel. While most of the world and many Palestinians applauded the famous handshake between Yasser Arafat and Yitzhak Rabin on the White House lawn on September 13, 1993, significant elements in the Palestinian community were deeply troubled by the occasion and particularly by subsequent Israeli-Palestinian agreements. Militant extremists, including both Islamic and nationalist organizations, vowed to carry on the violent struggle against Israeli occupation until they liberated Palestine. In the short term, their suicide bombings and other terrorist acts are the greatest Palestinian threat to the Arab-Israeli peace process. But opposition also came from disaffected al-Fatah members and Palestinian intellectuals such as Haider Abdel-Shafi, a Palestinian negotiator at Madrid and now a member of the Palestinian Council, and Edward Said, a prominent Palestinian-American professor. While they claim to support a negotiated solution to the conflict, they reject what they see as an imbalanced, Israel-dominated process that produced agreements full of Palestinian concessions.

Their opposition illustrates the continuing hesitation of many Palestinians who focus less on the process and more on the results; they have yet to be fully convinced that the peace process is leading to a legitimate Palestinian state with East Jerusalem as its capital.[37] These lingering doubts could prevent a resolution of the Israeli-Palestinian conflict if, in fact, a two-state solution does not emerge from the Arab-Israeli peace process. Palestinian popular support for suicide bombings has declined; but the perception of a humiliating and asymmetrical negotiating process in which Israel pulls the strings and avoids a Palestinian state makes many mainstream Palestinians unwilling to fully renounce the armed struggle and to embrace a nonconfrontational approach to relations with Israel.[38] The ultimate direction of the Netanyahu gov-

ernment will help resolve the debate in the Palestinian community over the Oslo process. Palestinian leaders feel that their differences with Israel form the core of the peace process.[39] If Likud
opposition to a Palestinian state is unyielding, Oslo critics will have
further ammunition and the ramifications of an Israeli-Palestinian stalemate will extend far beyond Gaza and the West Bank.

PALESTINIAN SUPPORT FOR THE OSLO PROCESS

Despite this hesitation, each Israeli redeployment has been
greeted with singing and dancing. In spite of the violent and pointed opposition to the process, Arafat and the Palestinian Authority (PA) have enjoyed significant Palestinian support in the West
Bank and Gaza. Arafat's personal standing, the activities of multiple Palestinian security forces, and the sense of greater freedom
created by Israeli military redeployment helped counter opposition in the period 1993-96. By 1997, however, increased criticism of Arafat and the Palestinian Authority's top officials was
voiced by many moderates, including members of the Palestinian Legislative Council.

The Oslo process and the Palestinian Authority are very much
Arafat's show. After leading the Palestinian movement for so many
years, Arafat had an immense amount of political capital. No other
Palestinian figure enjoyed anything even close to Arafat's stature:
his picture is widely displayed in the West Bank and Gaza, and
he received 88 percent of the January 1996 vote for *raes* (president or chairman). Moreover, the Palestinian Authority remains
a major employer, giving Arafat more leverage and creating more
positions for his key supporters inside and outside the territories. However, the economic condition of Palestinians was severely harmed by the months-long border closure carried out in
response to the bombing attacks in early 1996. In the end, the
suffering economy and charges of corruption may prove to be
Arafat's Achilles heel.

Of course, Arafat has not relied on his stature alone. Palestinian security personnel, said to number some 50,000, provide
the regime with another means of ensuring support and curtailing the activities of the opposition (especially the Islamist opposition).[40] Critics have called into question the Palestinian Authority's
commitment to human rights, a fair question, given the pressure
it puts on opposition organizations and the Palestinian media not
to criticize the official line or the tactics of Palestinian security personnel. There are many reports of human rights abuses in Gaza

and the West Bank, including the use of torture and the absence of due process, by both Palestinian and Israeli forces.[41] Each new call for a Palestinian crackdown further increases the likelihood of human rights abuses.

Implementation of the Oslo I and II agreements has, to some extent, created support for the peace process, since these have improved the lives of Palestinians by giving them a taste of freedom and self-rule. The removal of Israeli troops from day-to-day policing in many populated areas (especially in Zone A as defined in Oslo II; see chapter 1), the absence of curfews and the consequent ability to enjoy leisure time, and the general freedom from years of occupation contribute to a more open atmosphere and a partial normalization of life. The daily interaction of Israeli patrols and Palestinians had a corrosive effect on the Israeli-Palestinian relationship even on days without violent confrontations. Such feelings will not last indefinitely for they cannot replace deeply held demands for independence, sovereignty, and the removal of Israeli soldiers beyond just the municipal borders. Yet coupled with Palestinian control of many civilian departments (which means that Palestinians are now running a large part of their own affairs, with significant and well-known exceptions) there is a fair amount of unspoken support for Arafat and the Palestinian Authority. Although Arafat has not allowed unfettered political space for opposition and criticism, there is more freedom to conduct social activities; being Palestinian is no longer an automatic blemish in the eyes of the security forces and the governing authority as it was under Israeli rule.

Despite some positive signs, much of the economic news has not been helpful to Arafat's government. There is a large amount of housing construction, and some infrastructure projects have begun to improve roads, sidewalks, parks, and squares. Tax collection has improved, a significant challenge in a society accustomed to avoiding tax and utility payments as a sign of political protest against the occupation. In addition, Palestinian coffers have been helped by the agreement with Israel to transfer value added taxes (VAT) collected from Palestinians back to the Palestinian Authority. However, this leaves the PA vulnerable to Israeli decisions to withhold transfering the VATs.

Trade is potentially one of the most important factors in the Palestinian economy. There has been some direct trade via the Israeli port of Ashdod, isolated Palestinian businesses (such as flower-growers) have the right to export directly to the European Union (EU), and duty-free access to the United States is emerging.[42] Relations between the Palestinian Authority and donor countries are more stable, and donors are now better able to coordinate the flow of aid to the Palestinians. The international community (including the United States and many European countries) pledged $2.4 billion in aid to the PA; by late 1995, almost $850 million had been disbursed.[43] Much of this aid has been used for operational expenses, limiting the funds available for capital investment in Gaza and the West Bank.

These early signs of economic progress contrast sharply with the unemployment, poverty, and dependence that are Gaza's trademark.[44] Unemployment is approximately 50 percent (or as high as 60 percent according to some Palestinian claims);[45] GNP per capita has continued to drop (it is now roughly half the pre-Intifada figure from 1987); and dependence on external aid from Israel and donor countries continues. Much existing employment is nonproductive and nonsustainable. By spring 1995, nearly one out of eight Gazans, or about 100,000 Palestinians, depended on food and cash handouts; 40 percent of them had been newly impoverished since Oslo I in September 1993. In summer 1996, some Palestinian leaders expressed fear that the severe effects of the prolonged Israeli border closure would result in starvation among the poorest Palestinians.[46] The charge was repeated again in August 1997, following another closure of the border in the wake of the July 30 suicide bombing in Jerusalem.

Meanwhile, private sector development is constrained by the absence of political stability and the overall poor investment climate; repeated Israeli border closures and reductions in Palestinian work permits; tenuous trade relations; a weak regulatory and legal environment without an administrative infrastructure; weak physical infrastructure that needs billions of dollars of improvements; and uncertainty about Israel's willingness on any given day to facilitate the transfer of people and goods. Arafat claims that the hundreds of Israeli closures have cost Palestinians at least $6 million per day.[47]

Ironically, for a long time Israeli measures to separate Gaza and reduce the terrorism threat played into the hands of Hamas; only in the last year or two have the closures and restrictions had a detrimental impact on the Islamic opposition. Hamas builds much of its support at the grassroots level through social welfare agencies that provide food, housing, clothing, education, religious activities, and other staples. In the past, a weak economy forced more people to depend on Hamas. Thus the greater the level of misery in Gaza, the more the social services of Hamas were needed to fill the gap. In the last couple of years, with the suicide bombings and the resultant Israeli closures, some Palestinians began to hold Hamas responsible for the problems caused by closure. Israel succeeded in linking the economic drawbacks of closure with the militant bombing campaign against Israelis, and this has helped sap support for violent opposition against Israel.

At the rhetorical level, Israeli leaders understand the dangers of a weak Palestinian economy, but there have been few policy changes that reflect this awareness. Former Prime Minister Peres argued that "[i]f you want to fight fundamentalism, try to reduce poverty. How can you reduce poverty without helping to build a different economy? So a contribution to the Palestinian economy is indirectly but clearly a contribution to reduce the danger of terror and fundamentalism."[48] Meanwhile, in practice, the traditional understanding of Israeli security still operates, and Israel's closing the Gaza and West Bank borders and denying the majority of Palestinian laborers entrance to Israel appear to be enduring features of the Israeli-Palestinian economic landscape.[49] It remains to be seen to what extent business passes, offloading of goods, convoys escorted by the Israeli military, industrial parks on the Gaza-Israel border, and other measures tailored to this environment can both improve the Palestinian economy and satisfy security-conscious Israelis.

REJECTIONIST VIOLENCE

Against this backdrop of lowered expectations and economic hardship, violence by Palestinian militants is the most serious Palestinian threat to the peace process, at least for the short term. Although the process has weathered numerous terrorist attacks, a string of deadly bombings against Israeli civilians can still bring the talks to a grinding halt. As extremists fight marginalization and sense the growing difficulty in reversing or even stopping the process, massive violence could increase.

Both Islamic and nationalist extremists object to Arafat's compromises with Israel, since they still believe that the objective of the Palestinian movement must be the destruction of the state of Israel. They differ on whether Palestine should become an Islamic state or, as the more traditional Palestinian nationalists argue, a binational secular state. Clearly, this debate among the extremists will continue for many years, but at this point in time, and for the foreseeable future, they are united in their effort to liberate Palestine by violent means from Israeli occupation. Ibrahim

Ghawshah, Hamas spokesman, explained that "we must unite all sincere, honorable, nationalistic Palestinian factions—Islamists and non-Islamists—to confront this serious conspiracy."[50]

Hamas (and especially the military brigades carrying out the suicide bombings), Islamic Jihad, the Democratic Front for the Liberation of Palestine, the Popular Front for the Liberation of Palestine (PFLP)–General Command, and other Palestinian groups based in Damascus do not accept peace with Israel or any process that includes peace among its objectives or accepts Israel as a legitimate member of the region. In such circles, Israelis and Israel are still referred to as Zionists and the Zionist state. It is important to note, however, that Hamas, for instance, is not monolithic and lacks a single perspective on the peace process.[51]

Rejectionist organizations continue to use terrorism to oppose the peace process. As one Hamas spokesman explained, the Oslo agreement is "a conspiracy against the Palestinian people's land, destiny, and future."[52] It has failed to stop continued Israeli occupation and expansion. According to this view, Arafat sold out the true and just rights of the Palestinian people for a few crumbs of power. Moreover, he gave Israel cover to continue the creeping annexation of Jerusalem and the West Bank. Ghawshah charged that Arafat and the Palestinian Authority lost everything: "Actually they lost Palestine, they lost their land, and they lost their people."[53] Israel has proven that it is untrustworthy through its negotiating stance, delaying tactics, and resistance to even minor concessions. In the end, Arafat always caves in to Israeli concerns about security. Israel even has Arafat doing its bidding as Palestinian security forces are now the primary modes of repression in the self-rule areas. One Hamas communique asked "[w]hat sort of national authority is this which seeks to subdue our people to the abominable Zionist occupation under false banners?"[54] In attacking Oslo II, Ahmed Jibril, secretary general of the PFLP, highlighted the U.S. role by stating that Oslo II is part of the U.S. program to control the region.[55]

Palestinian opponents of the status quo want to continue the war against Israel; the late secretary general of Islamic Jihad, Fathi Shiqaqi, told an interviewer in early 1995 that the "war continues . . . What is going on inside Palestine now is a real war that will witness an escalation."[56] Shiqaqi's successor, Ramadan Abdallah, maintained the same line: "Our plans are summed up in one sentence, as they always have: the continuation of jihad, liberation of Palestine, and resisting any compromise until achieving total victory."[57] Ghawshah added that "[w]e in the Islamic Resistance Movement-Hamas declare and stress that there is no retreat from the jihad objective."[58] Suicide bombers remain popular among some Palestinian people, even if the Israeli tactic of closing Gaza every time there is an attack has reduced support among the average Gazan for such attacks. Imad Falouji, publisher of a Hamas newspaper, commented on the bombings in a favorable religious light: "We don't call this suicide, which is forbidden in Islam. These are martyrdom operations. We are commanded to wage holy war for the sake of God. Here the attacker is assured success, he avoids arrest, inflicts heavier casualties on the enemy and gains martyrdom."[59]

Despite their rhetoric, some groups are not totally locked into opposing accommodation with Israel, and the Palestinian elections in 1996 put the rejectionist organizations to the test in the West Bank and Gaza. Some more accommodating members of Hamas might, under certain circumstances, eventually pull the organization toward accepting co-existence with Israel. In late 1995, a new party, the Islamic National Salvation, formed to run in the elections. Numerous positions were attributed to Hamas, including calls for and against an election boycott, but Palestinian turnout was high. Hamas did not run any official candidates, but several candidates, including a handful of successful ones, are considered to be pro-Islamist. However, the resumption of the suicide bombing campaign against Israelis in late February 1996 demonstrated that militant leaders in Hamas still have not changed their perspective on the role of violence and terror in Israeli-Palestinian relations. The question of how they would react and how long they would continue their opposition if the peace process succeeds—and there are many different definitions of a successful process—remains to be answered.

Even as they oppose the peace process, some members of the Palestinian secular-nationalist opposition recognize that it is the only game in town. Inside the territories, in contrast to Damascus, Democratic Front for the Liberation of Palestine and PFLP supporters are involved in Palestinian NGOs and social organizations and must, therefore, establish some type of relationship with the Palestinian Authority. The ideals of the rejectionist Palestinian outsiders are harder to uphold when an individual or organization is confronted on a daily basis by opportunities for direct interaction with Arafat's regime. Those that choose to ignore or attack the PA run the risk of political retribution and significant interference in their operations.

POLITICAL OPPOSITION

The arguments of Edward Said, Haider Abdel-Shafi, and some others are more sophisticated. They are not opposed in principle to a compromise settlement, but believe that the deal that Arafat has struck is like a deck stacked in Israel's favor and controlled by the United States. The massive imbalance in the proceedings will short-change Palestinians. At best, the Palestinians will only get a statelet, a puppet regime with the trimmings of independence but none of the realities. Arafat will be at the beck and call of his Western donors and the Israeli government, which will still control virtually all national security and defense issues.

Clovis Maksoud, former Arab League representative to the United Nations, charged that during the interim period, "Israel will be able to 'cantonize' the West Bank and Gaza Strip and preclude the emergence of a Palestinian state or even a viable national Palestinian entity in the occupied territories."[60] Abdel Shafi added: "In the Gaza Strip, Israel withdrew from cities, villages and [refugee] camps, but they remain in the area in force and they are the real authority. So what we have are cantons of Arab population that are divested of any authority, with restricted movement, with roads and big stretches of the [Mediterranean] shore out of bounds to Palestinians. That's not anywhere near the requirements of peace that everyone is talking about."[61] To Said, "Arafat and his Palestinian Authority have become a sort of Vichy government for Palestinians. Those of us who fought for Palestine before Oslo fought for a cause that we believed would spur the emergence of a just order. Never has this ideal been further from realization than today."[62]

Most important, the critics argue, neither Oslo I nor Oslo II ensures that the peace process will result in a Palestinian state, with East Jerusalem as the capital.[63] With the signing of Oslo II, Abdel-Shafi explained: "I believe that the issue of our right to self-determination and the establishment of an independent state has become more difficult than ever before. . . . I tell those who are for the agreement that what is going on does not indicate that we will achieve our objective of an independent state."[64] Most Palestinians regard this as the minimum acceptable compromise now that they have formally rejected the notion of a binational state including Jews and Arabs. It is far from clear that a Likud-led Israeli government, at this point in time, is willing to formally accept a Palestinian state and even if they are, it would be a state in name only. This leads to the inevitable analogy with the

Bantustans in South Africa, and Edward Said uses this analogy in his vociferous criticism.[65]

From a broader perspective, the current process is seen as an imposed and heavy-handed American and Israeli effort. It is another form of colonialism where outsiders seek to impose their vision of peace, harmony, and justice on the region without taking account of regional needs, rights, and desires. On all tracks of the peace process, decisions are not based on the Arab people's needs but rather on the narrow interests of Arab leadership that is for the most part beholden to the United States. In mid-1995, before Oslo II was signed, Abdel Shafi, also the former head of the Palestinian negotiating team, explained that the current peace process "has lost all credibility as peacemaking." He suggested that Palestinian negotiators should suspend the talks and "tell the world the peace process is dead."[66] Given this predicament, Edward Said concluded after the signing of Oslo II that "it is absolutely legitimate to suggest that no negotiations, and no agreement, would be better than what has so far been determined."[67]

At times, even Arafat's own supporters criticize Israel and the peace process. Yasir Abed Rabbo, a PA minister, noted: "What we see is not a roll-back, but an expansion of settlement[s]. . .The basic supports of the Palestinian-Israeli agreement have collapsed. The Israeli bulldozers have bulldozed the agreement itself."[68] Israeli rhetoric notwithstanding, the actions of the Israeli government fail to demonstrate a serious commitment to the peace process. Farooq Qaddumi, PLO member and once a close Arafat aide, cited Oslo II as "more proof of the Israeli rulers' disavowal of the principles on which a settlement was based."[69]

Meanwhile, Israel continues the absorption of Jerusalem, the expansion of settlements, and other measures to consolidate Israeli control. While negotiations continue and the Palestinians get little, Israel has made no effort to slow actions that serve as obstacles to peace. As Said sees Oslo II, what "Israel got was official Palestinian consent to continued occupation."[70]

This group of critics does not reject all accommodation. According to Maksoud, "Mainstream Palestinian and Arab opinion strongly favors a negotiated, just peace with Israel. It opposes an imposed and humiliating peace of the sort that the current flawed process and assumptions are seen to be constructing."[71] This peace process is flawed and inequitable, but if the Arab leaders are willing to start again and build a balanced relationship with Israel and the West, a fair and just settlement can be found that includes acceptance of Israel, albeit a smaller Israel than many Israelis would like to see. Said sums up: "The peace process as now understood is a process with no true peace at all. In its present form, I am convinced, it will not stand the test of time; it must be completely rethought and put on a fairer course."[72]

Some critics focus on Arafat himself and the highly autocratic methods by which he governs. They call for more democracy within the Palestinian movement and for less clamping down on civil liberties. They believe that Israel is sending contradictory signals: calling for Palestinian democracy at the same time as calling for a major security crackdown to alleviate Israeli security concerns. Arafat's high-handed behavior, according to the critics, includes his complete control over sources of money, limited accountability, and the roughshod way he deals with human rights. Hanan Ashrawi, a member of the Palestinian Council and former head of a Palestinian human rights organization, charged that "the freedom of the press has been targeted in many ways. There has been a certain amount of intimidation, self-censorship and reticence."[73] She added that the overall record has been mixed: "There have been signs that there is a willingness by the Authority to address issues democratically while at the same time there were signs that there were violations of rights and freedoms and excesses—particularly by the security apparatus and systems."[74]

In the coming years, the Palestinian Council could play an increasing role in Palestinian decision making. The Council has been wary of directly attacking Arafat; it has, instead focused on building its strength behind the scenes.[75] In July 1997, the Council strongly criticized almost all of the PA ministers, charging that corruption and the misallocation of funds are rampant. This may be an important sign in the development of an alternative center of power in Palestinian areas.

As Israelis and Palestinians wrestle with permanent status issues, economic possibilities, and extremist violence, other tracks of the peace process will not be dormant. Chapter 4 discusses the two front-line states that have already made peace with Israel.

CHAPTER FOUR

EGYPT, JORDAN, AND THE PEACE PROCESS

E gypt and Jordan share the distinction of having signed peace treaties with Israel, but each state plays a different role in the peace process. Egypt sees itself as the leader of the Arab world and, consequently, as the central Arab interlocutor on the direction of the peace process and relations with Israel. Jordan has fostered a warm peace with Israel, to the chagrin of many Jordanians, and lies solidly in the U.S./Israeli political camp. Both states are wrestling with popular opinion that is often at odds with pathbreaking government policies, as well as varying degrees of economic trouble and political dissent.

EGYPT AND THE PEACE PROCESS

E gypt's relations with Israel remain the cornerstone of the current peace process. Egyptian officials insist that Cairo's pivotal role be acknowledged. Should anything happen to threaten the structure of the Egyptian-Israeli peace, it would have profound and dangerous consequences for the entire region. Since Camp David, the relationship between the two countries has been proper but with little official warmth. Egypt has been reluctant to embrace Israel as a close friend. Egyptians consider Egypt's role as key peacebroker to be a natural consequence of their country's role as the center of Arab culture, intellectual activity, and politics. Egyptian civilization has a long history and is on par with India, China, and other great civilizations; it deserves recognition and respect commensurate with this status. Suggestions that either the United States or Israel can determine Egypt's role are considered insulting.

Yet, ironically, as the peace process has expanded, Egyptian leaders have been concerned about the possibility of their own marginalization and secondary status in several areas. Since the Camp David Accords in 1978, Egypt has believed that a cold peace with Israel is the best that could be expected until comprehensive peace comes to the Middle East. Instead of comprehensive peace serving as a harbinger of Egypt's status and importance, Egyptians have pondered and fretted over diplomatic demotions and a sense that on major issues they are playing second fiddle to Israel; at the same time, they confront awesome and dangerous internal political and economic difficulties. This sense of frustration reached a peak during the Rabin-Peres government. In short, Egyptian leaders fear that comprehensive peace may undermine rather than bolster Egypt's regional and international standing, especially its claim to leadership in the Arab world. They believe that because of widespread Arab suspicions of Netanyahu, the Likud government in Israel will need to be more solicitous of Egypt.

Since Camp David, Egypt has experienced highs and lows in its effort to recapture its traditional leadership role. Sadat's trip to Jerusalem in 1977 and the subsequent 1979 peace treaty with Israel incurred the wrath of Arab states and various Arab and Islamic multilateral organizations. Most Arab countries severed diplomatic relations with Egypt, which was also expelled from the Arab League and other organizations. In 1981, Sadat paid the ultimate price for peace with Israel when he was assassinated by Islamic radicals. Israel completed its withdrawal from the Sinai peninsula on schedule in April 1982, and in June 1982 Israel invaded Lebanon. This was a humiliating experience for Egypt, since it was correctly perceived that the invasion would not have taken place so long as Sinai remained unresolved. Seen through Arab eyes, the first demonstration of the completed Egyptian-Israeli peace agreement was a "green light" for Israel to attack another Arab country.

The Lebanon War persuaded President Hosni Mubarak and other Egyptian leaders to work hard for re-acceptance into the Arab world and the opportunity to once again assume a leadership role. In 1984, the Islamic Conference Organization accepted Egypt back into its fold, and Egypt restored diplomatic relations with Jordan. In November 1987, at a summit meeting in Jordan of many Arab leaders, attendees passed a resolution formally allowing states to re-establish bilateral diplomatic relations with Egypt. In May 1989, the Arab League once again opened its doors to Egyptian representatives.

In 1990, the Iraqi invasion of Kuwait threatened to split the Arab world. Egypt denounced the Iraqi move, supported the U.S. position in opposition to Iraqi aggression, and joined allied forces in the Gulf. Egypt's efforts were handsomely rewarded when the United States cancelled $6.7 billion in debt and the March 1991 Damascus Declaration gave Egypt a future role in Gulf security. The Declaration, agreed to by Egypt, Syria, and the GCC states, called for Egyptian and Syrian troops to help provide security for the GCC states against Iran and Iraq. However, the Declaration was never implemented because the Gulf states preferred to rely on the United States for their external defense.

THE NEED FOR RELEVANCE

The political turmoil in the Middle East following the 1996 Israeli elections demonstrated once again Egypt's central role in achieving peace. Egyptian leaders worried that they were being marginalized in two key areas: in the Arab-Israeli peace process and in the Persian Gulf. Ironically, Netanyahu's election has boosted their status once more, as Israel again recognizes Egypt's contribution to the diplomatic process. When Arabs expressed deep concern about Netanyahu's philosophy and prospective policies, Mubarak played a leading role in bringing Arab leaders together for a summit, clarifying Israel's position through a Mubarak-Netanyahu meeting, and presenting Israel with a realistic picture of Arab expectations.

Though Egypt was the first to make peace with Israel, the Madrid peace process appeared to relegate Egyptian concerns to the margin. From 1993 to 1996, Israel, Jordan, and the PLO assumed center stage. The leaders of Israel and Jordan have established warm relations, even though Jordan's peace with Israel came fifteen years later than Egypt's and despite trepidation among many Jordanian citizens. The rhetoric from Jerusalem and Amman from 1994 to 1996 contrasts sharply with Israeli bitterness over the "cold peace" with Egypt. The Palestinians, too, moved closer to Israel; although Egypt continued to assist in negotiations between Israel and Palestinians, there was less room for Egyptian input than in years past (such as at Camp David autonomy talks, when Egypt essentially negotiated on behalf of Palestinian interests).

However, since the change of government in Israel, both the Palestinian and the Jordanian leadership see it in their interests to seek Egypt's help to save the peace process and their exposed positions. Egypt has attempted to drive home the message to Israel that peace is a strategic choice for much of the Arab world; that land for peace must be the basis for negotiations; that a comprehensive peace must include a mutually satisfactory resolution of the Palestinian question; and that Egypt will be Israel's biggest help as Israel attempts to integrate into the Arab world.

The Persian Gulf is the second area where the Egyptian role has been minimized and Egypt feels slighted. Egyptians had high hopes in the aftermath of the Gulf War that Egypt and the Gulf states would cooperate on security issues. These hopes peaked with the issuing of the Damascus Declaration in March 1991, when it appeared that Egypt and Syria might maintain a permanent military presence in the Gulf in exchange for financial payments from the vulnerable Gulf states. However, the Gulf states opted to turn to the United States for protection because they do not believe Egypt can provide security against the threat from Iran or Iraq. Moreover, the Gulf states undoubtedly feared that Egypt and Syria would use their military presence as financial and even possibly political leverage. In May 1991, Egypt announced the withdrawal of most Egyptian troops from Saudi Arabia and Kuwait. One cost for Egypt was the loss of the payments originally envisioned as part of an Egyptian-Gulf security arrangement.

RELATIONS WITH ISRAEL

Egyptians are sensitive both to the special status the United States accords Israel and to Israel's powerful military and economic position in the Middle East. The Arab-Israeli peace process has failed to alter or even confront Israel's special status. If anything, the process has enhanced Israel's special standing. Between July 1992 and May 1996, Israel and Washington had virtually identical policies. As a key American ally, Israel receives the most foreign aid of any country and better access to advanced U.S. military technology.

Israel's GDP is twice the size of Egypt's, even though Egypt has ten times the population of Israel. The Israeli economy and defense industry are more advanced technically. With Israel's diplomatic gains since the Oslo I agreement in 1993 and as Israeli leaders have begun to focus on integrating Israel into the Middle East, Egyptians and some other Arabs are concerned about Israeli economic hegemony. They fear that a new Israeli economic threat will replace the old Israeli military threat. The Labor government repaired relations with the U.S. government damaged by Bush-Shamir confrontations and by Israel's lack of enthusiasm for the peace process in 1991-92—events that had increased Egypt's appeal to the United States. With Israel's relations also improving with Jordan and the PLO, Egyptians have wondered how long until Syria's Asad also engages in warm relations with Israel. Netanyahu's election may have reduced some of those Egyptian fears.

88

The nuclear asymmetry between Israel and Egypt is perhaps the most important variable in Egyptian-Israeli relations and is symptomatic of the deep-seated ambivilance many Egyptians still feel toward Israel. Except on the nuclear issue, the United States has treated Egypt and Israel with rough parity since Camp David. The two countries receive the largest U.S. military and economic aid packages. Israel receives more aid on both an absolute and a per capita basis, but Egypt has received about $2 billion per year since Camp David from the United States. No Egyptian government can live indefinitely with an Israeli nuclear monopoly. For many, Israeli nuclear weapons embody the ultimate humiliation of Arabs by Israel. It is not enough that Israel has emerged victorious from most Arab-Israeli battles, built a powerful military and economic machine, and curried the favor of many of the world's industrial powers. But Israel now also controls nuclear weapons, the most destructive military weapon yet invented.

No issue better symbolizes the political and strategic barriers between Israel and Egypt than the discussion of weapons of mass destruction in the Middle East Arms Control and Regional Security (ACRS) talks. ACRS was one of five multilateral working groups that grew out of the 1991 Madrid Peace Conference. Its purpose was to focus on arms control issues and explore ways to reduce violence and promote strategic stability in the Middle East. From the beginning, ACRS talks were constrained because Syria and Lebanon refused to participate, and Iran and Iraq were excluded. Nevertheless, in the early meetings, considerable progress was made on developing an agenda for confidence and security building measures (CSBMs). A number of meetings considered issues ranging from maritime safety to problems of transparency to procedures for military-to-military contacts and information exchange. The talks eventually broke down when it became clear that Egypt and Israel had very different objectives and ideas about the purpose of the ACRS. For Egypt, the most important issue was to engage in serious negotiations concerning Israel's nuclear weapons and to persuade Israel to sign the Nuclear Nonproliferation Treaty (NPT). For Israel, this was unacceptable in the absence of a comprehensive Arab-Israeli peace and the inclusion of countries such as Iraq and Iran in multilateral arms control talks. Egypt became convinced that Israel was using the ACRS forum to extend its diplomatic contacts with other Arab countries and become more accepted in the Middle East. Israel was convinced that Egypt wished to use the ACRS forum to undermine and embarrass Israel on both nuclear matters and

Israel's qualitative edge in conventional military forces. By the end of 1996, it was not clear that the talks would ever resume without an understanding between Israel and Egypt.

Not just the military potential of the Israeli program, but also the symbolism of Israel as the lone nuclear power in the region, is problematic to Arab states. Israel's nuclear program creates ambiguity and uncertainty for the Egyptian military given the lack of Israeli transparency. Egyptians do not believe that Israel actually intends to use nuclear weapons, but they fear that Israel could utilize the weapons as a tool to impose its political will on the region. Egyptians argue that nuclear weapons are the most destabilizing weapons in an already unstable region, and that the Israeli program hampers efforts to stem proliferation in countries such as Iran.

Egypt voiced these and other concerns about Israel's nuclear program in early 1995 before the April 1995 NPT extension and renewal conference. No new conditions relating to the Israeli program were added to the NPT, but Egypt succeeded in turning some attention to Israel's program. Egypt accuses the United States of having a "double standard" on this issue, since Washington is willing to ignore Israel's nuclear capabilities while pushing a strong anti-proliferation agenda in the Middle East as a whole. The 1996 election of Netanyahu is bound to generate fears that Israel could resort to more explicit forms of nuclear blackmail. Like many Middle East states, and in contrast to larger countries such as the United States and Russia, Egypt could be wiped out by one or two nuclear bombs. Moreover, even if Israel uses a nuclear weapon in a battle that does not include Egypt, it will have negative ramifications for Egypt.[1] There have been no signs from Israel of any willingness to change its position on nuclear matters.

This said, the Netanyahu victory in May 1996 may have some benefits for Egypt. After all, Egypt negotiated its peace treaty with past Likud leaders and weathered countless controversial policies under Likud governments in the 1980s. A slower peace process might even help Egypt's standing if the spotlight is removed from the Israeli-Palestinian and Israeli-Syrian tracks.

ECONOMIC TROUBLES

Political irritations and challenges to Egypt's leading role might be more manageable if the Egyptian economy was strong, but its continual poor performance has been the most threatening long-run problem for the Mubarak regime. Economic difficulties in Egypt are related to demographic, economic, and political constraints. Fouad Ajami, a noted Middle East observer, laments the weakening of Egypt, much of it in the economic realm:

> The sorrow of Egypt is made of entirely different material: the steady decline of its public life, the inability of an autocratic regime and of the middle class from which this regime issues to rid the country of its dependence on foreign handouts, to transmit to the vast underclass the skills needed for the economic competition of nations, to take the country beyond its endless alternation between false glory and self-pity.[2]

1996 might come to be seen as the year the Egyptian economy finally turned the corner. Some interpreted Mubarak's installation of a new prime minister, economist Kamal al-Ganzoury, in January 1996 as a sign that Mubarak recognized that the reform program to date had been slow and inadequate.[3] While much of our review of Egypt's economic performance is pessimistic, the prognosis looked better in mid-1997 than it had for many years. Without suggesting that Egypt is the next Hong Kong or South Korea, it is worth noting that the economy has picked up and has some chance for a take-off if reform and privatization are at least partially successful.[4]

Egypt has had some success limiting population growth, but the population is still projected to increase from 62 million in 1995 to 98 million in 2025.[5] Like India and, more recently, Iran, Egypt has been the focus of major family planning efforts, since unchecked growth is a problem for any Egyptian government, regardless of its political view. The population growth rate in Egypt has slowed from a high of 3 percent per year in 1985 to 2.3 percent in 1993,[6] but it takes a generation for reduced population growth rates to have an impact on food, water, housing, and other resources. In the meantime, serious efforts are needed to meet the basic needs, including food and jobs, of a growing and young population.

Pressure on resources and demands for basic services are a continuing concern. According to a report prepared for the Ministry of Economy and Foreign Trade by the U.S. Agency for International Development (USAID), Egypt will need economic growth rates of 7 percent and higher in order to meet the challenges of population and job creation.[7] Between 1990 and 1994, Egypt fell short, with economic growth rates, according to the USAID report, of 5.7 percent, 1.1 percent, 4.4 percent, 1.0 percent, and

2.0 percent.[8] The Egyptian government claimed that growth rates were higher (3.9 percent in 1993/94 and 4.5 percent in 1994/95).[9]

In the past, Egypt has counted on foreign remittances from Egyptian workers, U.S. aid, and internal productivity to generate revenue to keep the economy afloat. These sources of income are not assured. U.S. aid is under increasing attack from budget cutters and foreign aid opponents. The U.S. Congress may have to provide further financial support to other Arab countries and the Palestinians for new peace agreements, and it may be argued that Egypt has had its turn. The Gulf War demonstrated the vulnerability of Egypt's expatriate workers since many had to leave Iraq. From 1974 to 1993, Egyptian remittances from the Gulf totaled $72 billion. Closer to home, Egypt struggles to balance political demands on its relationship with Libya (e.g., U.S. and U.N. pressure to isolate Libya for alleged involvement in international terrorism) with the fiscal benefit of Egyptians working in Libya. In addition to foreign remittances, Egypt counts on tourists and investments from the Arab Gulf, as well as the use of the Suez Canal, as a tie-in to Gulf economies.[10]

The Egyptian government is often criticized for excessive corruption, inefficiency, and bureaucracy. Economic reform has been slow, inconsistent, and lacking in follow-through, and criticism of Egypt's slow privatization policies and timetables has been widespread. According to the USAID-prepared report, Egypt needs—in addition to general economic reform—wider deregulation, stronger protection of intellectual property rights, and better information networks.

What, then, led observers in 1996 to suggest that Egypt is improving economically? The same USAID report notes that Egypt has a large labor force with competitive wage rates; climate and lands suited to a wide variety of crops; a central location offering easy access to Europe, North Africa, and the Far East; a large (and growing) local market; and preferential access to the EU.[11] In mid-1996, an Egyptian institute described Egypt's economic prospects as "fairly bright" because of governmental deregulation, private sector confidence that bureaucratic reform will proceed, incentives offered to the private sector such as extended tax holidays, infrastructure improvements, declining population growth rates, and a cheap labor force.[12] It remains to be seen whether this much-anticipated growth spurt will materialize, though in April 1997, Egypt's progress in attracting foreign investors was front-page news.[13]

ISLAMIC FUNDAMENTALISTS

The Egyptian government and Islamic militants have clashed sporadically since the 1970s, but the violence has intensified in the 1990s. Using both political and violent means, Islamic militants have been at war with the Mubarak regime over the nature of the Egyptian state and the future leadership of the country.[14] The militants have called for the establishment of a theocratic Islamic state in Egypt in direct repudiation of Egypt's efforts over the last twenty years to become more secular, modern, and capitalist. They have also waged terrorist attacks on tourists, government officials, and the Christian Copt community, which makes up approximately 6 percent of Egypt's population.[15]

The Egyptian tourism industry has been hit hard by the Islamist campaign, which regards Western tourists as yet another intrusion into Egyptian society. Tourism is an important element of the Egyptian economy and a major employer. Scaring off tourists weakens the economy and infuriates ordinary Egyptians who are dependent on tourism for work. After some uncertainty in the early days, Egyptian government forces appear to have contained the insurgency.[16] The government's campaign of repression, including cracking down on the once-tolerated Muslim Brotherhood, has been successful in the short term.[17] As the government has become more effective with its crackdowns, tourism has rebounded. During 1995, tourist arrival, tourist night (in hotels), and occupancy rates all climbed significantly. Regional discrepancies remain, and tourist levels in Upper Egypt are still low. In 1992, tourism peaked at approximately 3.2 million tourists, who spent $3 billion. In 1995, Egypt again approached the 3 million mark.[18]

Sadat and Mubarak's opening to Israel, and their pro-American and pro-Western stance, have fueled much of the Islamic militancy. But the militants benefit from the fact that Egypt is a "have-not" country that does not have sufficient natural resources to generate immense wealth akin to the Gulf states. Moreover, the weak economy, population pressures, and insufficient services provide fuel for widespread dissent and increase the number of poor and indigent Egyptians dependent on nongovernmental social welfare agencies.

The regime's efforts to counter the militant Islamic threat influence broader foreign policy decisions. The battle is tied to the nature of the regime and its political outlook. The basic dilemma for Egypt is that while the peace process and relations with Israel have helped fuel the Islamic movements, the main benefit from making peace with Israel has been close ties and military and economic aid from the United States. This further encourages the extremists who paint Mubarak as a puppet of Uncle Sam.

Government crackdowns have brought the Islamic threat under greater control than two or three years ago. However, an assassination attempt on Mubarak in Addis Ababa in June 1995 served as a reminder that Islamic militants still hope to topple the regime. With no vice-president in place, the attack also highlighted the absence of a distinct chain of command in the event of a crisis. It was perhaps not surprising that the attack took place close to Sudan. Mubarak and other government officials have repeatedly alleged that Sudan and Iran are involved in fomenting and supporting Islamic militants in Egypt, although Iran and the Sudan have denied such involvement. Still, by mid-1997, some top Islamist leaders openly talked of a truce with the Egyptian government. Much of this talk was probably due to the government's successful containment of the Islamist militants.

JORDAN AND THE PEACE PROCESS

The Gulf War and the Arab-Israeli peace process have forced the Jordanian leadership to make difficult decisions about the future of the Hashemite Kingdom. King Hussein and his supporters have chosen to break close relations with Iraq and enter into a full-scale rapprochement with Israel. As a result, the divisions between the King's forward-looking perspective and the more hesitant and hostile feelings of much of the Jordanian population have come to the surface.

King Hussein, his brother Crown Prince Hassan, and other members of the government have pushed for full implementation of the treaty with Israel. Members of the Islamic opposition opposed the treaty in parliament while average Jordanian citizens are waiting for the economic dividends of peace to materialize. In addition—in a country where the majority of residents are Palestinians and virtually every family has relatives in the West Bank and Gaza—many Jordanians, including many government officials, are disappointed about the lack of progress in the Israeli-Palestinian negotiations.

The peace treaty with Israel is a direct result of Jordan's effort to recover from its disastrous performance during the Gulf War. After being ostracized for refusing to break with Iraq after the Iraqi invasion of Kuwait, Amman has now allied with the West. At the same time that it has improved relations with Israel, Jordan has adopted a more critical policy toward Iraq. It gave asylum to Saddam Hussein's sons-in-law (and their entourage, which included two of Saddam Hussein's daughters) when they broke with Saddam Hussein and fled from Iraq in August 1995; a few weeks later, King Hussein criticized Baghdad in a widely reported speech.[19] This new Jordanian approach has not hampered Iraqi-Jordanian economic ties, which are essential to Jordan's economy; it has helped repair relations with Kuwait and Saudi Arabia.[20] Most important, King Hussein has now been fully redeemed in the eyes of American decision makers and as a result Jordan will receive increased economic and military assistance.

JORDAN'S PREDICAMENT

Insecurity is a familiar mindset for the Jordanian leadership. With the legitimacy of the regime and the state frequently challenged and surrounded by larger, well-armed states, the leadership sees the peace process as a way to extricate Jordan from an uncertain, insecure future.

Challenges to the state and regime come in at least three forms. The first set of challenges involves the regime's legitimacy. From the founding of the independent Jordanian state in 1946, some have seen the Hashemite monarchy as no more than a creation of the British colonial powers. The successive Arab-Israeli wars have created tension between East Bank Jordanians and Palestinians from the West Bank, due, in part, to the large number of refugees fleeing to Jordan in the wake of Israel's military victories.

The Hashemite monarchy envisioned a major role for itself in the Arab world and Britain's actions partially fulfilled that vision. In a region where colonial powers have had a lasting impact in determining the rulers and shaping the borders, and where sensitivity to colonialism still runs strong, some see the Jordanian monarchy as an artificial relic of the colonial era. As one analyst explains, "The Hashemite monarchy—transplanted from Saudi Arabia by the British as a means of resolving the intricate machinations of the late colonial period—is an inherently vulnerable institution."[21] The question of King Hussein's legitimacy lingers event though he has spent over forty years on the throne.

A second set of challenges stems from differences over the definition of the Jordanian state. Both the 1948 and 1967 Arab-

Israeli wars sparked a significant exodus of Palestinians to Jordan. In 1948, many stayed in the West Bank, but the 1967 movement was exclusively into Jordan proper since Jordan lost the West Bank to Israel. Today Palestinians are a majority in Jordan, with some estimates suggesting that they are 70 percent of the population. Much of the struggle between the two groups (Palestinian and non-Palestinian) is over the question of loyalty and identity. Does the Jordanian regime truly represent Palestinians of West Bank origin? How much of a stake do Palestinians of West Bank origin have in the Jordanian state?

The issue was at its most dangerous point in September 1970, when Jordanian forces loyal to the king fought PLO militias in a civil war that almost toppled the Hussein regime. In the aftermath of the massive Israeli triumph in the 1967 war, the PLO sought not only to dominate the Palestinian refugee community in Jordan but also to topple the Hussein monarchy. Despite Syrian intervention on behalf of the Palestinians, the Jordanian army rapidly crushed Palestinian resistance. To this day, King Hussein and his supporters are highly sensitive to matters involving the Palestinians since the reverberations could have such a profound impact on Jordanian society. For instance, a permanent settlement between Palestinians and Israel that fails to address the Palestinian refugee question would affect Jordan's future demographic balance and might turn Palestinian refugee camps in Jordan into a permanent source of tension for Jordan. The current peace process again raises the issues of whether Palestinians can be represented by Jordan and of the ultimate status of the West Bank. Jordan's leadership appears less convinced than the PLO leadership that an independent Palestinian state is in Jordan's best interest; perhaps Jordan fears that a Palestinian state would try to undermine the king's regime. Such decisions have a direct bearing on Jordanian stability and Jordan can be expected to watch all Israeli-Palestinian developments very closely.

A third type of challenge to the Jordanian regime comes from right-wing Israelis who regard Jordan as the solution to Israel's Palestinian problem. Ariel Sharon, a top member of the Likud party in Israel, has made numerous statements that typify this approach. Sharon has frequently stated that Jordan is the one and only Palestinian state:

> Also, surely, we must expose the lie of "the rights of the Palestinians." It must be explicitly and loudly proclaimed by the government and the Knesset that Jordan has been and is the

Palestinian state in the Land of Israel. It is enough that this Land of the Jews has been partitioned and we have lost its overwhelming portion to Arab sovereignty.[22]

On occasion, Sharon also has also subtly challenged King Hussein's leadership: "Whether King Hussein or anyone else heads this Palestinian state, Jordan, is their decision."[23] Former Prime Minister Yitzhak Shamir of the Likud Party dropped the "Jordan is Palestine" mantra, but it can still be heard in some circles in Israel.

Jordan's inferior strategic position in relation to its neighbors compounds its problems. Jordan is surrounded by four states, all with better military forces: Israel to the west, Syria to the north, Iraq to the east, and Saudi Arabia to the east and south. Jordan has a smaller population than Israel and less than one-third the populations of Syria and Saudi Arabia. Iraq has more than four times as many people as Jordan. In area, Jordan is smaller than all these states except Israel. Israel and Jordan fought in 1948 and again in 1967; Syrian forces moved against Jordan in 1970 and 1980.[24] In 1970, Syria supported Palestinian forces in their battle against the Jordanian army.

Jordan faces additional threats in the form of radical subversion, particularly from Syria and Iran. The Jordanian government is concerned that Iran might attempt to bolster Islamic opponents of the government and foment unrest led by Islamic groups. It is also concerned about terrorists infiltrating from Syria and using Jordan as a base of operations to attack Israeli targets. Jordan has uncovered individuals, weapons, and explosives that apparently originated in Syria. It is hard to believe that the Asad regime is unaware of such operations in Jordan, and Jordan has protested privately to Syria and more publicly at the August 1996 Cairo summit.[25]

Finally, Jordan's insecurities are compounded by economic vulnerabilities. In 1994, trade with Iraq accounted for over 13 percent of exports and 12 percent of imports, including about 70,000 barrels of Iraqi crude oil each day.[26] Jordan has resisted Western pressure to cut economic ties with Iraq, especially as long as Kuwait and Saudi Arabia do not restore pre-Gulf War aid levels. At home, unemployment may be as high as 20 percent,[27] and the post-Gulf War building boom has slowed. With limited natural resources and a large foreign debt, Jordan has limited options with regard to its economic future. Because of these circumstances, the much anticipated peace dividend has been a driving force behind Jordan's interest in the peace process.

WILL PEACE BENEFIT JORDAN?

While the rapid pace of Israeli-Jordanian negotiations took diplomats by surprise, it is understandable in the context of potential benefits the process could provide to Jordan. The Jordanian leadership is counting on the benefits of peace to help win over its ambivalent citizens.

The provisions of the 1994 Israeli-Jordanian treaty put to rest many security concerns and laid the groundwork for future cooperation. In Article 4, the parties agreed to refrain from the threat or use of any kind of force against each other, including subversion; to ensure that "violence against the other Party do not originate from, and are not committed within, through or over their territory" (a response to historical Israeli fears of an Arab coalition attacking from the east); to cooperate on combating terrorism; and to work toward a Middle East free from weapons of mass destruction. In Article 11, they went so far as to agree "to abstain from hostile or discriminatory propaganda against each other." On the subject of cooperative ties, the treaty is full of calls for economic development, cultural exchanges, increased transport links, tourism promotion, and other aspects of warm relations. In addition, Jordan secured recognition of its border with Israel, a major boost to overall Jordanian legitimacy, and its "special role" in the Muslim holy shrines in Jerusalem. The treaty also contained novel land-leasing arrangements that allowed Israel to concede Jordanian sovereignty over several areas of farmland along the border without uprooting Israeli farmers.[28]

More generally, the peace process reduces Jordanian isolation within Western-Israeli-moderate Arab circles. In the past, Jordan was often overlooked in regional discussions because it is a small state with little political or military clout. Its role in the peace process has brought Jordan increased recognition and respect, and increased its regional standing. In the long run, the process could help put challenges to Jordanian legitimacy to rest. If Israeli-Palestinian talks are successful, tension with West Bank Palestinians and Israeli right-wingers should ease. Moreover, a full peace now with Israel ensures that Jordanian interests are not sold out by Israel and other Arab leaders in the future while Jordan stands on the sidelines. By participating early, Jordan has ensured that it is part of the process and has a credible voice.

In the security realm, a successful peace process could alleviate Jordanian concerns about the military strength of its neighbors. The treaty with Israel has reduced the Israeli threat and may help Jordan use Israel as a counterweight against Iraq or Syria. In fact, in August 1995, Israeli sources implied that the Israeli government would not accept Iraqi moves against Jordan as a result of the defection of Saddam Hussein's sons-in-law. This is related to a long Israeli tradition of regarding Jordan as a buffer state and opposing the presence of foreign forces in Jordan. As the process moves forward, greater conflict resolution can only benefit Jordan. Similarly, an arms control agreement would benefit a weaker state like Jordan, since Jordan will have little to cutback, unlike several of the neighboring states.

Peace also brings the advantages of friendly relations with the United States after a period of disagreement surrounding the Gulf War. U.S. debt relief will alleviate a portion of Jordan's foreign obligations (over $700 million). Alignment with the United States, the world's only superpower, is an attractive option for a vulnerable state such as Jordan.[29]

Economic help goes beyond American debt relief. Jordanians hoped for additional U.S. military and economic aid, much like Israel and Egypt received after Camp David. (However, little such aid had materialized by mid-1997, and it does not seem likely in the more austere fiscal climate prevailing in Washington.) Peacemaking should also help increase private foreign investment. With the fear of conflict removed, tourism should grow. In 1995, Jordan saw such an increase in foreign visitors that, at sites like Petra, limited capacity became a constraint; according to Jordan's Ministry of Tourism, the number of tourists rose 25 percent from 1994 to 1995.[30] Ties with Israel could increase economic contact, and trade with its neighbor could lead to a variety of economic gains, including increased tourism, and development of the Jordan Valley and the Aqaba-Eilat area, two border areas that have not been developed because of ongoing tensions. Jordan's position in the region could make it a major transit point for goods. The government has made several major proposals that would enhance Jordan's infrastructure and its role as an economic bridge.

If some of these hopes come to pass, Jordan will have gained significant benefits from the peace with Israel. In the meantime, however, while the king and government supporters talk of the theoretical benefits, more skeptical Jordanians are concerned that the Hashemite Kingdom moved too fast and will not achieve nearly the return that the palace has claimed.

PROBLEMS WITH THE PROCESS

Many Jordanians are far more hesitant than the government leadership about the peace treaty with Israel, in part because Israel has not moved as fast as expected on follow-through with the Palestinians. Jordanians, including the leadership, regard the Palestinian track as an important barometer of Arab-Israeli peace and assumed that the Israeli-Palestinian process would move faster. They are disturbed that little progress has been made on several core issues, including Israeli settlements and further Israeli withdrawals from occupied territory. Among the public, Netanyahu's election in May 1996 enhanced these fears.

The economic dividend also has been slow to bear fruit. King Hussein and his advisors oversold the economic benefits of the treaty to create popular support. The resulting high expectations, however, were dashed when progress was slower than promised. The government also lost support for the treaty when Jordanian security forces surrounded the parliament on the day of the vote; this heavy-handed approach was regarded by some as intimidation.

Relations with the United States provide another example of how expectations and reality diverged. Aid from the United States has been less than Jordan hoped for. Unlike Egypt and Israel, which received large U.S. aid packages after Camp David, Jordan's aid has been mostly limited to debt relief. Even this relief ran into brief trouble with some Republican budget cutters in the U.S. Congress in 1995, although in the end the relief package was not cut. Economic benefits are coming to Jordan slower and on a smaller-scale than Jordanians expected. As a result, many Jordanians who were not enthusiastic at first are even less supportive now. The overly optimistic visions meant to win their support have actually contributed to greater skepticism.

There will continue to be ups and downs in the process as King Hussein struggles to find the proper pace of change. Another Israel-PLO agreement and the continued, measured pace of Israeli-Jordanian implementation should help erase doubts among some Jordanians. The key question is whether or not the Jordanian regime can find a way to balance various concerns while proceeding in a consistent direction on the peace process. The leadership has been enticed by the prospects of moving forward in the peace process and sitting in the American camp, but it remains to be seen how well the government can bring along the people. King Hussein is counting on this approach to ease Jordan's insecurities and bolster its political and economic standing in the region, a tall but plausible order from a regime and state with so many question marks and concerns.

Jordan's approach is vulnerable to Israeli policies under Netanyahu. If Israel undermines the entire peace process by increasing settlement building in the West Bank, King Hussein will be hard-pressed to continue in a pro-Western, pro-Israeli direction. The crisis between Jordan and the Netanyahu regime that erupted in fall 1996 and the early months of 1997 over the opening of a tunnel in Jerusalem and the construction of Israeli apartments in East Jerusalem at Har Homa (Jebel Abu Ghneim) provided additional fuel to the domestic critics of the Jordanian regime, an unwelcome prospect for King Hussein.

CHAPTER FIVE

SYRIA, LEBANON, AND THE PEACE PROCESS

Although Israeli-Palestinian relations remain at the heart of the Arab-Israeli conflict, the Israeli-Syrian front is important to achieving peace both among the front-line states (Egypt, Israel, Jordan, Lebanon, and Syria) and throughout the region. Because of Syria's dominant role in Lebanese decision making, talks between Israel and Syria are essential to resolving the discord between Israel and both Syria and Lebanon. Since the peace process began in Madrid, Israel and Syria have talked at length, but no agreement has been concluded. Though the probable outlines of an agreement are not difficult to ascertain, the two sides had failed to progress further as of mid-1997 for both specific technical and broad strategic reasons. Meanwhile, Lebanon grapples with a host of internal issues even as the future of Israeli-Syrian relations seemingly holds the key to Lebanon's future.

SYRIA AND THE PEACE PROCESS

A peace treaty between Syria and Israel would be a major milestone in the search for a comprehensive Middle East settlement. Once Hafez al-Asad or his successors have signed a treaty, Lebanon would quickly follow suit, and then most of the North African and Gulf Arab states would follow. Despite U.S. and international pressures to achieve this breakthrough, Israeli-Syrian talks have stalled repeatedly. Syria's domestic situation, the status of economic reform, and its relations with Iraq, Turkey, and the wider Arab world affect Syrian foreign policy and national security considerations as well as relations with Israel. They help shape the atmosphere of the negotiations and Syria's calculation of whether peace with Israel is in its interests.

In late 1995 and early 1996, new negotiations between Israel and Syria once again generated initial optimism, despite the remaining gaps between the parties. Unlike his predecessor, Shimon Peres expressed an interest in restarting substantive talks and moving toward a peace agreement.[1] But the subtleties and complexities of the Israeli-Syrian relationship made an imminent breakthrough implausible, and then the election of Netanyahu— who had vowed in the campaign never to return the Golan Heights—put any hope for early progress on hold. Furthermore, the nuts and bolts of an Israeli-Syrian agreement will take many months to negotiate even after a general framework is agreed upon.

The difficulties were highlighted during the April 1996 Israeli offensive in Lebanon. On April 11, Israeli forces launched a large-scale attack in response to Hizbollah rocket attacks against northern Israel. Although life in northern Israel was totally disrupted, Lebanon suffered the heaviest casualties, with 160 killed during the weeks of fighting. The deadliest incident came on April 18, when 100 Lebanese were killed after Israeli shells hit a U.N. peacekeeping base at Qana that had been housing hundreds of refugees. Though Israel claimed that the attack was accidental and that Hizbollah guerrillas were attacking Israeli forces from the area, a later U.N. report suggested that it may have been intentional.[2] A U.S.-brokered ceasefire went into effect on April 27. The agreement barred attacks on civilian areas, but each side retained the right of self-defense. Since that time, sporadic fighting has broken out between the hostile military forces.

In assessing Syria's political stance in 1997 in light of the Israeli elections, it is essential to remember the role that the downfall of the Soviet Union played in encouraging a new Syrian tack. Syria's current approach to relations with Israel and the United States was shaped in part by Mikhail Gorbachev's decision that the Soviet Union, a key ally of Damascus, no longer supported Syria's quest for strategic parity with Israel and that it would begin to require Syria to pay for Soviet weaponry, including past shipments involving billions of dollars of Syrian debt. In late 1991, with the collapse of the Soviet Union, Syria was threatened with isolation from most centers of global power. During the long and bitter Iran-Iraq war, Syria had been one of the few countries to support the Iranian position. Syria's subsequent alignment with the United States during the Gulf War, though inspired by the historic rivalry between Saddam Hussein and Hafez al-Asad and Syria's friendship with Saudi Arabia, paved the way for a less antagonistic, and potentially beneficial relationship between Damascus and Washington. Nonetheless, as of mid-1997, Syria remained on the U.S. list of terrorist countries, where it had been since 1979.

Peace talks with Israel following the Madrid summit in 1991 gave Damascus an opportunity to improve relations with the United States. For Syria and the other parties to the Arab-Israeli conflict, regional peace would bring significant security gains. But while Asad may hope to use the peace process to reposition Syria within the international community, he understands that he is a vital piece of the puzzle and therefore will play his hand carefully. On the important issues of arms control and regional security, no serious multilateral progress can be made without Syrian involvement. In addition, if Syria and the Damascus-based Palestinian groups are at peace with Israel, the countries of Iran, Iraq, and Libya will have a harder time opposing the process.

This highlights one area in which Israel very much wants a peace agreement with Syria. Although many Israelis oppose relinquishing the Golan Heights, they recognize the important role that Syria plays in national security calculations. Israelis' sense of personal security was in the spotlight after the signing of the Declaration of Principles and the string of suicide bombing attacks against Israelis, but personal security is related largely to Israeli-Palestinian relations. In contrast, national security depends largely on reaching a deal with Syria, the key holdout. A new war with Syria could have devastating consequences for both countries. Israel would certainly "win" the war but at a cost in Israeli lives considered unacceptable at this time. While terrorism is a ghastly reality to Israelis, the real threat to their survival has been from Arab states and Iran. Again, if Syria and Israel can come to an agreement, the maneuvering room for Iran, Iraq, and Libya will be reduced, strengthening prospects for greater regional security.

WHAT SYRIA WANTS

The outline of an Israeli-Syrian deal is no mystery. What is needed is a new catalyst to implement it.

Syria's major demand is that Israel withdraw from the Golan Heights to the line held by Israel on June 4, 1967. This involves withdrawing from slightly more territory than if Israel only withdrew to the international border established in 1923 (although at this point, the Israeli public considers withdrawal to either the 1923 or the 1967 border as tantamount to full withdrawal). In return for Israel's withdrawal, Syria offers Israeli negotiators the measures mentioned in U.N. Security Council (UNSC) resolution 242 of 1967: an end to the belligerency, recognition of Israeli sovereignty, and respect for Israel's territorial integrity. According to Syria, Israel must withdraw not only from the Golan but also from

105

southern Lebanon, as stipulated in UNSC resolution 425 approved in March 1978.

Although both Rabin and Peres emphasized that Israel expects "full peace" with Syria, including normalization of relations, the Syrian government has stated that open borders and diplomatic and economic relations cannot occur until there is also substantial progress on the Israeli-Palestinian track. Thus far the Oslo process has not produced enough to meet Syria's definition of progress. Syria is looking for full Palestinian control of the West Bank and advanced negotiations on Jerusalem, borders, and Israeli settlements. The key question for Asad is whether a clear majority of Palestinians back and support the policies of Yasser Arafat and the Palestinian Authority.

Syria offers both historical and pragmatic reasons for its interest in the Palestinian cause. Syria and Lebanon have viewed Palestine as part of natural Syria,[3] and have been involved in Palestinian issues since the 1930s. Lebanon and Syria both house hundreds of thousands of Palestinian refugees. This has not been a problem for Syria on either demographic or security grounds, but the refugees and the Palestinian question have been a central factor in Lebanese instability over the last twenty-five or more years. This creates an added impetus for ensuring that Israeli-Palestinian talks lead to a genuine solution that encompasses the Palestinian diaspora as well as the Palestinians in the occupied territories.

It is understood that any Syrian regime would insist on these basic principles for peace with Israel. To yield to anything less would be equivalent to political suicide. After all, as most Syrians insist, the "Golan has been Syrian territory since time immemorial."[4] Any plausible post-Asad regime would likely adhere to the same conditions, with perhaps minor variations.

No Syrian regime can accept the continued Israeli occupation of the Golan Heights. Not only is the Golan regarded as Syrian territory but Israeli military occupation poses a direct and immediate military threat to Damascus, which is only thirty-seven miles from the ceasefire line.[5] The Golan is a "critical natural defense against Israel. . . .The Golan in Syrian hands would provide crucial defensive depth for the country's security."[6] Without the Golan and lacking natural barriers to the east, Syria's strategic situation is dubious at best. Israeli military contingents are in direct line of sight of Damascus, and their sophisticated electronics on Mt. Hermon can eavesdrop on the city. Israeli control of the Golan is both a strategic threat and an unending source of humiliation. The Golan Heights issue is important not only to Syria's security, but also to Asad's personal standing among the Syrian people and in the Arab world. Continued Israeli control undermines Syrian aspirations for Arab leadership; thus far, Egypt—not Syria—regained all it lost, including both its territory and, after some time, its clout in the Arab world.[7]

Despite this strong stance, Syria may be more flexible than its current position suggests. First, it is possible that Syria would accept some steps toward normalization once an agreement on full withdrawal is signed—rather than waiting until the withdrawals are completed. These steps will not be as farreaching as Israel would like, but could include a meeting of foreign ministers or an official exchange of academics and journalists. Even if Syria is willing to consider these and additional steps toward normalization after a withdrawal agreement is signed, it would be reluctant to admit so at this time for tactical negotiating reasons.

Second, Asad is likely to be more flexible on the Palestinian issue. Although the calls for withdrawal from the Golan Heights and Lebanon have set a concrete benchmark for successful agreement and implementation, the Palestinian track lacks a clear and specific threshold for measuring success. Syria is able to adjust its position on the Palestinians both because of on-the-ground changes in the West Bank and Gaza and because of other, perhaps more important, considerations in Damascus. For instance, Syria could use progress at the Israeli-Palestinian final status talks as a pretext for a policy adjustment, especially if advances lead to a broadening of Palestinian support for the Oslo process. Syria was resentful of the separate Palestinian deals with Israel (Oslo I and II) and may feel less inclined to stand up for Palestinian interests at the expense of Syrian ones.

The absence of a specific marker for Israeli fulfillment of Syrian positions on the Palestinian cause may be no accident. One wonders to what extent Syria's inclusion of the Palestinians is a genuine concern rather than a fig leaf for delay or an attempt to stake out a tough bargaining position with Israel. Syria argues publicly that its emphasis on success on the Palestinian track is legitimate, but it is easy to be cynical about such claims. Only time will tell how deeply Syria feels for the Palestinian cause.

ISRAELI-SYRIAN HESITANCY

A number of additional factors contributed to the slowdown in negotiations between Israel and Syria even before Netanyahu came to power. However, these factors do not preclude Israeli-

Syrian progress (except perhaps for the overriding importance of other Syrian interests); they merely suggest why delays and false starts have been an enduring feature of Israeli-Syrian talks. At the right moment, or with the right catalyst, this slowness could quickly dissipate. These factors also are indicative of what issues need to be addressed for a complete Israeli-Syrian peace.

STRATEGIC STALEMATE

Syria now recognizes that it does not have the offensive capabilities to achieve a military victory in a limited war on the Golan. The end of the Cold War ended Syria's quest for the type of strategic parity that might have given Syria a more effective offensive force. At the same time, Syria possesses sufficient defensive capabilities to deter Israel from a major military assault along the Golan front. Syria has deployed a surface-to-surface missile force armed with chemical warheads.

The military standoff means that neither side is in a position to compel the other party to submit to its conditions for a settlement. Syria cannot threaten Israel with a military option to retake the Golan, and Israel cannot use the threat of force if Syria refuses to agree to Israeli demands for a peace settlement. This stalemate is not permanent. Both Syrian and Israeli leaders have hinted that a failure to achieve peace could lead to a continued struggle and possibly war.

There is little domestic pressure on the Asad regime to change course and either speed up the talks with Israel or abandon them altogether. Asad's domestic power base is the security establishment and the Baath Party and includes the support of Alawites, peasants, and lower-middle-class Syrians. This support legitimizes the regime, and there are no signs that the support is crumbling or declining. Although corruption and mismanagement continue, the economy has improved since the mid-1980s. Liberalization, good agricultural harvests, rising oil export revenue, and post-Gulf War investments in infrastructure and industry are all pushing the Syrian economy in a positive direction. Foreign relations in general are good with the countries that matter most to Syria's security and financial well-being: Saudi Arabia, the United States, and the European Union.

In contrast to this relatively comfortable status quo, greater concessions to Israel could spark a strong domestic backlash both within the government and from the general population—which is why Syrian officials are in no hurry to conclude a deal that is not entirely on their terms. Syria is ready to make a peace deal, but only an unadulterated version of the one outlined by Syrian negotiators. At this point, the risk to the regime is too great to justify a change in stance.

Secondary concerns about Lebanon only bolster this approach. Although Lebanon is not publicly cited by Syria as a major concern, the effect of the peace process on the ultimate disposition of Lebanon is important to the Asad regime. In particular, Asad is concerned about the effect of the peace process on Syria's military and business leaders who benefit from Syrian control of Lebanon. They fear that a deal with Israel could increase Lebanese political independence.

In September and October 1989, the Arab League facilitated an agreement—the Document of National Understanding— among sixty-two Muslim and Christian members of the Lebanese parliament who met in Taif, Saudi Arabia. The agreement called for the transfer of executive power from the Christian president to a cabinet with an equal number of Christians and Muslims. Initially the Taif agreement was rejected by many Lebanese, and a bitter dispute between the Christian factions led to a military stand- off between General Michel Aoun, who rejected Taif, and the new President Hrawi, who accepted Taif. The Lebanese constitution was amended in September 1990 in order to bring about the imple- mentation of the Taif agreement, which also called on Syria to help the armed forces of the Lebanese government re-assert control over Lebanon. For up to two years (starting from the time the con- stitution was amended) Syrian armed forces would assist the Lebanese government in implementing the Taif security plans before withdrawing to eastern Lebanon; the Arab League committee that helped negotiate the Taif agreement also disclosed an annex to the agreement in which they pledged to ensure that Syria would ultimately withdraw from Lebanon. In October 1990, Syrian troops defeated General Aoun, who was exiled to France. In May 1991, Lebanon and Syria signed a bilateral treaty establishing formal economic, military, and political links and confirming Syria as the guarantor of the Taif security plans.

Syrians have reason to fear that the peace process could even- tually break the Syrian hold on Lebanon, even if the United States and Israel agree to accept the Syrian military and political presence in the short run. Peace could allow Lebanon to achieve economic growth, renew ties with the West, and develop its own ties with Israel. Such developments would contribute to Lebanon's re-emergence, perhaps returning it to the glory years of the

1950s and 1960s. For some Syrians, the prospect of a Lebanese renaissance has troubling implications and they prefer to see Lebanon remain in the Syrian shadow.

Some observers reject the idea that Syria can indefinitely bide its time. They argue that the stability of the Asad regime, the state of the economy, and the type of transition likely in the case of Asad's death challenges the status quo. If the regime is less secure or the economy is in need of a boost from external investment and greater foreign trade, the drawbacks to inaction increase. In fact, pessimistic assessments of both regime stability and the state of the Syrian economy leave plenty of room for other interpretations of the cause of Israeli-Syrian delays.

OTHER SYRIAN CONCERNS MORE IMPORTANT

Another possible reason for stalemate is that the leadership might regard even a deal entirely adhering to Syria's current negotiating position as detrimental to its survival. According to this view, other issues are simply more important to the regime than the supposedly negotiable issues that are blocking an Israeli-Syrian breakthrough. These more important issues include ensuring the Asad regime's survival in general, maintaining Alawi supremacy and the control of Lebanon, and avoiding normalization with Israel—all seen as more important than reclaiming the Golan. Daniel Pipes, one analyst who sees the stalemate this way, writes that Asad "is likely to avoid any compromise unless essential to ensure the stability of his rule."[8]

The prospect of normalization with Israel raises perhaps the gravest concerns in Damascus. Thus far, Syria has argued that the act of defining peaceful relations should follow an Israeli commitment to full withdrawal from the Golan. On January 16, 1994, Asad told President Clinton in Damascus that Syria was ready for "normal peaceful relations" with Israel, but gave no further details. On September 10, 1994, Asad told the Syrian parliament that "Syria shall meet the objective requirements of peace that are agreed upon."[9] This was widely seen as a reference to security arrangements and normalization.

The Israeli definition of normalization with Syria includes diplomatic relations, open borders, and trade. Rabin emphasized the importance of normal relations: "This government wants to reach a peace which will provide us with real peace—a peace which every Israeli will recognize as such, wherein every Israeli will be able to travel to Syria, to Damascus or anywhere else, in order to forge commercial or cultural relations."[10] He considered it as important as withdrawal or security arrangements:

> The third component is our desire, our demand for a crucial component: Following a very limited withdrawal—because the entire Golan Heights is very small—after a token withdrawal really, we would like to have a period that would also last years, during which full normalization would develop. That should include embassies, borders open to the movement of people and goods. Without these elements we will be definitely unable to consent to any peace treaty.[11]

Rabin (and then Peres) stressed normalization as a necessary component that is desired by all Israelis; indeed, withdrawal from the Golan would not pass a referendum or Knesset vote unless linked to normalization.[12] However, for Hafez al-Asad, normalization entails a high degree of transparency and openness. It would involve greater interaction with the outside world. Open borders would still leave border controls in the hands of the Syrian government, but the government would be unable to refuse entry to Israelis simply on the basis of their passport. Jordan, which has limited the number of Israelis who may enter the country since the treaty with Israel was signed, nevertheless has hundreds of Israelis crossing at each checkpoint on a daily basis.

The reverse possibility of Syrians traveling to Israel is also a drawback for an authoritarian regime. Visits to a Westernized, democratic country like Israel might push some Syrians to lobby harder at home for more economic benefits or political rights. To some extent, Asad's fear of normalization is a rational fear based on specific possibilities that can be described and delineated. Yet there is also an intangible element solely based on the general fear of ties with a Zionist democracy that was once his arch-enemy. Israel's traditional role as Syria's primary foe distinguishes it from other democracies with which Syria already has relations. At a minimum, the Asad regime would have to shift its focus from an anti-Israel base in which legitimacy is derived from the conflict with Israel, a process that has already begun. Both the concrete fears and the impalpable ones contribute to Syrian apprehension about the process.

U.S. officials have made clear that they are completely behind Israel's call for full peace and normalization with Syria. In a speech on May 17, 1994, Anthony Lake, then national security adviser, said the Clinton Administration "will insist" that peace include "full diplomatic relations, and [sic] end to the boycott, open borders for people and trade, and promotion of joint economic projects."[13]

Critics of this analysis contend that the contamination by democratic forces that allegedly scares Asad into slowing the peace talks already exists. Syria has widespread contacts with other countries, companies, and regimes. There are few restrictions on travel, and foreigners—including Westerners—regularly visit Syria. Extensive commercial and cultural contacts are in place, and foreign companies, especially U.S. oil companies, already operate in Syria. Foreign films, books, and newspapers are available, and active U.S. and European cultural centers exist. In short, Syria already has the same level of openness that would be associated with normalization with Israel, even if it is an authoritarian country overall. Critics contend that the normalization argument stems from a misunderstanding of Syrian hostility toward Israel. It has not been caused by fear of Israel as a democracy or open society, but rather by historical and nationalist enmity toward the Zionist state and Zionism. Rather than precluding a deal with Israel, Syria's long-held struggle with Israel necessitates that Asad achieve enough of Syria's objectives in a negotiated settlement to justify and vindicate the decades of human and financial sacrifices by the Syrian people.[14]

U.S. PRESSURE INEFFECTIVE

The United States is not in a strong position to facilitate an agreement by exerting pressure on the parties. In theory, the United States could offer incentives to Syria such as removal from the U.S. State Department's list of international sponsors of terrorism, but this would cause anger in the United States and is likely to be opposed as long as Syria continues to harbor terrorist organizations and their notorious leaders.

U.S. pressure on Syria's financial supporters like Saudi Arabia also is unlikely to work. Syria could react to such heavy-handed pressure and abandon the peace talks altogether, the opposite of the result desired by the United States. In extremis, strong U.S. pressure could lead an indignant Syria to join and/or mobilize the rejectionist countries and organizations, including Iran, Iraq, Libya, and several Palestinian organizations.

The Clinton administration was highly unlikely to exert serious pressure on Israel as long as a Labor government was in power;

even under a Likud government, serious pressure is likely only if Israel blatantly disregards the peace process. Also, the Israeli-Palestinian track is demanding much of the Israeli government's attention and political capital, leaving less flexibility for talks with Syria at the present time.

ISRAEL CAN WAIT

Syria is not the only party in these bilateral talks with reasons to hold off on concessions or further agreements. Netanyahu was elected in part because he promised not to withdraw from the Golan, a sine qua non of peace from the Syrian perspective. After his election, Netanyahu and his advisors suggested that Israel and Syria should focus on understandings on specific issues rather than a comprehensive peace treaty. They claimed that this incremental approach would take advantage of existing areas of common interest and would avoid the all-or-nothing nature of past Israeli-Syrian talks.[15] One possibility mentioned was an initial focus on southern Lebanon.

In the meantime, Israel is reaping major benefits from other Arab-Israeli advances. Oslo II, ties with Jordan, the economic summits in Casablanca and Amman, and a host of new diplomatic and economic relations have been a boon to the Israeli economy and, except for Oslo II, the Israeli psyche across-the-board.

Even for an Israeli government willing to compromise and part with all or most of the Golan, the bottom line calculation would be that the Israeli public cannot accept too many major concessions at once. The bridge can only bear so much traffic, as Israelis are fond of pointing out. The Israeli public is bitterly divided over the best course of action with regard to the Palestinians. Israeli officials privately related similar concerns in 1994-95, when Egypt pressed Israel to sign the Nuclear Nonproliferation Treaty (or at least set up a specific timetable to do so), although at that time Israeli-Syrian issues were lumped with Israeli-Palestinian talks and considered in the basket of issues on which concessions might be forthcoming. With the implementation of Oslo II, including large-scale changes on the West Bank, and the start of Israeli-Palestinian final status talks on issues such as borders, Israeli settlements, Palestinian refugees, Jerusalem, and the exact nature of the future Palestinian entity, the agenda is already full of controversial and complex issues. Although Israel might accept a breakthrough roughly on its own terms, the rapidity of other developments precludes offering major concessions to Damascus.

The irony is that Israel and Syria do agree on one point: both sides see potential domestic drawbacks to proceeding unless it is done without concessions, an obvious impossibility for both parties given the incompatibility of the official positions.

DELAYS ON THE ISRAELI-PALESTINIAN TRACK

One final factor worth noting is that Israeli-Palestinian talks have not progressed on schedule. Oslo II was signed more than a year after the initial deadline. To the extent that the disposition of the Palestinians is a fundamental Syrian concern, delays on this track add to the stalled Israeli-Syrian track. Advances in the Oslo process—or wider acceptance of Arafat in the Palestinian community, including the diaspora—would make this less of a factor in the Israeli-Syrian talks.

THE DANGERS OF WAITING INDEFINITELY

If no agreement is signed between Israel and Syria, military confrontation could re-emerge. Low-intensity skirmishes in Lebanon, such as those in April 1996, could become more common. In this kind of action, Syrian forces may not be directly involved; Syria may take a behind-the-scenes approach, exerting influence over both Hizbollah and the Lebanese government. But if a peace agreement is indefinitely postponed, more significant clashes that involve direct Israeli-Syrian confrontations could become possible.

While Syria currently does not have the offensive capabilities to confront Israel's armed forces, this could change or at least the gap could be narrowed,[16] and Syria could think about a limited offensive strike to reclaim the Golan. Rabin recognized this in June 1994, when he said that without an agreement with Syria, Israel should "prepare for war 3, 5 years or 7 years from now, or 10 years from now."[17]

Syrian military planners are aware that in a future confrontation a Syrian military victory is unlikely. As one Arab commentator has written, "Syria is no match for Israel in terms of economic development and military prowess. Israel is a nuclear power whose security and well-being are guaranteed by the United States."[18] Israel's occupation of southern Lebanon poses another military problem for the regime. Although Syria itself has used Lebanon to fight a proxy war against Israel through Hizbollah, in a future confrontation, Syrian military planners fear that

Israel could outflank Syria through Lebanon. As a result, Syrian military planners believe that the most logical approach would be a casualty-intensive strategy that counters Israeli military strength by attempting to inflict heavy human losses on the Israeli side. Syria retains the benefit of a much larger standing army than Israel, but once Israel achieves full mobilization, Israeli troops could possibly traverse the short distance to Damascus. While Israel relies on air power and flanking maneuvers in part to avoid high Israeli military casualties, Syrian military leaders know that a bloody groundwar is the surest method to sap Israeli domestic support for continued fighting.

The Syrian military has been unable to match Israel's air superiority and is alarmed by Israel's continuing efforts to improve its own arsenal. Publicly, the Syrian regime alleges that Israeli weaponry demonstrates Israel's militaristic nature. A commentary published in *Tishrin,* a state-run Syrian newspaper, explained that "Israel's determination to acquire and stockpile additional weapons and military hardware shows that the Israeli mind-set rooted in aggression, war, and tension is unchanged, and that Israel is not pursuing a policy aimed at promoting peace efforts."[19]

Although the Israeli nuclear program has not been as high on the Syrian agenda as the conventional threat from the Golan, Damascus is also concerned about Israeli weapons of mass destruction. Syria was not displeased to see Egypt push the issue of Israeli nuclear weapons—yet another example of Israel's dominating and threatening posture—in relation to the April 1995 NPT renewal. Syria may consider its missiles and chemical weapons to be a bargaining chip in negotiations and discussions of weapons of mass destruction.

OTHER SECURITY THREATS TO SYRIA

In addition to the Israeli threat to Syrian security, the Asad regime faces a number of other issues that influence Syrian security and stability. The Israeli-Syrian talks do not take place in a political and military vacuum, but rather in the context of Syria's domestic situation and relations with its other large neighbors, Iraq and Turkey. Religious and ethnic splits in the Syrian population, the state of the Syrian economy, and the situation in Lebanon all help shape, at least indirectly, the possibilities for an Israeli-Syrian agreement. The opposite is also true: the pathway of the Israeli-Syrian peace process affects these matters and contributes to Syria's overall security posture and political approach.

Moreover, even if these issues are not threatening at the moment, they could serve as the fuel for a crisis or confrontation in the future. Some will remain as non-issues indefinitely but the potential for trouble exists in all these areas.

RELIGIOUS AND ETHNIC DIVISIONS

Asad's dictatorship thus far has provided protection for the Alawites, a Moslem sect shunned by mainstream Shiite and Sunni Moslems, but it could also generate deep resentment among disempowered Syrians, particularly Sunni Arabs. In terms of religion, Sunni Moslems are 74 percent of the Syrian population, Alawites are under 16 percent, and Christian sects 10 percent. About 90 percent of the population is Arab, while Kurds, Armenians, and other non-Arab groups account for close to 10 percent of the population.[20] Thus one can imagine a scenario in which Asad and other Alawites have good reason to fear that the fall of the regime could mean the repression of Alawites by Sunnis, partially out of revenge for the years of Alawite strength under Asad, but also because the Alawites are, after all, a minority. As the favored group, Alawites would be the target of disgruntled Syrians looking to blame someone for the years of subservience to Asad and a disproportionate number of Alawite officials. Asad has worked hard to appease a variety of constituencies, but such efforts by a dictator are not a fail-safe method of avoiding future bloodshed and divisions.

In the past, when faced with internal dissent in the form of the Muslim Brotherhood, an Islamic religious and political movement, the Asad regime moved aggressively to dismantle the Brotherhood organization. The Brotherhood in Syria has sought to introduce greater adherence to Islam in the face of the largely secular Asad regime. Asad's ruthless murder of thousands of Islamic fundamentalist opponents at Hama in 1982, which included the destruction of large parts of the city, was the most publicized event of an internal crackdown on regime opponents. This kind of confrontation, if repeated, can spark severe problems for a regime. While usually successful, aggressive attempts to maintain stability and order have also been known to backfire and shorten a regime's tenure.

THE ECONOMY

As already discussed, the economy is a relevant factor in peace process calculations, security concerns, and regime stability.

The peace process could provide an opening for greater foreign investment and give the government the opportunity to focus on economic reform. It could, however, also take away trade and business from some Syrians operating in Lebanon. It could contribute to continued stalemate at the Israeli-Syrian negotiations, where Israel expects to secure significant economic access to Syria (and other Arab states). Despite the prospects for economic improvement, opinions differ about the current state of the Syrian economy.

Throughout the 1980s, the Syrian economy was very weak. Syria had a high foreign debt, low foreign exchange reserves, and a limited amount of oil revenue. The economy picked up in 1990, but it is unclear how far this will carry Syria. Outside observers express a variety of views about Syria's economic future.

Some see the 1990s as the beginning of a more stable situation: "Syria's domestic economic crisis, therefore, appears to have ameliorated as the post-Cold War era opened."[21] Positive developments include oil revenues of about $2 billion per year, a real GDP growth rate of over 6 percent per annum from 1991 through 1994, and an increase in imports from $2.1 billion in 1989 to $5.5 billion in 1994.[22] Asad has been able to please key military officials and commercial interests in economic terms, and this will help keep the economy afloat. But it is uncertain whether the recent recovery will persist.

Others observers, particularly Western analysts, are more negative. One observer writes:

> Syria's economy is in shambles. Assad's faithful supporters now must hold two and three jobs to be able to put ever more expensive bread on their tables. . . . inflation that's running between 15 percent and 20 percent annually. . . . What industry there is is almost worthless. . . . Syria's debt to Russia, which Assad refuses to pay, stands at over 412 billion dinars.[23]

Baath party socialist management and heavy spending on arms have taken a severe toll on the Syrian economy, and per capita income is only about $1,000 despite the boost from Syrian oil fields.[24] The 600,000 barrels per day of oil bring in about $2 billion annually, but little oil money has trickled down to the general populace and current oil reserves are expected to last only for another decade or less.[25] The Syrian government has held back in essential areas of economic reform. It has taken only a par-

117

tial step toward privatizing state entities, failed to overhaul the interest rate system or modernize the banking system, and accumulated significant foreign debt. Without a "realistic" interest rate environment, foreign investment is likely to be limited, including among the Syrian expatriate community that may control $25 billion or more. Syria may be counting on debt relief from Russia and other countries as part of a peace agreement with Israel, the easy way out of large-scale financial obligations. Other economic problems include rising inflation (20 percent in 1994), unemployment, and an overstretched water and power infrastructure.[26]

This more pessimistic outlook increases the importance of progress at the peace talks. Peace with Israel would open the doors to greater foreign investment and might lead to the lifting of U.S. limitations on dealing with Syria (e.g., inclusion on the U.S. list of sponsors of international terrorism). When business leaders around the globe begin to sense that the conflict is winding down, they will be more likely to enter Syrian markets; only then can Syria reap the benefits of a post-conflict boom. But the threat of economic domination by Israel, the loss of Lebanon as a source of funding and salaries for the regime's officials, and continuing vulnerability on water issues with Turkey complicate the political calculus. The peace process cannot operate in an economic vacuum. For an economy characterized by central planning and bureaucracy to maximize the so-called peace dividend, political advances must be coupled with economic reform and liberalization.[27] The economics of the era of peace are appealing, but one wonders how long they would take to get off the ground and how much would be lost in peace-process-related economic setbacks.

SYRIA AND LEBANON

One fear shared by many members of Syria's establishment is that a full peace may ultimately lessen Syria's control of Lebanon. Ever since Lebanon declared independence on November 26, 1941, most Syrians have considered it an artificial French colonial creation that is rightfully part of Syria. In the last few years, Syria has solidified its control over Lebanon, and the current Lebanese government makes no major move without Syrian approval. Over the past decade, Syria's political and military influence in Lebanon has resulted in close economic ties. Syrian workers, who have traditionally worked in Lebanon, now occupy a larger share of the workforce and a greater proportion of skilled jobs than in the past. Syria earns $1-$3 billion annually in remittances from Lebanon.

Equally important to the Asad regime, however, are the rewards that Syrian army and secret police officers are able to reap; they run "thriving trades in vegetables, cigarettes, clothing, and other commodities." Families and friends of the Asad regime are deeply involved in the reconstruction of Lebanon and are amassing fortunes as a result. Loss of political influence in Lebanon would endanger this financial bonanza; although Syrian workers would remain in Lebanon, the ability of Syrian elites to secure major contracts and demand hefty commissions would be lost or at least seriously decreased.[28] *(Ed. note: see below for more detailed discussion of Lebanon situation.)*

SYRIA AND TURKEY

Tension between Syria and Turkey over borders, water, and opposition movements has not yet caused significant conflict but creates fertile ground for future disputes and contributes to Syria's security calculations. Although the two countries have kept their disputes in check, it is not difficult to imagine a dangerous escalation under the right circumstances. Syria is not concerned with a specific Turkish military threat but rather with a number of underlying sources of tension in their relationship. Syria, which already has forces deployed in Lebanon and against Israeli and Iraqi threats, cannot put adversarial forces on every front.

One issue between the two countries is Syria's potential to get involved in Kurdish separatist issues. Turkey spends $8-$10 billion annually, or 30-35 percent of government revenues, fighting Kurdish separatism in southeast Turkey and on occasion has carried the war into the Kurdish enclave in northern Iraq. Turkey's main opponent is the militant Kurdish Workers' Party, the PKK. Although Syria's Kurdish population is small, the risk of greater entanglement over Kurdish issues is nonetheless significant. The Kurdish minority in Syria could constitute another source of opposition to Asad's Alawite-dominated regime. For years, Syria has given aid and comfort to the PKK, which operates paramilitary bases in parts of Syrian-controlled Lebanon, if not in Syria itself.[29] Syria denies that the PKK operates from its territory. Syrian support for the PKK has angered Turkey and the two governments have discussed the matter repeatedly, with periodic agreements to change the status quo. To date, however, Syria still appears sympathetic toward PKK militants. As Syrian leaders in Damascus watched Turkey strike against Kurds in Iraq once again in 1995, the possibility of a similar Turkish incursion in Syria must have crossed the minds of observers. Syria has used the Kurdish issue as an instrument in relations with Turkey, particularly in its effort to counter Turkish threats in other areas, such as Turkish control of the Euphrates. Based on Syria's actions, it appears that its leadership either does not perceive a long-term threat of the PKK mobilizing Syrian Kurds, or it believes that the best way to contain such a threat is to work with the PKK.

Another source of tension is Turkey's ability to control the flow of the Euphrates River. The massive new system of dams in southeastern Turkey is rapidly increasing Turkish control of the waters, which affects both Iraq and Syria. The Southeast Anatolia Project is expected to include twenty-one dams at a cost of $32 billion.[30] The new dams give Turkey the ability to shut-off a key source of Syrian water without even consulting Damascus, leaving Syria vulnerable to blackmail. Iraqi, Syrian, and Turkish officials have discussed the water controversy without reaching a satisfactory settlement.

The dispute over the Hatay Province is an additional irritant that could spark a Syrian-Turkish clash. Syria still lays claim to Turkey's Hatay Province, an area given to Turkey in 1939 by France and discussed in chapter 8. In short, Turkish-Syrian relations are characterized by a number of seemingly manageable disputes that could, however, lead to a broader confrontation under certain circumstances.

In recent years, Syria has noted with concern the growing ties between Israel and Turkey. The possibility of an Israeli-Turkish alliance, or even friendship, is daunting to the Syrians. A more formalized military relationship between Israel and Turkey would be a significant threat to Syrian security. In 1996, Israel and Turkey signed a military training agreement that includes the use of Turkish airspace for Israeli air force training. The deal was not received well in Syria or much of the Arab world.

SYRIA AND IRAQ

Iraq and Syria, two states led by Baathist dictatorships, are each concerned about the other state's intentions. Asad and Hussein hate each other, and their troubled relationship mirrors the state-to-state ties. In the effort to balance its rivalry with Iraq, Syria has cultivated relations with Iran. Syria also contributed to the allied effort to expel Iraq from Kuwait.

Syria and Iraq are both former client states of the Soviet Union, but they dealt with the Soviet dissolution differently. Asad saw it as an opportunity to develop better ties with the West, a policy he pursued in supporting the allied coalition against Iraq. Saddam Hussein took almost the opposite tack; instead of reaching out to the West, he looked for an opportunity to challenge the United States. The end result was the invasion of Kuwait by Iraqi forces in August 1990.

The two countries avoided coming to blows despite repeated regional crises and confrontations in the 1970s and 1980s. Iraq is now weaker than at any time in its recent history, but Damascus still considers a resurgent Iraq a concern. Nevertheless, Syria does not wish to see Iraq fragmented and does not fully support the international sanctions still levied against Iraq. Syria engages in some illicit trade with Iraq but has not denounced the sanctions regime in a forthright manner. At a routine meeting of Iranian, Syrian, and Turkish foreign ministers, the officials took a partial swipe at the sanctions by saying that "any international punitive measure against the government of Iraq should not be to the detriment of the people of that country."[31] The fear of Iraq's fragmentation has influenced Syria's rhetoric on postwar Iraq in two ways: first, the Asad regime consistently has called for maintaining Iraq's territorial integrity, and second, Syrian leaders regularly criticize meddling in the internal affairs of a sovereign state.

While Syria has often been on the opposite side of Iraq in wars and military confrontations, a future alliance is possible, although unlikely. If Syria seeks counterweights to the U.S.-Jordanian-Israeli peace-process axis, natural allies sit in Iran and Iraq, among other places. Such an alliance has many problems, including the Baath rivalry and Saudi-Syrian ties, but the idea may influence Syrian policy toward Iraq.

THE APPEAL OF PEACE WITH ISRAEL

Syria would stand to gain from an Israeli-Syrian agreement if the terms are acceptable to the majority of Syrians. Renewed Syrian control over the Golan (and Lebanese control of southern Lebanon) would secure Asad's place in history. He would successfully restore Syrian honor after over thirty years of Israeli occupation of Syrian soil and vindicate past sacrifices made in the effort to confront Israel. In the international arena, the Arab mainstream is now identified with the pro-peace-process camp, and thus a deal would allow Syria to compete with Egypt and others on equal terms. When considered along with other potential benefits such as better relations with the United States and the European Union, a decrease in defense spending in the long term, and increased investments that would give a boost to economic development, a peace agreement with Israel—on the right terms—has significant appeal.

This vision of an Israeli-Syrian agreement is also the missing piece in Israeli-Lebanese relations, for without an Israeli-Syrian breakthrough, Israel and Lebanon will remain at odds. Lebanon has just begun to rebuild from a long and destructive civil war. Whether or not this physical reconstruction is matched by significant and positive political change depends in part on internal Lebanese changes, but a host of Israeli and Syrian factors undoubtedly will help shape any change.

LEBANON AND THE PEACE PROCESS

Although much of Lebanon's recent stability can be traced to Syrian enforcement efforts, most citizens yearn for true independence—a yearning that only increases after violence such as the April 1996 confrontations. The Israeli occupation, civilian casualties from Israeli-Hizbollah battles, and Israeli bombings that roll back reconstruction efforts serve as a reminder that the pattern of the last twenty years has not brought much comfort to Lebanon. As the Arab-Israeli peace process moves forward, it offers some hope to those who remember Lebanon before its civil war and wish to return to the period of economic and social elegance of the 1950s and 1960s, when Beirut was called "the Paris of the Middle East."

In the 1950s and 1960s, Lebanon was a religiously heterogeneous society that successfully accommodated a myriad of religious faiths—including Maronites, Greek Orthodox, and other smaller Christian sects, as well as Druze, Shiite, and Sunni Muslims. An unwritten national pact in 1943 agreed to by Maronite and Sunni leaders, representing the two largest sects at that time, allocated political power among the various religions and sects and on the surface seemed to keep all parties content. According to the pact, the president would be a Maronite and the prime minister, less powerful than the president, would be a Sunni Moslem. Yet the seeds of future discord were planted in the decades after Lebanese independence in the early 1940s. Thousands of Palestinian refugees from the Arab-Israeli wars ended up on Lebanese territory and lived in refugees camps, mostly located in southern Lebanon. As Palestinian activism increased in the 1960s, first with the formation of the PLO in 1964 and then with fedayeen raids against Israel in 1968, Lebanon became increasingly entangled in

the plight of the Palestinian people. Israel retaliated against fedayeen based on Lebanese soil, and the flow of Palestinian guerrillas from Jordan in 1971, following King Hussein's crackdown in
September 1970, exacerbated an already escalating problem.

Christian, particularly Maronite, Lebanese objected to the
uncontrolled Palestinian activities. In 1974-75, clashes occurred
between Palestinian guerrillas and Phalangist (Christian) militias.
The Lebanese government resigned in May 1975 as the violence
spun out of control and a full-scale civil war developed. Lebanese
Muslims generally sided with the Palestinians, at least in the early
days of the violence. Lebanese Muslims also objected to the system that apportioned power in ways that favored Christians
even though Muslims constituted a majority in Lebanon. Ironically, in mid-1976, Syria intervened, mainly to prevent an outright
victory by the Lebanese National Movement, a Muslim militia, and
its ally the PLO. At the time, Syria feared that a Maronite defeat
would spark a massive Israeli intervention in Lebanon. An October 1976 ceasefire brought 30,000 Arab, mostly Syrian, troops
into Lebanon to deter further conflict. But tensions between the
combatants remained. PLO forces used Lebanon to conduct
raids against Israel, and Israel supported a small Christian militia in Lebanon in the hopes that the militia would halt the Palestinian attacks. In 1978, when lesser measures failed to stop
PLO terrorist attacks, Israel moved against the PLO (Fatah) forces
in the south. In the face of extreme U.S. pressure, Israel eventually withdrew and the United Nations moved in several thousand peacekeepers (the U.N. Interim Force in Lebanon or UNIFIL).

UNIFIL did nothing to stop the growing power and strength
of the PLO, and in June 1982, Israel invaded once more with the
support of the Phalangist leader, Bashir Gemayel. At a minimum, Israel intended to eradicate PLO forces in southern
Lebanon and redraw the map of Lebanon.[32] In late August 1982,
a U.S.-brokered agreement led to the dispersal of thousands of
PLO fighters trapped in Beirut by Israeli forces to various Arab states
as well as the introduction of a multinational peacekeeping force
into Beirut. In May 1983, Israel and Lebanon signed an agreement that among other provisions called for the withdrawal of
foreign forces, but Syria did not recognize the agreement and Israel
only withdrew to south of the Awali River; by the end of the year,
Israel had cut its troops in Lebanon by two-thirds to 10,000. Late
1983 also saw fighting between Arafat's PLO militants and Syr-
ian-backed Palestinians; Arafat eventually left Lebanon with tens
of thousands of Palestinian fighters. The peacekeepers were

drawn into the fighting and came to be seen as pro-Christian by Muslim militias. Devastating suicide bombing attacks were carried out against American, French, and Italian forces in October 1983. As fighting dragged on, the multinational peacekeepers withdrew the following February and March.

In spring 1984, the remnants of the Lebanese government formed a national unity government and allied with the Syrians. By June 1985, Israel had withdrawn to its self-declared security zone in the south. Syrian troops were mostly left in the Bekaa Valley. Over the next few years, Syria backed several failed ceasefire agreements and increasingly clashed with Maronite General Aoun. Aoun's rejection of the October 1989 Taif agreement between Syria and Lebanon helped lead to his defeat at Syrian and Lebanese hands a year later. Syrian and Israeli forces remain in Lebanon to this day. There are also about 350,000 Palestinian refugees, including approximately 220,000 who live in desperate conditions.[33] Today Lebanese society is approximately 38 percent Christian and 62 percent Muslim.[34]

Syria has long charged that Lebanon was created by colonial powers and actually is part of Syria. Asad once noted that, "Throughout history, Syria and Lebanon have been one country and one people."[35] Syrians raise the issue of Syria's right to Lebanon on a regular basis—talk that is unsettling to the many Lebanese who have little interest in becoming part of Syria. The Syrian claim also raises concerns about Syria's military presence in Lebanon. Syria's troops are the symbol of Asad's commitment to retain control of Lebanon, even if Lebanon is technically a sovereign, independent state and not part of greater Syria.

Since the Taif agreement, political decision making in Beirut has been largely controlled by Damascus. Today, few if any major decisions are made by the Lebanese government without the approval of the Asad regime. Lebanese and Syrian officials regularly travel between the two capitals in order to consult on matters of Lebanese policy.

This Syrian influence has dictated Lebanon's approach to major issues such as the peace process. Whenever Israeli-Syrian talks have broken down, Israeli-Lebanese talks also have suffered or been canceled. Syria has declined to participate in the multilateral track of the Arab-Israeli peace process; Lebanon has done the same. Objective analysts recognize that Lebanon and Israel have much to talk about and without the Syria factor might come to an agreement on many issues that divide them. But the Syria factor complicates the issues themselves as well as Lebanon's

124

ability to maintain contacts and participate in negotiations with Israel. As long as Syria retains the final word and Israeli-Syrian negotiators are unable to cut a deal, Lebanon is unable to proceed in talks with Israel.

Syria's major role in Lebanese affairs also extends to economic matters. Syrian officials and business representatives have been able to take financial advantage of Lebanon's rebirth and reconstruction. Syrian companies are deeply involved in rebuilding roads and buildings. Many Syrian officials, both from the army and from the secret police, control markets for some consumer goods or receive handsome commissions during contract negotiations. These Syrians could lose their privileged economic status if Syria's special relationship with Lebanon ended.

Some Lebanese are resentful of Syria's economic presence and would welcome the opportunity to challenge Syria. Syrian laborers have squeezed poorer Shiite Muslims and Palestinians out of occupations they once held. Lebanese merchants would like to reclaim Syrian-controlled markets in consumer goods such as vegetables and clothing. Lebanese, from small merchants to big-time businessmen, are vulnerable to Syrian commissions and bureaucratic fees (i.e., corruption). The peace process could provide an opening for Lebanon to reduce Syrian involvement in Lebanese political, military, and economic affairs, but whether Lebanon will be party to the peace process is more likely to be decided in Damascus, Washington, or Jerusalem than in Beirut.

RECENT RELATIONS WITH ISRAEL

Since 1985, much of the Israeli-Lebanese relationship has focused on Israel's occupation of a wide strip of land in southern Lebanon. The Israeli-declared security zone is three to nine miles wide and used as a buffer by Israel to safeguard communities in northern Israel from attack. Lebanon rejects the Israeli occupation and demands that Israel withdraw from the area, a demand highlighted during Israel's military assault against Lebanon in April 1996.

The northern border of the security zone functions much like an international border. Israel and its ally, the South Lebanon Army (SLA)—a Christian militia—limit access to the security zone; barbed wire fences and fortified checkpoints are used to enforce the division from the rest of Lebanon. Israeli and SLA forces repeatedly clash with Hizbollah and other militants intent on both driving the Israelis from the zone and striking at northern Israel. Economically, exports from the zone to Israel are rare and the process

125

of moving goods to the rest of Lebanon is bureaucratic and rife with corruption. The SLA is a small militia by Lebanese standards and would have a difficult time surviving without Israeli patronage.

As Lebanese have been quick to note for years, Israeli activities have never been confined to the southern strip of land. In retaliation for attacks on Israeli and SLA forces, Israeli aircraft have attacked alleged bases and guerrilla-controlled villages. For some time, Israeli/SLA ground forces have made periodic forays north of the zone to take on their militant rivals, usually claiming the need to retaliate against Hizbollah attacks on the security zone or northern Israel. The Israeli attacks are unpredictable and broaden the impact of the Israeli occupation of Lebanese territory. The zone contains about 1,000 Israeli and 3,000 SLA soldiers.[36]

Lebanese sources charge that part of Israel's interest in the zone is to achieve greater water security. The Hasbani River emerges from southern Lebanon and feeds the Jordan River; the zone gives Israel greater control over that water source. Another, although far less substantiated, charge is that Israel somehow depletes the water of the Litani River.

In the future, even if Israel no longer occupies any Lebanese territory, Israel's economic capabilities raise concern in Lebanon. Israel's GDP of $57.4 billion (1992 estimate) is many times greater than Lebanon's GDP of $4.8 billion (1991 estimate).[37] Per capita income in Israel is close to nine times that of Lebanon. Israeli leaders, most notably Shimon Peres, have talked about strong economic ties as part of a regional era of peace, a thought that has created some fear that Israeli economic hegemony could replace Israeli military hegemony. Depending on the timing of Lebanese reconstruction and Israeli-Lebanese peace, Lebanon still may be involved in a period of substantial rebuilding and growth as a peace agreement opens up Israeli-Lebanese relations; such a period could provide ample opportunities for Israeli businesses to develop a noticeable—and potentially troubling—presence in Lebanon.

PEACE BENEFITS

Even after suffering more than $15 billion in damages to its physical capital, Lebanon retains many features that made it such a hub of social and business activity.[38] The strong merchant class, beaches and other tourist spots, location near Europe and the Middle East, and other factors still could serve as the framework for a 1990s rebirth. The country has been rebuilding, and relative stability has allowed some progress to be made.

Unlike many of its neighbors, Lebanon has ample water supplies, an advantage for both internal and external relations. The government need not worry about a water shortage that could undermine an otherwise healthy economy. The surplus also gives Lebanon an asset in its relations with Israel and Syria, two countries that do not share Lebanon's advantageous hydrological status.

In the political realm, peace might allow Lebanon to emerge from under Syria's shadow. While a matter of great concern in Damascus, such a change would be welcome in much of Lebanon. As a state with a moderate climate and strong economy, Lebanon could become a rising star despite its insignificant position in the current political scene. This assumes, of course, that Lebanon can overcome the religious and ethnic divisions that turned the country into rival fiefdoms for much of the 1970s and 1980s. If the Syrian forces leave Lebanon, the re-emergence of Druze, Maronite, Shiite, Sunni, and other militias would quickly dash any hope of a new Lebanon. The Lebanese people are aware of the risks, but sometimes conflict fatigue and popular sentiments are not enough to defuse military and political power grabs.

The peace process could potentially allow Lebanon to return to the bountiful 1950s and 1960s. It is a dream cherished by many Lebanese. The economic and political implications are important not only for Lebanon, but also for Syria and Israel. Many Lebanese are far more ready than the Asad regime to open relations with Israel and focus on economic growth instead of military power, a change in emphasis that would play to Lebanon's strengths.

THE ALTERNATIVES

If Lebanon regains a measure of independence and full control of its land, Lebanon has the opportunity to rein in divisive forces. Freedom and renewal will only arrive if Lebanon returns to peaceful multi-confessionalism. If, however, the peace process only serves to lock-in Lebanese subservience to Syria because the United States and Israel have more important priorities than Lebanese independence, or if Lebanon's release from foreign control only unleashes the same old militias and violent forces, there is little hope for a peaceful and independent Lebanon. The Lebanese recognize that the peace process has great potential, but they fear that their needs could go unheeded and they could miss their last opportunity for independence.

127

CHAPTER SIX
THE ARAB GULF COUNTRIES

The countries of the Persian Gulf and Arabian peninsula— Iran, Iraq, Yemen, and the six Gulf Cooperation Council (GCC) states (Bahrain, Kuwait, Oman, Qatar, Saudi Arabia, and the United Arab Emirates)—and their off-shore economic zones contain close to two-thirds of the world's proven petroleum reserves.[1] For the foreseeable future, access to these resources will remain vital for the industrial world, giving the region great strategic importance and making several countries extremely rich. Equally relevant, the Persian Gulf is one of the most highly armed regions in the world, and its infrastructure is extremely vulnerable. Political leaders run the gamut from brutal totalitarian dictators (Saddam Hussein) to corrupt mullahs (Iran) to enlightened monarchs (Sultan Qabus of Oman).

A stable and secure Persian Gulf bolsters the prospects of the Arab-Israeli peace process; similarly, the Arab-Israeli peace process greatly affects the stability of region, even though the most challenging issues facing the GCC countries relate to the ongoing crisis with Iran and Iraq and the internal social and economic problems facing each regime. In short, the Arab-Israeli front-line states and the Persian Gulf states do not operate in isolation from each other. Since 1993, the GCC has taken on an important role in Arab-Israeli normalization. This chapter focuses on some of the Arab Gulf states; chapter 7 discusses Iran, Iraq, Libya, and the Sudan—the so-called rejectionist states.

Gulf issues connect with the peace process in a number of ways. Like the GCC states, Egypt, Israel, and Jordan benefit from a successful U.S.-led containment of Iraq and from a reduced Iranian threat. As the wealthiest Arab states, the GCC countries have the opportunity, along with the United States, Japan, and the EU, to provide financial backing for Arab front-line states that make peace with Israel. On the negative side, conflict in the Gulf can spill over into the Arab-Israeli arena, as Iraq's attacks on Israel during the Gulf War demonstrated. Weapons of mass destruction affect all states in the region; they have too large an impact to be confined to one subregion. Not only military but also other issues link the Middle East's subregions: water scarcity, demographic growth, and economic dependence in the form of aid and remittances ensure that the people and countries of the region have interacting relationships that in turn lead to both cooperation and conflict.

A successful resolution to the Arab-Israeli conflict would have positive benefits for the GCC, especially in dealing with the Iranian and Iraqi threats. Arab-Israeli peace would remove many irritants that have harmed U.S. cooperation with the GCC in the past—the pro-Israel stance of various U.S. administrations has complicated relations with Arab states. Alternatively, a setback in the peace process could once more put the United States in the awkward position of working with Israel on the one hand and moderate Arab states on the other hand. In the past, this was a divisive, time-consuming exercise that no U.S. administration would want to repeat. Since the United States is crucial for GCC external security, better U.S.-GCC ties would strengthen the overall security environment by counterbalancing the power and outreach of Iran and Iraq. Arab-Israeli peace would also weaken the effectiveness and appeal of Islamist and nationalist opposition to the U.S. military presence in the Gulf. Furthermore, since a comprehensive Arab-Israeli peace will almost assuredly be preceded by an Israeli-Syrian peace treaty, Iran and other rejectionist countries would be further isolated; Iran's ability to create trouble in Lebanon and Israel would be significantly curtailed without Syrian acquiescence. Limitations on Iran's ability to cause trouble will enhance the stability of the Gulf.

All the GCC countries have participated in the Arab-Israeli multilateral talks that began in 1992.[2] Since Oslo I was signed in September 1993, Bahrain, Oman, and Qatar have hosted multilateral meetings that included an Israeli delegation. The governments of Oman and Qatar have established low-level diplomatic ties with Israel. In 1994, the GCC formally ended observance of the secondary boycott of Israel under which Arab states blacklisted companies that dealt with Israel. Businesses from various Gulf countries have gone one step further and made direct contacts with Israeli companies. In 1995, Israel and Qatar signed a major natural gas agreement.[3] The first meeting of a multilateral working group after Netanyahu's May 1996 victory was held in Oman.[4]

Similar diplomatic and economic ties have been established between Israel and Mauritania, Morocco, and Tunisia. Israel and Mauritania signed a mutual recognition pact in November 1995. Former Israeli Prime Minister Yitzhak Rabin visited Morocco in 1993 after the signing of Oslo I. In 1994, the two countries agreed to direct air, postal, and telephone links, followed by the announcement in September of low-level diplomatic relations. Israeli and Tunisian foreign ministers announced the establishment of low-level relations in October 1994; in November 1995, these countries signed a tourism agreement allowing group visas.[5] Algerian and Israeli officials have had tentative contacts.

These improvements in bilateral relations between individual Arab countries and Israel are especially relevant at a time when some in the Arab world have suggested that Arab-Israeli normalization could be a casualty of intransigent Israeli policies. The Arab summit in Cairo in June 1996 did not directly threaten Israel but did link continued progress on normalization with advances in the peace process. If the larger Arab countries began to make explicit calls to halt or reverse normalization with Israel, the small Gulf states would be in an awkward position. Even if they wanted to maintain their new links with Israel, would they defy the larger Arab powers such as Egypt and Syria? Arab unity is often more rhetoric than reality, but if all the larger Arab powers stand together, it is doubtful any GCC states would unilaterally have close ties with Israel. All of Israel's fledgling ties with Arab countries in the Gulf and North Africa have been more limited since the election of Netanyahu in Israel.

HOW STABLE ARE THE GCC COUNTRIES?

The most challenging issues facing the GCC countries do not concern the Arab-Israeli peace process but their internal social and economic problems and continuing confrontation with Iran and Iraq. Nevertheless, the GCC countries would be adversely affected if the peace process regressed.

The Gulf countries, which have enormous riches, are conservative and income is not well distributed. Lower-class residents and the expatriate work force do not benefit as much as others from the countries' wealth. Discontent is growing, especially in Bahrain and Saudi Arabia, and the economic systems are permeated by corruption at the highest levels.

Because the GCC states cannot come close to matching Iranian and Iraqi military power, they rely on U.S. and other Western forces for external protection. But the GCC states are also vulnerable to subversive Iranian and Iraqi efforts at destabilization; closer U.S.-GCC ties, therefore, can exacerbate and/or provide a catalyst for domestic upheavals. Yet the GCC countries must risk such turmoil, because the military power of Iraq and Iran is an even greater threat to their security than domestic subversion, and this threat can only be neutralized by U.S. military power. As long as the United States maintains a strong military presence in the region, neither Iran nor Iraq is capable of exercising classical hegemony by deploying military forces into the Gulf or the Arabian Peninsula.

The oil market is essential to assessing the competing powers and security positions of various countries in the region. The long-term forecasts suggest that world demand for Persian Gulf oil will continue to grow, particularly as Asian economies increase their energy needs.[6] At the same time, incoming revenue is offset by huge entitlement programs that provide cradle-to-grave social security for citizens; enhanced defense budgets for which the United States has pushed; and arms purchases from the United States to offset the cost of the U.S. deployment. Hence to varying degrees, any serious disruption in the oil market could affect the internal stability of the Gulf states.

Reviewed here are the security challenges facing Saudi Arabia, Kuwait, Oman, and the United Arab Emirates. Qatar and Bahrain face similar and equally important problems, which are particularly imminent in the case of Bahrain.

SAUDI ARABIA: WILL THE SPOTLIGHT TURN TO THE DOMESTIC SITUATION?

In the more than six years since Iraq invaded Kuwait, Saudi Arabia's external security situation has improved immeasurably. On August 2, 1990, Saudis wondered how far Saddam Hussein's forces would push into the Arabian peninsula; today the Saudi kingdom is well-protected and faces weakened foes in both Baghdad and Teheran. The U.S. presence and commitment to Saudi Arabia greatly enhances Saudi security. But for the Saudi leadership, the appropriate direction of Saudi policy in the coming years remains ambiguous in the face of internal tensions and the potential implications of the peace process.

On the positive side, the effective removal of the Palestinian problem from the Arabian peninsula to the Mediterranean will take from Saudi Arabia and its Gulf neighbors some of their political and moral obligations toward the Palestinian diaspora. In the past, the Palestinian confrontation with Israel was a pan-Arab problem, and Arab countries' moral obligations complicated their relations with the United States, Israel's strongest supporter. If the peace process succeeds, the Palestinian question will no longer haunt Arab gatherings and cast a pall over relations with the United States. Palestinian acceptance of Israel in face-to-face negotiations and compromise agreements greatly reduces the need for widespread Arab unity against Israel; most Arab leaders recognize that the Palestinians' future is now out of their hands and under the control of Arafat and his negotiators. Except for the so-called Jedda Yuppies, a small, well-educated group based in the Red Sea city who still support Arab nationalist causes, most of the Saudi elite has little interest in meddling in affairs to the northeast. They have more than enough to worry about within the Kingdom itself and the Gulf.

Saudi Arabia's internal situation is in flux. King Fahd is ill and Crown Prince Abdullah now deals with many day-to-day issues; the resulting ambiguity surrounding the locus of decision-making power may mean that the Saudi government is not operating from a strong position as it grapples with internal dissent. In November 1995 and June 1996, U.S. bases in Saudi Arabia were bombed by militants opposed to the U.S. presence and to what they regard as the Saudi regime's lax interpretation of Islamic law. The dilemma for the regime is that the U.S. military presence is essential for the defense of the Gulf from conventional military threats from Iraq and Iran. However, setbacks in the Arab-Israeli peace process strengthen the radicals who speak so bitterly about the foreign presence.

Alternatively, the emergence of an Arab-Israeli peace could turn the spotlight on Saudi Arabia's human rights abuses and the general lack of openness in the Kingdom. Pressure for democratization and adherence to international human rights standards is not new for the Saudi government but a consistent focus on such issues is likely to exacerbate existing domestic tensions. Until now, there have always been larger, more urgent issues for the survival of Saudi Arabia or for the good of the Arab states. Although Iranian and Iraqi threats remain issues of concern for Saudi Arabia, both are less threatening than in the past. Iraq was subdued by the U.S.-led Gulf War coalition, and postwar U.N. restrictions continue to hamper Iraq's civilian and military recovery. While not subject to such stringent measures, Iran is also monitored carefully by international powers and their intelligence agencies; the United States has taken the lead in containing Iran's revolutionary zeal. If the peace process succeeds, Saudi Arabia may find itself under pressure to open up its society.

Different views can be found on this subject. Some argue that as long as the Saudi regime is able to adjust its policies of dispensing perks and rewards to its population, there is little reason to suppose the streets of Riyadh will be full of Saudi citizens demonstrating for human rights, including more representative government. Of course the regime's ability to provide such benefits depends upon its oil revenues. If proceeds from oil sales declined significantly, the impact of the relative deprivation on Saudi society would pose a new set of problems for which there is no ready solution.

Others question whether the regime is capable of adapting to change without at the same time relinquishing its fundamental power base, which is the control of oil revenues by the extended royal family. Saudi society is sufficiently large, flexible, and stable in the short term to withstand the sorts of social pressures that are bound to come if other areas in the Middle East adopt more Western forms of government and accept Western notions of universal human rights. Over the longer term, however, the Saudi leadership will no longer be able to balance the technocrats who want reform against the Islamists who want a more conservative regime. Moreover, the future of the Kingdom is bound to be influenced by its immediate neighbors, which include Iraq, Iran, the small GCC states, and Yemen. If several small GCC states cease to be viable entities, this could upset the delicate balance in the Gulf and provide opportunities for troublemaking by Iran and Iraq. Alternatively, if either Iran or Iraq or both evolved toward more open, liberal societies, this, too, could have significant implications for the sheikdoms of the Gulf.

A STRONG BASE: OIL AND THE U.S. PRESENCE

As the largest oil producer and exporter in the world, Saudi Arabia is the model of the wealthy, well-endowed Gulf monarchy. This has given the Saudi government a strong base from which to conduct foreign and domestic affairs. Since the 1970s, money has been available for virtually any policy or alliance.

Saudi oil exports are the linchpin of the Saudi economy. Saudi Arabia has the largest proven crude reserves in the world, just over 23 percent of the world total, not including shared oil in the Neutral Zone (with Kuwait).[7] At a production rate of 8 million barrels per day (b/d), current reserves could last for ninety years. Output *capacity* has risen from 9.3 million b/d in 1990 to 10 million b/d in 1995; this figure is expected to rise to 12 million by the year 2000, nearly 17 percent of the world total. The industrialized world is the major recipient of Saudi oil, with the United States estimated to import 1.26 million b/d, Europe more than 2 million b/d, and Japan 1.2 million b/d[8]—at least partially explaining why developed countries demonstrate a strong interest in Saudi security and stability. Saudi Arabia plays a major role in the Organization of Petroleum Exporting Countries (OPEC). During the Gulf crisis and war, it increased oil output in order to compensate for the loss of oil from Iraq and Kuwait.

Despite Saudi oil wealth, recent years have seen greater fiscal difficulty and a resultant challenge to the implicit Saudi trade-off between democracy and economic prosperity. Saudi Arabia, which has been running a deficit for a decade and has an enormous debt, is trying is to cut government spending, but privatization is unpopular among Saudi citizens accustomed to generous government programs. In Saudi Arabia, as in other oil-rich Gulf states, the government has subsidized utilities, goods, and services for decades. Concern about the political consequences of privatization is acute in Saudi Arabia. Though the Saudi government has approved privatization measures, no significant steps were taken by the end of 1996. [9]

In Saudi Arabia, the combined fiscal deficit for 1990-92 was $48 billion, compared with $39 billion for the previous three years. The deficit and the unwillingness of the government to curb expenditure or impose taxes to pay for the war has led one expert to conclude that the Gulf War "made a bad situation worse."[10] In addition, the Saudi economy relies on about four million foreign workers employed in sectors like oil and banking. Real growth in GDP was 1 percent in 1993, the inflation rate was also 1 percent, and the unemployment rate was 6.5 percent (1992 estimate).[11] In 1994, the economy grew at under 1 percent; it decreased by 0.8 percent in 1995.[12] For 1996-97, real GDP growth is expected to be only 1.5 to 2.0 percent annually.[13] These economic problems, combined with a rapid population growth rate of 3.7 percent (1995 estimate) and concern about water supply, have exacerbated Saudi Arabia's other domestic problems.[14]

EXTERNAL SECURITY THREATS

Saudi Arabia and the smaller Gulf states see Iraq as a potentially dominant power that has been contained by U.S. and allied military activities. It was not so long ago that Iraqi troops rolled through Kuwait and appeared poised to go after the biggest oil prize, Saudi Arabia. Iraq has been greatly weakened by the Gulf War and the postwar sanctions regime, but could return to its status as a regional military power if sanctions are lifted (though sanctions have now been in place since Iraq's invasion of Kuwait in 1990). Under an agreement reached with the United Nations (UNSC resolution 986), Iraq began exporting about 700,000 b/d to pay for food, medical supplies, and U.N. inspections and reparations.[15] Nevertheless, most Iraqi oil remains off the market, and Saudi Arabia continues to receive extra oil revenue as a result. If Iraq finally emerges from sanctions and resumes production at 1.5 to 3 million b/d, Saudi oil revenue would likely drop, at least in the short run, aggravating Saudi Arabia's fiscal difficulties.

Saudi Arabia also worries about Iran's attempts to foment unrest among Saudi Shiites. Iran's neighbors, as well as states throughout the region, fear that local Shiites will become a fifth column that provides an entry point for Iranian terrorism and subversion. In Saudi Arabia, the Shiites live mostly in the Eastern Province along the Persian Gulf, and estimates of the Shiite population range from two to eight percent.[16] The Shiites are frequently mistreated, so the possibility of unrest, or Iranian-sponsored unrest, is real. General discrimination and unfair employment practices against the Shiites are entrenched in Saudi society. Incidents of unexplained sabotage of oil facilities in the early 1980s and periodic disturbances have been attributed to disgruntled Shiites.[17] The Shiites are systematically harassed and denied full religious freedom. Some changes in Saudi policy in 1993 led to marginal improvements for the Shiites.

INTERNAL SAUDI MATTERS

Inside Saudi Arabia, democracy, human rights, and the general level of openness are a potential problem for a regime that appears unwilling to become more open or more tolerant of dissent. The sixty-man consultative council, instituted in 1993 in response to domestic pressure but given little substantive power, is not enough either to placate critics or to channel dissent. Among Saudis, criticism of the regime comes from many quarters. Some dissident *ulema*[18] members, including hardline preachers and students, espouse xenophobic, anti-Western, anti-Shiite views; they are highly critical of the ruling family for allowing a strong Western military presence and for failing to adhere to a strict interpretation of Islam. Many have been arrested by the regime, but the government has also tried to appease conservatives by enforcing tough policies on women's issues and granting wide autonomy to Saudi religious police (i.e., officials who enforce Islamic law with regard to personal conduct). At the other end of the spectrum, reformist and liberal Saudis criticize the government for not being open and democratic enough; these liberal critics have little influence over decision making and public opinion. One vocal opposition group operating out of London, the Committee for the Defense of Legitimate Rights, combines elements of both opposition tendencies, calling for more religious influence and an end to what they see as the closed and corrupt Fahd regime. Finally, Saudi Shiites, located mostly on the Gulf coast and Eastern Province, oppose the government for its systematic discrimination against them.

For a long time, the government has counted on economic development to placate the Saudi people and indirectly serve as a substitute for democracy. As the 1990s have witnessed a growing need for government cutbacks, the possibility that the people may have to get used to a less generous welfare state has not been received well.

KUWAIT, OMAN, AND THE UNITED ARAB EMIRATES

While Saudi Arabia may have the cohesiveness and national identity to ride out pressures for a more open and "democratic" society, the future of the smaller Gulf countries is less clear. Bahrain and Qatar are so small and vulnerable that they may have difficulty surviving without a security agreement with their neighbors or an explicit commitment by the United States to assure their independence. Thus considered here are three GCC countries, Kuwait, Oman, and the UAE. These states have some similarities and are usually spoken of together, but they also have many noteworthy differences.

KUWAIT

As the victim of an Iraqi invasion, Kuwait's security problems are obvious and real. In fact, the sense of insecurity among Kuwaitis is said to be so pervasive that many keep foreign bank accounts and packed bags in case the events of August 1990 are repeated.

Kuwait is within striking distance of the three largest Gulf powers, Iran, Iraq, and Saudi Arabia—all three of which have bigger economies, more people, and much larger armed forces. There have been well-known territorial disputes with Iraq as well as land and maritime differences with Saudi Arabia (see chapter 8). Iranian forces are also just a short distance from Kuwait by air,

137

land, and sea; Kuwait and other small Gulf states suspect that Iran (as well as Iraq) has expansionist designs on parts of the Gulf and the Arabian peninsula. Kuwait has no natural borders with these countries, and no strategic depth.

The one area in which Kuwait can compete with its more powerful neighbors is in oil resources, but rather than equalizing the relationships it feeds Kuwaiti insecurities. Kuwait's oil reserves are both abundant and much-coveted. The lack of natural borders and strategic depth, however, make Kuwait's natural resource base a starting point for Kuwaiti vulnerability rather than a defensive asset.

In addition, the post-invasion political situation has raised questions about maintaining a stable order. About 15 percent of Kuwaitis, so-called first-class males, have the right to vote for parliament. In the last few years, the rejuvenated Kuwaiti legislature has become an assertive voice on certain matters, including budgetary decisions and government corruption. The al-Sabah leadership has reluctantly accommodated criticism and alternative policy suggestions but seems unwilling to allow too strong a legislative voice on key matters; defense, foreign affairs, and interior portfolios have remained in the control of the al-Sabah regime. In 1992, however, the government relaxed press censorship laws. The open debates in Kuwait contrast sharply with the limited (to non-existent) commentary in several other Gulf states, including both Iraq and Saudi Arabia.

In the past decade, Saudi Arabia has put behind-the-scenes pressure on the Kuwaiti regime to limit the opening up of Kuwaiti society, apparently fearing that calls for democratization and greater legislative rights might spill over into Saudi Arabia. Kuwait is surely conscious of the concerns of its neighbors. Thus the democratic element adds both internal pressure on the regime and a possible irritant in external relations. Given the opposite directions of the domestic and Saudi pressure, the Kuwaiti government has a difficult time satisfying either side: the more the al-Sabah regime allows democratic elements in Kuwait to develop, the more likely democratization will be a continuing and growing source of friction with Saudi Arabia.

Unlike some GCC members, Kuwait does not face a serious succession crisis. Although the al-Sabah regime and the legislature disagree about the distribution of power, Crown Prince Sheikh Saad al-Abdullah al-Salim al-Sabah will be the next ruler barring an unlikely change in plans.

The presence of foreign workers and the limited willingness of Kuwaiti citizens to join the military add a demographic dimension to Kuwaiti insecurity. Only 39 percent of Kuwait's population are citizens.[19] Even decades-long residents of Kuwait are often not considered first-class citizens because they cannot trace their family roots in Kuwait back to the 1920s and before. Although the number of foreign workers has dropped substantially since 1990, the foreign contingent in Kuwait is still sizable and the poor treatment many of these workers receive has drawn some international attention.

The small number of citizens who can be conscripted or who would be willing to volunteer for military service makes expanding Kuwait's armed forces a difficult task. The army has only 11,000 soldiers that form six under-strength brigades. But the small number of Kuwaiti citizens (616,000), combined with the general disinterest in serving in the military, provides little hope for expanding the already small armed forces.

While the opening up of Kuwaiti society could have some significant positive effects, it may prove to be a destabilizing factor—and hence a matter of concern for the al-Sabah family—for relations with Saudi Arabia or even internally in Kuwait. Kuwait's summary expulsion of thousands of non-Kuwaiti workers after the Gulf War demonstrated both that the large-scale importation of labor causes concern and that the government is prepared to quickly alleviate those fears when necessary.

OMAN

There have been no significant challenges to either Sultan Qabus' leadership or to Oman's existence as a sovereign state, but Oman periodically struggles with discontent and insecurity among its population. Oman is neither as poor as Yemen nor as wealthy as Kuwait or the UAE, but its economy is a continuing concern, especially as oil reserves are rapidly depleted.[20]

Part of Oman's security problem stems from the relatively recent consolidation of the state. The interior was not brought under national control until the late 1950s, when Sultan Said bin Taimur, father of Sultan Qabus, defeated his last rival. Said bin Taimur relied on personal rule and prevented the development of modern political institutions. He was overthrown by his son in a bloodless coup in 1970.[21] In Dhofar, in the south, national control did not come until the mid-1970s, when an insurrection led by Marxist guerrillas was put down. Thus the cohesion and unity of Oman as a state is still in the early stages. The national government under Sultan Qabus has tried to bolster centralization and state identity with large-scale development and infrastructure programs.

Like many governments in the Gulf and elsewhere, the government must cope with internal discontent. The regime has monitored militant Islamic forces. Because of suspicions that Islamists were plotting against the regime, the government initiated a crackdown in 1994; some 130 alleged Islamists—including several government officials—were arrested; they were later released to avoid creating a public backlash against harsh security measures. Although the Islamists were advocating stricter adherence to Islamic law, they were probably motivated as much or more by economic discontent. Furthermore, people are angry about the intertwining of politics and business, fearing that ministers are using their influence to get rich.

In response to criticism, the government agreed to the creation of a *Majlis al-Shura,* or consultative council. Inaugurated in January 1992, this council is made up of notables who basically rubber stamp government decisions. It has not served as an outlet for airing grievances or stating opposition to government policies; yet some have called it a stabilizing influence.[22] Most Omanis are apparently satisfied with the overall leadership of Sultan Qabus and the direction of his domestic and foreign policies (except for economic concerns), and there has been little known pressure for more participatory institutions. In terms of modernization, Qabus has been effective in his twenty-five-year rule; he has added hundreds of schools and a national university and fostered the growth of industry and more modern political institutions. For the future, no clear line of succession has been established, although Sultan Qabus has suggested that senior government officials should choose his successor; Qabus has several cousins in government.

Oman is concerned about balancing the potential threat from its larger neighbor on the Arabian peninsula, Saudi Arabia, with other alliances. Like other GCC members, Oman is sensitive to what it perceives as Saudi bullying or domination. Oman has not called for Saddam Hussein's ouster, perhaps to maintain Iraq as a counterweight, and it has sought good relations with Iran. At the same time, Oman maintains friendly ties with the West, including the United States, with whom it has a defense cooperation agreement and extensive military contacts. In the last couple of years, Oman has also improved its ties with Israel, in part through the Arab-Israeli multilateral peace talks. Even Oman's view of GCC defense relations—Oman is in favor of a strengthened joint defense force—reflects Oman's penchant for reaching out to and working with many parties simultaneously. Oman has long avoided dramatic diplomatic shifts; it broke relations neither with Egypt after Camp David nor with Iraq after the invasion of Kuwait. Outside parties are interested in strong ties with Oman for a variety of reasons, especially its location on one side of the Strait of Hormuz.

Oman's armed forces are notably larger than those of Bahrain, Kuwait, or Qatar, but they are small compared with bigger players such as Iran, Iraq, and Saudi Arabia. Oman can take some solace in its geographic location, situated at the edge of the Gulf region rather than in the midst of the three most powerful armed forces in the area. In fact, much of Oman's history has been influenced by its insularity since it is surrounded by mountains, deserts, and seas. It is also helpful that military service among Omani nationals carries some prestige and is considered more palatable than in some wealthier Gulf states, where there is little enthusiasm for leaving life's comforts behind even temporarily in order to serve in the military.

Although to a lesser extent than in other Gulf states, foreigners have a large presence in Oman. Approximately 27 percent of the population of just over two million are expatriates.[23] Two points about its economy are particularly important. First, Oman benefits significantly in terms of business and trade from its proximity to the Gulf region, just as it benefits in security terms from not being in the heart of the Gulf region. It is close but not too close. Second, although not poor, Oman lacks the capital base of the wealthier states in the region, such as Kuwait, Saudi Arabia, and the UAE. Its known oil reserves may run dry in only seventeen more years.[24] With high birth rates, free education and health care, and large military spending, Oman may significantly increase its debt and unemployment rate if it is not careful in managing its resources and reducing government spending.

THE UNITED ARAB EMIRATES

For the United Arab Emirates, the key security questions revolve around the extent to which the emirates are truly united and Arab. The federation of seven emirates was formed in 1971 and the relationship between the national government and the individual emirates has yet to be fully defined. No unified state has emerged.

141

In addition, the UAE's wealth has allowed it to import foreign workers for low-skilled and less desirable jobs.

Close to three-quarters of UAE residents are foreigners; estimates range from 70 to 76 percent of the UAE population of 2.4 to 3 million.[25] The vast majority of these foreigners are from South Asia: workers come from India (30 percent of total UAE population), Pakistan (16 percent), other Asian countries (12 percent; e.g., Bangladesh, Sri Lanka, Philippines), and other Arab countries (12 percent; e.g., Egypt).[26] The foreign workers send about $2.5 billion in remittances to their home countries.[27] In total, immigrants constitute 90 percent of the UAE work force.[28]

Combined with limited enforcement of the few existing weak labor laws, the presence of so many non-citizens creates a dangerous situation ripe for abuse. Foreign workers tell countless horror stories of abuse, unfairly low salaries, fraud, and other schemes operated to the detriment of the laborers. Some observers believe that the situation could fairly rapidly erupt into protests or riots against the government or UAE nationals. Non-citizens may come to demand the enforcement of existing laws and rights in UAE decision making. One former senior UAE official with close ties to the ruling al-Nahyan family warned that, "Existing labour and immigration laws are not being applied. It is just a matter of time before the crisis boils over."[29] Periodically, the stories of abuse draw unfavorable international publicity.

The majority population of expatriates—and the particular distribution of nationalities in the UAE—creates security problems as well. Antagonisms and rivalries that do not involve the UAE may be played out among the various groups of expatriates living and working in the UAE. This was vividly demonstrated to UAE authorities in December 1992, when Hindus and Muslims rioted in the UAE after the Ayodhya mosque in India was destroyed by Hindu nationalists. The government, therefore, must be highly attentive to issues and events occurring in the home countries of the foreign workers that could lead to unrest and instability in the UAE. If two countries in South Asia were to go to war, for instance, UAE authorities would need to be on guard against hostility and confrontation in the UAE among the nationals of those countries. The problem is further complicated by the estimated 30 percent of UAE military forces, or perhaps 18,000 personnel, who are themselves expatriates and may be more susceptible to the influence of events at home than to their local UAE command.[30] This makes putting down unrest even more challenging. To some degree, this same problem exists in other labor-importing countries with a similar mix of nationalities.

In addition to these demographic concerns, the UAE still struggles with state consolidation. The state was formed just twenty-five years ago and still lacks complete state cohesion. Two emirates, Abu Dhabi and Dubai, maintain separate military forces that are not fully integrated into the UAE armed forces. A Federal National Council has representatives from all the emirates, but the real power lies with the Federation President and Abu Dhabi ruler, Sheikh Zayed bin Sultan al-Nahyan.

While the UAE as a whole is a wealthy state, the resources are distributed unevenly. Abu Dhabi, the main emirate for oil, and Dubai, a commercial center with key markets in other emirates, Iran, and South Asia, subsidize the poorer emirates (Fujairah, Ajman, Ras al Khaimah, Umm al Qayam). Such subsidies increase the importance of maintaining strong economic relations with Dubai's main trading partners, including Iran. The UAE (particularly the emirate of Sharjah) and Iran disagree over the disposition of three Gulf islands (Abu Musa, Greater Tunb, and Lesser Tunb), but Dubai cannot afford to let the dispute escalate into a political and economic war with Iran for this could jeopardize the amount of resources available for redistribution in the UAE.

The succession of Sheikh Zayed also hinges on relations among the emirates. His son, Sheikh Khalifah, the Crown Prince of Abu Dhabi, is the most likely successor to the federal presidency; but other emirate leaders are interested as well. Sheikh Khalifah is vulnerable to such challenges because he has not been as adept as his father at managing the affairs of Abu Dhabi. Whoever it is, Sheikh Zayed's successor will need to do a careful job of lining up support throughout the UAE.

The government has attempted to build a capable military force in order not to have to rely on Saudi Arabia or the GCC for security. Partly for this reason, thousands of expatriates are members of the UAE armed forces. If it had a strong, independent force, the UAE could not only provide for its own defense but also pursue its broader interests with more confidence in the military option. As long as the UAE must rely on a questionable military alliance like the GCC, insecurities will remain high (this is not to say, however, that the UAE could actually build up an independent force that would greatly enhance security). It should be noted that even a strong, independent, well-armed UAE force will be no match for the much larger Iranian or Iraqi militaries.

The presence of so many foreign workers coupled with the low level of state cohesion make the emergence of a strong, independent UAE unlikely. The wealth and geographic location of the UAE, island disputes notwithstanding, may help mitigate some fears, but there will still be nervousness over the disposition of the foreign communities and the potential for discord in the relationship between the seven emirates and the national government.

The UAE and the other GCC states share a central feature of foreign relations in the Gulf: the presence of Iran and Iraq. To some degree, the nature of relations with Iran and Iraq is an important consideration for all the GCC members. The GCC members are not alone; in both positive and negative ways, most states in the Middle East are affected by the stability in and foreign policies of Iran and Iraq. Supporters of the peace process are no exception. Whether through small-scale meddling in the process or as long-term impediments to regional security and arms control, the rejectionists in Iran and Iraq cannot be ignored.

CHAPTER SEVEN

THE REJECTIONIST STATES: IRAN, IRAQ, LIBYA, AND SUDAN

The most important Middle East countries that continue to reject Israel's right to exist are Iran, Iraq, Libya, and Sudan, of which Iran and Iraq have the greatest potential to contribute to a failure of the peace process. President Saddam Hussein has occasionally hinted that Iraq would be prepared to recognize Israel in exchange for the lifting of international sanctions. At the same time, however, Iraq is the one Arab country with the capacity to develop nuclear weapons; his threat to "make the fire eat up half of Israel" in April 1990 helped lay the groundwork for the crisis that followed.[1] At the time, Iraq had only chemical weapons but it had already demonstrated willingness to use these systematically against Iran. Now all Iraq's weapons of mass destruction programs—nuclear, chemical, biological— have been or are being dismantled. Iran also has a chemical weapons capability and is supporting nuclear and biological weapons programs. As long as Iran and Iraq remain implacably hostile to Israel and the peace process, they will remain a high priority on both the U.S. and Israeli agenda, and the U.S. policy of dual containment—the effort to restrain both Baghdad and Teheran—will continue. Libya, too, may be developing chemical weapons.

But a stable Gulf—and indeed Middle East—will not come about until Iraq and Iran change their ways. In Iraq, this will require a change in leadership; in Iran, it will require significant changes in government behavior. The dual containment policy outlined in the early days of the Clinton administration was in fact a misnomer. Although the policy was tough on Iraq, it was easier on Iran, even calling for a dialogue with the Iranian government and stating explicitly that the United States did not challenge the right of the Islamic Republic to exist. In 1995, the dual containment policy was made tougher on Iran, both because of Iran's continued intransigence and because of pressure on the Clinton administration from the U.S. Congress and Israel. But further isolating Iraq and Iran is problematic for it assures that they cannot be brought into the regional security arrangements that are necessary for long-term stability in the region.

IRAN

On May 23, 1997, the landslide winner of Iran's presidential elections was Mohammed Khatemi, a moderate cleric whose victory was quite unexpected. Khatemi's support came from a diverse group of disaffected Iranians, especially women and young people. Whether his victory will lead to changes in Iranian foreign policy will depend upon his ability to use his impressive mandate to challenge the entrenched power of the conservative clergy, including the Supreme Leader of the Revolution, Ayatollah Ali Khamenei and the majority in the *Majlis* (the Iranian parliament). It will also depend on the response of the United States and Iran's neighbors to his victory. Within Iran, the conservative opposition still wields great power and remains hostile to the West.

The conservative leaders believe that the most serious threats to their survival are the military and cultural challenge posed by the West in general and the United States in particular. In April 1995, when the Iranian regime decided to begin enforcing a ban on satellite television dishes, then Interior Minister Ali Mohammed Besharati was explicit about its importance in Iran's battle with the West. "The ban," he said," will immunize the people against the cultural invasion of the West."[2] At the forefront of the Iranian regime's concerns is the struggle to insulate the Iranian people from the seductive cultural reach of the "Great Satan," the United States. Normalization with the West is perceived by the conservatives to be a dangerous threat because it could open the floodgates of Western culture, unleashing movies, soaps and other television programming, music, magazines, and celebrities on the Iranian people, the ultimate perversion of the Khomeini revolution. Perhaps most important, such contact would end the mullahs' monopoly of power. Many of them have become very rich as a result of the revolution.

Through the mechanism of the Arab-Israeli peace process, the United States and its supporters, including Israel and moderate Arabs, are attempting large-scale political manipulation and control of the region. Iran has therefore worked to undermine the peace process, as well as the notion of Israel's legitimacy and acceptance into the region. The conservatives believe the peace process is forcing an American/Israeli vision of stability in the region

146

that will increase Iran's isolation. The United States and Israel dictate the terms of the negotiations as, one after another, the Palestinians and Arab countries submit. They are concerned that Syria will eventually sign an agreement with Israel and downgrade its links with Iran. An Israeli-Syrian deal would open the door for full diplomatic relations between Israel and the Arab Gulf states, perhaps even Iraq. Without Syrian acquiescence, Iran's role in Lebanon and support for Hizbollah would be limited.

Iran has become a factor in Arab-Israeli relations. The Persian Gulf and the Arab-Israeli arena are interconnected, and a comprehensive resolution of the Arab-Israeli conflict must take into account a large number of states, including Iran. Iran's military and political support of Hizbollah and other Arab and Islamic groups such as Hamas and the Islamic Jihad that continue the armed struggle is evidence of its openly rejectionist role. Iranian and Israeli leaders regard each other as a military threat, particularly with respect to weapons of mass destruction. Iran fears Israel's nuclear weapons and long-range aircraft and missiles, and Israel recognizes that Iran is moving toward developing similar capacities. The arms race in the region feeds off such fears and will be difficult, if not impossible, to contain as long as Iranian-Israeli relations do not improve. To make matters more difficult for Iran, during 1995-96, Israel developed diplomatic and economic ties with several smaller Arab Gulf states. The peace process not only threatens to reduce Iranian influence in Israel's neighborhood, but could allow further Israeli penetration of Iran's backyard.

Despite the conservatives' focus on the threat from the West and the peace process, a wide array of strategic, demographic, and economic issues confront Iran at home. The Iranian state faces military threats or unrest on all sides. Its internal demographic mixture leaves the country vulnerable to separatist tendencies and intervention by other states on behalf of one group or another. And the health of the economy is ultimately tied to the price of oil and the country's ability to finance its huge but underdeveloped natural gas reserves.

THE ISLAMIC REGIME

The Iranian mullahs came to power in 1979 and established a new model of government in which revolutionary Islam was to play the central role. It has not worked out as planned; not only has the Iranian model had limited success outside Iran, but Iran now finds itself needing to defend Khomeini's legacy among its own people. The regime has become defensive and is widely disliked. This in part explains the extraordinary results of the 1997 presidential election.

The regime's underlying fear is that the West seeks to overthrow the Islamic Republic. It has good cause to be wary, given the U.S. policy of dual containment of Iran and Iraq. U.S. military power poses a direct military challenge to Iran and dilutes potential Iranian influence in the Gulf. American naval vessels in the Gulf, defense cooperation agreements with and pre-positioned equipment in Arab Gulf states, and allied aircraft enforcing the no-fly zones over Iraq are regular reminders of U.S. military hegemony in the region. The Iranian leadership is acutely aware of past U.S. military actions against Iran—both direct actions such as the so-called "tanker war" (Iraqi and Iranian attacks on third-party ships and oil tankers began in 1984 and led to direct U.S. naval intervention in the Gulf in 1987) and indirect actions such as Operation Staunch (the U.S.-led campaign to block arms from reaching Iran during much of the Iran-Iraq war). In addition, after being defeated by Iraq, Iran had to watch with humiliation as the United States and its allies trounced Iraq in Operation Desert Storm, which reminded Teheran of its extreme vulnerability to U.S. military power. Iran also fears Israel's strategic reach, which includes long-range aircraft, ballistic missiles, and nuclear weapons. It is further constrained by the U.S. global campaign to stop nuclear cooperation with or sales to Iran, at the same time that the United States vetoes efforts to curb Israel's nuclear program.

The mullahs' obsession with the United States—matched, it must be said, by a parallel U.S. preoccupation with the "pariah" state—obscures other security issues that would otherwise concern any Iranian regime. Iran faces a number of potential security threats that have little to do with the United States or the West. Coupled with Iran's economic difficulties, these issues help foster long-term insecurities in Iran.

EXTERNAL AND INTERNAL CHALLENGES

Iran faces strategic threats on all sides, with the most obvious, significant threat emanating from Iraq. The two countries fought an eight-year war that cost at least 200,000 Iranian lives and did significant damage to infrastructure and to the Iranian regime's standing. Most Iranians both fear Iraq and have a desire for revenge. The "war of the cities" (a part of the Iran-Iraq war in which both sides targeted and killed civilians in enemy urban areas), the heavy casualties, the POWs, Iraq's use of chemical weapons, and the brutal fighting on the front lines all took their toll. Iraq only accepted the 1975 Algiers Accord—a resolution of their territorial dispute considered favorable for Iran—in August 1990, when the allied mobilization against Iraq's invasion of Kuwait forced Iraqi President Saddam Hussein to settle on the Iranian front (after the settlement Iraq moved troops from the Iranian border to the Kuwaiti theater). Iraq also hosts the most aggressive and well-known Iranian opposition group—the People's Mojahedin and its National Liberation Army (NLA). Although the NLA does not pose a threat to the Iranian military, the mullahs are not happy that Baghdad hosts a militant opposition movement.

In general, Iran is better off with even the risky status quo than such alternatives as the break-up or rehabilitation of Iraq. As long as Iraq is unable to sell much oil on the open market and thus generate revenues, the Iraqi military is deprived of arms and spare parts and thus poses less of a military threat. Moreover, in the face of Baghdad's potential belligerency, Saudi Arabia might be more inclined to develop relations with Iran. Post-Hussein Iraq could once more pose a threat, especially if Iraq re-emerges as a military power. For the moment, however, the lingering issues from the Iran-Iraq war—POWs, reparations, borders—serve as a reminder that the two dominant Gulf powers are unlikely to form a coalition in the near term.

Gulf relations are a second area of concern, and Iran has pursued a seemingly contradictory policy. On the one hand, the mullahs would like to lessen Iran's isolation and build stronger ties with its Arab Gulf neighbors. On the other hand, Iran's assertive, hegemonic tendencies appear especially strong while Iraq is contained, undermining efforts to strengthen relations with the Arab Gulf states. This has led to mixed results; relations are better with some states, such as Oman and Qatar, than others. Saudi Arabia was the key host of U.S. military forces during the 1990-91 Gulf crisis. Saudi Arabia's influence in OPEC and its ability to keep Iran out of Gulf security talks frustrates Iranian policymakers. The Islamic rivalry between the two pits Iran's Shiites (of the Twelver branch) against Saudi Arabia's Sunnis (of the Wahabbi branch), giving the political rivalry an added religious dimension. Both Islamic states hope that others will emulate their version of Islam.

Iran has differed with the United Arab Emirates (and the emirate of Sharjah in particular) over the control and sovereignty of the islands of Abu Musa and Greater and Lesser Tunbs, but trade relations with the emirate of Dubai have been strong. On their own, the Arab Gulf states pose no military threat to Iran, but agreements with large military powers like the United States create more of a problem. With the United States in their court, the Gulf states are able to act more brazenly toward Iran. The wealth of the Arab Gulf states also contrasts sharply with the situation in Iran, where fifteen years of mismanagement and population growth have squandered billions of dollars, much of it oil and natural gas revenue.

Unrest and civil wars in several neighboring states threaten Iran internally. Iraqi Kurds, for example, operate an autonomous safe haven in northern Iraq. The Caucasus mountains are a hotbed of civil strife, including the Armenian-Azerbaijani war and violence in Georgia and Chechnya. Afghanistan has been torn apart by a seemingly endless civil war. And further to the east, Iran has become embroiled in the chaos and fighting in Tajikistan, the one Central Asian country whose population is predominantly Persian speaking and of Shiite faith.

Iran's internal demographic balance is complicated. Iran has perhaps the most diverse population in the region. In addition to the majority Persian population, Iran has Azeris (24 percent of the total Iranian population), Kurds (7 percent), Arabs (3 percent), and Balochs (2 percent).[3] Each group is linked to other members of their ethnicity elsewhere in the region. Azeris in Azerbaijan; Kurds in Iraq, Syria, and Turkey; Arabs throughout the Middle East; and Balochs in Afghanistan and Pakistan mean that Iran must always be on guard against a fifth column. The fear that unrest in other states could set off brushfires in Iran is compounded by the presence of so many different minorities. From refugee flows to pressure for Iranian intervention, the possibilities are unsettling. Watching the fragmentation of Iraq must remind Iranian leaders of the dangerous possibilities associated with ethnic and religious splits. As a result, Iran has pursued moderate policies with its northern neighbors in an effort to foster stability. It has promoted Islamic unrest in places further from its own borders, like Lebanon or Sudan.

The economic realm provides little comfort as Iran faces population and petroleum challenges, insufficient foreign investment, and high levels of external debt. Iran's economic growth rate dropped from 6.8 percent in 1992, to 2.6 percent in 1993, and 1.8 percent in 1994.[4] The growth rate for 1995 and 1996 averaged about 3 percent.[5] Although Iran has been trying to attract foreign investment by offering long-term tax, import, and custom

duty exemptions, greater foreign investment faces several hurdles: the slow pace of economic reform, conservative parliamentarians ideologically opposed to foreign investment, and
continued U.S. sanctions. Iran also faces serious payment problems to regional and other creditors (like Japanese trading houses).[6] During an import consumption binge following the end of
the Iran-Iraq war, imports rose from $13.4 billion in 1989 to $25
billion in 1991; after Iran imposed stringent and unpopular
import curbs in an effort to stem the outflow of foreign curren-
cy, annual imports declined again to $13 billion in 1994.[7] These
import compression policies help explain the drop in the economic
growth rate because Iranian industry is unable to import sufficient
inputs. Between 1990 and 1994, Iran's total external debt rose
from $9 billion to $24.6 billion.[8]

Earnings from oil exports, a central element of Iran's economy, dropped in 1993/94 due to falling oil prices, but rebounded in 1994/95. In 1993/94, only about 55 percent of export revenue
came from oil and gas sales.[9] In 1994/95, oil alone provided 75
percent of total export revenue.[10] The role of hydrocarbons in the
Iranian economy is evident in the high proportion of revenue that
oil and natural gas provide: 64 percent of the 1995/96 Iranian
government budget ($8.9 billion out of $13.9 billion).[11]

Iran, which faces serious production and maintenance problems, is working to rebuild its deteriorating oil fields.[12] From
1993 through the end of 1996, Iran boosted production to an
average of 3.6-3.7 million barrels of oil per day, including pumping as much as 4 million barrels on some days to demonstrate
productive capacity.[13] Some have suggested that such high levels of pumping will damage Iranian oil reserves. At these high levels, Iran's proven oil reserves will last just over forty years. The
depletion or damaging of Iran's existing reserves makes expansion of Iran's proven reserves essential. As part of its effort to get
a larger share of the resource pie, Iran has attempted to be part
of deals in the Caspian Sea and has claimed large areas of
Qatar's Persian Gulf offshore North Field gas reserves.

Economic mismanagement and the large amounts spent on
arms imports and arms development have contributed substantially to growing deficits and high inflation. Consumer price
inflation has climbed from 7.6 percent (1990) to 31.5 percent
(1994) and reached 49.7 percent in 1995.[14] Ironically, during the
period 1996-97, there was an improvement in Iran's macroeconomic
indicators, with reduced inflation, a trade balance surplus, foreign reserves rising, the budget deficit falling, and debt serviced

as scheduled. The reasons had less to do with management reform in Teheran than with the unexpected rise in oil prices and the strength of the U.S. dollar.[15]

After his election in 1989, former President Rafsanjani attempted to enact a program of economic liberalization; he was not able to do so because of strong opposition from conservative Muslim leaders and a lack of adequate social support. Any attempt to free the economy from state control meets vehement political opposition and risks intensifying social and political instability. Yet, without economic reform, the economy is likely to deteriorate further, which in turn, will produce further domestic frustration, instability, and political violence. This is the most serious challenge facing President Khatemi.

In sum, the political situation in Iran is in a state of flux. Whether this will mean better relations with the region and the Western countries remains uncertain. As of mid-1997, it seemed possible that a gradual lowering of rhetoric in both Teheran and Washington could lead to an eventual dialogue. However, on the key issues so important to the United States—namely, abandoning support for terrorism, endorsing the Arab-Israeli peace process, and curtailing programs to develop weapons of mass destruction—progress will be very difficult to achieve. Nevertheless, if Iran's new strategy of improving its ties with its Arab neighbors, the countries of the Caucasus and Central Asia, Russia, Turkey, and South Asia succeeds, it will be more difficult for the United States to isolate the regime and will encourage a more open debate in Washington concerning the wisdom and viability of the strategy of dual containment and unilateral sanctions.

IRAQ

As long as Iraqi President Saddam Hussein remains in power, his aspirations for a stronger Iraq will be severely restricted by the United States, which does not want Iraq to participate in regional economic and political agreements or organizations. The Hussein regime's objectives of ending Iraq's isolation, exporting oil, and rebuilding the military, as well as broader hopes of achieving greater sea access and control of water resources, are blocked by the U.N. sanctions regime and the Western military presence and commitments. Especially significant has been Iraq's ambivalent cooperation with the United Nations Special Commission on Iraq (UNSCOM), established in 1991 to ensure the elimination of all Iraqi weapons of mass destruction. Until the head of UNSCOM certifies that Iraq is in full compliance with U.N. resolutions, sanctions will not be lifted.

The Arab-Israeli peace process presents a double-edged sword for the Hussein regime. If Iraq continues its current policy of hostility toward Israel by rejecting the peace process, it only contributes to its further isolation, especially given the central U.S. role in the Arab-Israeli negotiations. The process has further complicated Iraq's foreign relations, already muddled by the Gulf War in 1991. Although Jordan still maintains some ties with Iraq, the weakening of Iraqi-Jordanian relations has hurt Iraq's economy and demonstrated that the separation between Arab states favoring the peace process and those opposed is likely to grow wider in the future. Iraq needs integration into the regional economic infrastructure, at the very least to facilitate the export of its oil through pipelines and by tanker, yet it has few regional allies.

On the other hand, even if Iraq wanted to pursue peaceful relations with Israel—and there have been repeated allegations of secret Iraqi-Israeli contacts over the last few years—there are no guarantees that such an approach will yield beneficial results for Iraq. There is a deep suspicion of Saddam Hussein and his regime and little willingness to put much faith in his government's compromising policies. For instance, even though Iraq supposedly accepted the new and unfavorable Iraq-Kuwait border, many observers regard it as a tactical move that could be changed overnight. These skeptics say that Iraq's interest in the peace process cannot be taken seriously as long as Hussein remains in power. In fact, if Hussein were overthrown, continued non-participation in the peace process is one of the few policies his successors could use as leverage to regain international acceptance. Although the process is now moving forward without Iraq, over the longer term, a comprehensive peace, regional arms control, and full normalization all will require an Iraqi role.

The U.S.-led effort to maintain sanctions is aimed at Saddam Hussein and not the Iraqi people as a whole, although the hardest impact is felt by average Iraqis. From the beginning of the Gulf crisis in August 1990, U.S. President George Bush and other U.S. officials personalized the conflict and demonized Saddam Hussein.

The sanctions have led to widespread poverty and degradation of infrastructure and facilities in Iraq. The Iraqi people are suffering food and medical shortages and only an elite circle of Hussein's supporters are protected from the scarcity of goods. Rebuilding has proceeded, but Iraq has limited access to new parts, and thus repairs are probably at best temporary. Iraq has few financial resources, since the sanctions have kept Iraqi oil off the international market for close to five years.

In 1989, Iraq was pumping 2.8 million barrels per day when its OPEC-authorized quota was 3.1 million b/d. Some observers predict that once Iraq is permitted to sell its oil abroad, its output could rise to about 6.5 million b/d, primarily because of the new exploration done by Russian, French, and Italian companies.[16] Iraq's oil minister, Safa Hadi Jawad, has said that once the embargo is lifted his country will start pumping oil at full capacity until it reaches the production levels of Iran. Most Western observers consider such predictions premature. In 1994, Iraq had a provisional OPEC quota of 550,000 b/d, and Iran had a quota of 3.6 million b/d.[17] Even if Iraq is permitted to export oil, it will not be able to recover its full production ability right away due to poor maintenance of the fields and pipelines. Iraq will need to expend considerable effort to reach 3 million b/d, let alone higher targets.

The first significant break in Iraq's bleak economic picture came in May 1996, when UNSC resolution 986 allowed a food-for-oil deal. Under this plan, Iraq was permitted to sell $2 billion of oil for six months or about 700,000 b/d. Although some of the funds will be used by the Iraqi government for the purchase of food and medicine, hundreds of millions of dollars also go toward the Gulf War reparations fund, U.N. costs for the disarmament program in Iraq, and Kurdish needs in autonomous northern Iraq. If Iraq complies with the guidelines, the plan is renewable.[18] Iraqi oil exports began to flow in December 1996.[19]

At least until the plan takes full effect, the economy of Iraq will remain in crisis. Skyrocketing inflation, devastation of the economic infrastructure, lack of basic sanitary conditions, and shortage of food products all testify to acute economic weakness. Per capita domestic food production has been in decline for years and fell 32 percent from 1980 to 1991. The 1992 harvest covered only 20 percent of 1992-93 needs. Between 1965 and 1980, per capita income grew at an average annual rate of 0.6 percent. Though few current statistics are available, one can assume the long war with Iran, the Gulf War, and the embargo have resulted in negative economic growth and falling per capita income.[20]

Saddam Hussein faces a continual leadership struggle, never sure of the direction of the next challenge. In August 1995, two sons-in-law, Gen. Hussein Kamel Hassan and Gen. Saddam Kamel, defected along with their wives, demonstrating a deep split in the ruling family (they later returned to Iraq and were killed). Saddam Hussein's son and putative heir, Uday, has been criticized from many quarters; for instance, Saddam Hussein's half brother Barzan Ibrahim al-Takriti, Iraq's representative to the United Nations in Geneva, strongly criticized Uday in an interview with *Al-Hayat* in August 1995.

There is little the Iraqi president can do to avoid these problems. Iraq has been both cooperative and intransigent with regard to U.N. disarmament inspectors, and the regime makes every effort to circumvent the economic sanctions. Yet as long as Hussein remains in control, an easing of sanctions is unlikely. Saddam Hussein has lasted longer than many expected—and the United States desired—after the Gulf War. He may yet be around to see an opening for Iraq, but the United States will make every effort to put off that day as long as possible.

INTERNAL DIVISIONS

With or without Saddam Hussein, Iraq is plagued by a number of shortcomings that feed Iraqi insecurity. In the longer term, the Iraqi state still faces insecurities based on limited sea access, a vulnerable freshwater supply, ethnic divisions, and the large armed forces of neighboring states. If Hussein died tomorrow and was replaced by a more accommodating leadership, these concerns would remain unaddressed, even if sanctions were eased and oil exports resumed.

Iraq is primarily composed of Sunnis (32-37 percent; roughly half Arabs and half Kurds) and Shiite Arabs (60-65 percent).[21] These ethnic and religious splits are a significant issue for Saddam Hussein's Sunni Arab regime. Over the years, the regime has been in conflict with both Kurds and Shiites. Iraq may be able to stave off fragmentation, but it will have a difficult time achieving integration of these three major groupings.

Like several other groups in Iraq, the Shiites are oppressed; their leaders have been arrested and executed by the hundreds. In March 1991, after the Gulf War, Shiites rose against Saddam Hussein, but were brutally crushed. The Iraqi government continues to target the Shiites by draining and shelling the southern Iraqi marshlands, which is majority Shiite, but the Shiites in Iraq have received little international support. Neither neighboring states nor the allied coalition support Shiite separatism. Kuwait and Saudi Arabia are overtly hostile, and even Iran has done little to help. Many countries, including Saudi Arabia, fear the fragmentation of Iraq and the possibility of an Iranian-dominated Shiite entity in southern Iraq.

In the north, the Kurdish enclave raises similar fears for the Turks and Iraqis who would not like to see the formation of an independent Kurdish state on their border. The Iraqi Kurds have operated an autonomous safe haven in northern Iraq since just after the conclusion of the Gulf War in 1991. The safe haven has been battered by an Iraqi blockade, Kurdish in-fighting, and Turkish military incursions. Though allied planes patrol the no-fly zone over the Kurdish safe haven, there has not been a movement to grant independence to the Kurds. The pressure to keep Iraq from fragmenting is one of the few issues on which most countries, including probably Iran, see eye to eye with Saddam Hussein.[22]

NEIGHBORING STATES

Relations with Iran, Kuwait, and Turkey are central to Iraq's external concerns, and the key issues revolve around oil and water.

In the east, Iraq stands as an Arab bulwark against the Shiite Persians in Iran. At the geographic edge of the Arab world, Iraq sits next to Iran, a larger and more populous state. The two countries fought a bitter eight-year war from 1980 to 1988 that caused hundreds of thousands of casualties. With the Iran-Iraq war only over a couple of years, the allied response to Iraq's invasion of Kuwait presented a difficult choice for Baghdad. In 1990, Iraq decided to settle with Iran and accept the 1975 Algiers Accord, which favored the Iranian position on the division of the disputed territory (the Shatt-al-Arab River), in order to focus forces and resources in the Kuwaiti theater.

Much of the tension between Iraq and Iran is linked to the ongoing Iraqi quest to secure adequate access to the Persian Gulf. With a coastline of only 36 miles (58 km),[23] Iraqi leaders are obsessed with protecting, and in some cases expanding, their water access and port facilities. The Shatt-al-Arab, a disputed waterway along the Persian Gulf and the Iran-Iraq border, has been the focus of major disputes and conflicts. Among other benefits, control of Kuwait after the 1990 invasion gave Iraq another 310 miles (500 km) of coastline. Iraq's concern about access to water and ports is likely to continue even if the current regime is displaced. Iraq's coastline is shorter than the coast of Iran or any GCC state; even the tiny island state of Bahrain has a coast of 100 miles (162 km).

Iraq has long coveted Kuwait. Within a week of Kuwait's independence in 1961, the Iraqi president asserted that Kuwait constituted "an integral part of Iraq."[24] Since then, Iraq has maintained its claim to the tiny Gulf state, and Saddam Hussein's invasion of Kuwait temporarily fulfilled Iraqi hopes for absorption of the so-called nineteenth Iraqi province. Control of Kuwait gave Iraq far greater sea access and full control of naval and port facilities at Umm Qasr; this and more was lost when postwar border decisions around Umm Qasr by international arbiters adversely affected Iraqi naval assets and put Iraq in a weaker position than before.

Another motivation for the invasion was obtaining access to Kuwait's oil and its potential for increasing state wealth. Before the invasion, Iraq complained about Kuwaiti oil pumping from the Rumaila oil field that straddles the border between the two states. Kuwait's wealth coupled with the pre-war attitude of Kuwaiti leaders who refused to submit to Iraqi political pressure was not received well in Baghdad.

Iraq's forced expulsion from Kuwait returned Iraq to a weaker position than before the war. The U.N. Iraq-Kuwait Boundary Demarcation Commission produced results highly favorable to Kuwait, and Iraq is now under the most stringent sanctions regime in recent history. Thus Iraq not only failed to rectify past concerns, but made its long-held quest to improve access to the sea and to gain control of more oil fields unlikely.

In Iraq's relationship with Turkey, the central issues are the Kurds and water. Iraqi society is itself dependent on the Tigris and Euphrates rivers, both of which originate in Turkey and combine in southern Iraq to form the Shatt-al-Arab. Sitting downstream from Turkey and Syria leaves Iraq in a vulnerable position. Turkey's Grand Anatolia Project, designed to increase hydroelectricity and agricultural irrigation, has generated deep concern in Syria and Iraq,[25] which fear that the Turkish project will reduce their share of the river and give Turkey the power to shut off the flow altogether during a conflict or crisis. In fact, in 1990 Turkish President Turgut Ozal threatened to restrict the water flow to Syria over an unrelated political issue; Turkish officials later disavowed the threat. The geographic reality leaves no simple alternative for Iraq in its quest to prevent Turkish domination of vital Iraqi water resources.

Since the end of the Gulf War, the nature of the Kurdish dilemma has changed markedly. Before the war, Iraq was in full control of the Kurdish regions in northern Iraq. As a result of the war and protection of the Kurds, Kurdish leaders now control a section in northern Iraq. This Kurdish safe haven has allowed some Kurdish activity free from the control of Baghdad; it also means that Turkey can carry the war against the PKK into Iraqi territory. Turkey demonstrated this in late March 1995, when 35,000 Turkish troops, supported by tanks and combat aircraft, poured into northern Iraq and spent weeks tracking down PKK guerrillas and bases, according to the Turkish government. Turkey, which is glad to have a free hand to act against Kurds in the safe haven, would not be pleased if the Iraqi Kurds were able to build on their autonomous status and achieve either statehood or greater autonomy from Iraq.

Relations with Saudi Arabia, Jordan, and Syria also are important to Iraqi foreign relations. When Iraq invaded Kuwait in 1990, many wondered whether the Iraqi forces would continue on into Saudi Arabia. Although Saudi Arabian forces are unable to match the Iraqi military—especially without the help of sanctions and arms limits—the U.S. presence totally alters the balance of forces. To Baghdad, the United States may have coordinated and led the war, but it would have been a very different battle without Saudi Arabia's acquiescence to the presence of hundreds of thousands of foreign troops and their equipment.

Jordan and Iraq have had strong political and economic ties for many years, even during the Gulf War. This has changed in the past few years, as King Hussein has tried to make amends in the West for Jordan's Gulf War position. Jordan's embrace of the Arab-Israeli peace process and acceptance in 1995 of Saddam Hussein's defecting daughters and sons-in-law have soured the relationship. With Syria, the sense of rivalry runs deep, from the competing Baath parties to the personal rivalry between Hussein and Asad. Despite the rivalry, the two states have avoided military conflict.

IRAQ UNDER SIEGE

Since invading Kuwait in mid-1990, Iraq has been under siege. U.N. sanctions, backed by the United States and allied military and diplomatic muscle, have brought great hardship upon Iraqi society and prevented Iraq from exporting oil, its main source of revenue. Saddam Hussein wants to get the oil flowing, rebuild Iraq and his armed forces, and end Iraq's isolation, but he recognizes that the price for these goals is his own ouster. This is too steep a cost for him, even if it would mean that Iraq could once again be treated as a normal nation on the regional and international scene.

LIBYA AND SUDAN

Libya and Sudan are listed by the U.S. State Department as state sponsors of international terrorism. In August 1996, President Clinton signed legislation that mandated economic sanctions against Libya and Iran and prohibited certain types of U.S. foreign investment in these countries. The law aims to stop the development of oil and gas resources in both countries and the violation of U.N. sanctions against Libya. At the signing, Clinton called Libya and Iran "two of the most dangerous supporters of terrorism in the world."[26]

Libya has remained in the terrorism spotlight mainly due to lingering charges that Libyan agents were responsible for the downing of Pan Am flight 103 in 1988 and UTA flight 772 in 1989. In 1991, two Libyan intelligence agents were indicted for the Pan Am bombing. The U.N. Security Council has passed several resolutions calling for the trial of the agents and other measures and has imposed economic sanctions. Tripoli, generally hostile to Israel and the peace process, has also been linked to Palestinian rejectionist groups, including the Palestinian Islamic Jihad. Libya has denied most of these allegations, and like Sudan, participated in the June 1996 Arab summit in Cairo in which the final communiqué implicitly accepted Israel's right to exist within its pre-1967 borders.[27]

Sudan, an ally of Iran and a training ground for terrorists, also opposes the peace process and supports groups working to undermine it. Sudanese security services have been accused of providing direct assistance in the attempted assassination of Egyptian President Hosni Mubarak in Ethiopia in June 1995. Uganda and Eritrea have severed relations with Sudan over related security matters, and the Organization of African Unity called on Khartoum to extradite three suspects in the Mubarak assassination. According to the U.S. State Department, "Sudan's support to terrorist organizations has included paramilitary training, indoctrination, money, travel documentation, safe passage, and refuge in Sudan."[28] Hamas and Egypt's Islamic Group are just two of the many terrorist organizations said to have offices in Sudan, which also hosts one of the most-publicized alleged financiers of Islamist terrorism, Osama Bin Ladin, a denaturalized Saudi citizen.

CONCLUSION

Iran, Iraq, Libya, and Sudan stand in the way of the existing peace process and a successful Arab-Israeli peace. Truly comprehensive peace in the Middle East will remain illusive until these countries are part of the discussions. Their concerns and a variety of potential obstacles to comprehensive regional peace are explored in Part II.

PART II
OBSTACLES TO COMPREHENSIVE MIDDLE EAST PEACE

CHAPTER EIGHT

OTHER MIDDLE EAST TERRITORIAL DISPUTES

Many borders on the Arabian peninsula, particularly those in open desert areas, were never clearly defined by their colonial creators. In recent decades, the desire for greater control of oil and natural gas reserves has fueled numerous disputes. Because of the economic significance of many territories in this oil-rich region, national boundaries are widely disputed, with periodic escalation into violence. During the December 1994 summit of the Gulf Cooperation Council, the member states determined to try to resolve all regional border disputes by the time the leaders met again in Muscat the following year.[1] However, with some exceptions, many potentially explosive territorial disputes remain unresolved.

The border disputes in the Persian Gulf and Arabian peninsula range from the strategic, economic, and ideological disagreement between Iraq and Kuwait to the purely economic disputes on much of the Arabian peninsula (see map). In an area of such abundant natural gas and oil reserves, territorial disputes frequently have major economic significance. The Iraq-Iran and Iraq-Kuwait disputes are interesting examples of how many factors intermingle to create complex and long-running territorial quarrels. Not every regional dispute is included in this section.[2]

IRAN-IRAQ

In the Persian Gulf, the Shatt-al-Arab River has a long history as the meeting point of the Arab and Persian worlds. In more recent years, it has served as a vital waterway for Iraqi and Iranian ports and facilitated the export of oil by both countries. The Shatt-al-Arab defines the border between Iran and Iraq and has been the source of conflict between the two countries for many years. Control of the Shatt-al-Arab has major strategic implications for Iraq, which desires it as a way of rectifying its limited access to the sea, a serious disadvantage for an aspiring military power and major oil exporter. Iran, with its long coastline, is not dependent

Map of Persian Gulf/Arabian Peninsula Disputes

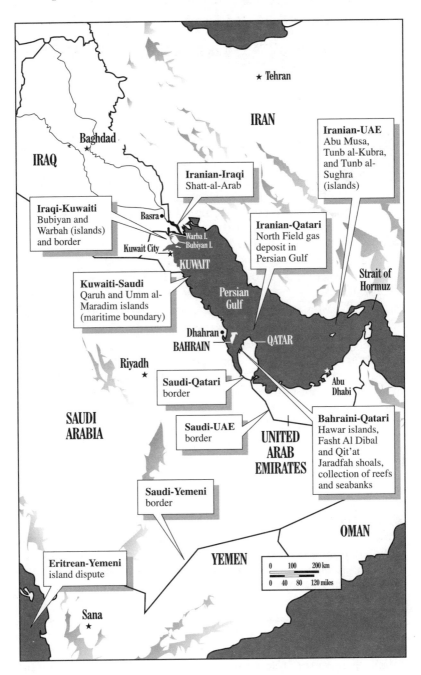

on the Shatt-al-Arab for sea access but enjoys the opportunity to limit Iraqi strategic assets in whatever way it can, including through a dispute over a waterway.

After many years of conflict, Iraq, in the 1975 Algiers Accord agreed to move the border to the center of the waterway, thus defining it more favorably for Iran, in exchange for an end to Iranian support for Kurdish rebels in Iraq. In 1980, after reporting multiple border incidents and Iranian incursions, Iraq abrogated the agreement and the eight-year Iran-Iraq war commenced; much of the fighting took place in and around the Shatt-al-Arab. In 1990, two weeks after Iraq's invasion of Kuwait, Saddam Hussein reversed his position and agreed to accept the 1975 agreement.

The Iranian-Iraqi dispute over the Shatt-al-Arab is of greater concern to Iraqi leaders for they have the most to gain from the ultimate disposition of the border. Although Iraq accepted the current border in 1990, Saddam Hussein or future Iraqi leaders may well revisit the issue at a more advantageous time. Unlike the Golan Heights, where both sides to the dispute gain immense strategic and economic benefits from control of the land, the Shatt-al-Arab confers little additional advantages to Iran other than denying its adversary strategic access. Iran has no shortage of coastline or ports. For Iraq, an advantageous settlement of the Shatt-al-Arab dispute could have major benefits, because Baghdad has such limited sea access. In any case, given the stakes involved, the dispute is unlikely to remain quiet in the coming years unless Iraq eventually succeeds in renegotiating its border with Kuwait.

IRAQ-KUWAIT

The dispute between Iraq and Kuwait is another manifestation of Iraq's quest for greater access to the Gulf. But it also involves economic and ideological considerations, including Iraq's long-standing claim that Kuwait is its nineteenth province.

The border between Kuwait and Iraq has caused friction between the two countries since 1961, when Iraq claimed sovereignty over the whole of Kuwait, a part of the Basra governorate under the Ottoman Empire before the British separated it in 1932. Territorial claims over the islands of Bubiyan and Warbah, which occupy a strategic position at the entrance to the Iraqi port of Umm Qasr, and a dispute over three miles of border between Iraq and Kuwait near the Rumaila oil field, brought the two countries to the brink of armed conflict in March 1973. The island and

165

oil-field disputes both figured prominently in Baghdad's justification for invading Kuwait in August 1990.[3] Iraq continues to seek sovereignty over the islands because of their strategic importance to its security and because of the economic benefit they would provide by increasing its share of seabed oil.[4] At various times, Iraq has offered Kuwait an exchange of Iraqi territory for either or both of the islands, an exchange of freshwater for Kuwait from the Shatt-al-Arab, or straightforward leasing. Kuwait has refused all these offers.

The U.N. Iraq-Kuwait Boundary Demarcation Commission set up after the 1991 Gulf War determined the border based on a 1963 agreement in which Iraq and Kuwait agreed to respect a common border described in a 1932 exchange of letters.[5] The Commission's recommendation was approved unanimously by the U.N. Security Council on May 27, 1993. It placed the official boundary almost 2,000 feet north of the previous frontier, effectively handing Kuwait an extra strip of territory and offering Kuwait a greater share of the Rumaila oil-field, eleven oil wells that Iraq had drilled into the Ratga oil field prior to the invasion of Kuwait,[6] and a portion of the Umm Qasr port, including some naval facilities.[7] Iraq vehemently refused to accept the Commission's decision; it especially opposed the ruling on Umm Qasr, which remains its only outlet to the sea, its only port, and its only naval base, as long as the Shatt-al-Arab remains closed. Paradoxically, Kuwait has never claimed Umm Qasr, and official Kuwaiti government maps showed the boundary line as south of the port even in mid-1992.

After an interim Commission report was released in 1992, Iraqi Foreign Minister Ahmed Hussein sent a letter to the U.N. Secretary General on May 21, 1992, calling into question the finality of the Commission's decision; denouncing the Commission's mandate, composition, and working methods; and suggesting that Iraq may dispute the very existence of Kuwait.[8] The demarcation undoubtedly has reinforced Iraq's sense of grievance and increased the probability of irredentist action in the future. Iraq formally recognized Kuwait's independence in 1994, but the recognition was given grudgingly, under acute international pressure, in the hope that it would lead to the lifting of international sanctions. Even if Saddam Hussein is replaced by a more conciliatory leadership, Iraq's antipathy toward Kuwait, grounded now in the issues of borders and access rights, will continue. Iraq remains a revanchist state until a formal Iraqi-Kuwaiti agreement on borders is openly and freely negotiated.

The territorial dispute between Iraq and Kuwait will be hard to resolve because it involves oil, strategic islands, water access, and Iraq's claim to the entire Kuwaiti state, a potent mix that belies an easy solution. Perhaps Iraq would be more accepting of Kuwait as an independent state if concessions were made with regard to oil fields and sea access. While the current Iraqi leadership might not be satisfied with such trade-offs, a different Iraqi leadership might consider some form of compromise. Of course no Iraqi leaders will accept the status quo without at least complaining about Kuwaiti oil riches, Umm Qasr, and other issues related to sea access.

IRAN-UAE

Iran has a major territorial dispute with the United Arab Emirates over the three strategically located islands of Abu Musa, Tunb al-Kubra, and Tunb al-Sughra (the Greater and Lesser Tunbs) on a tanker route at the entrance to the Strait of Hormuz. The location of the islands and Iran's military presence on them gives the dispute an important strategic element, and the possibility that the waters off the islands may have rich oil fields adds a significant economic element.

Claiming that the islands were Persian before the British transferred their sovereignty to the sheiks of the Trucial States almost a century ago, Iran landed troops on Abu Musa and the neighboring Tunbs in 1971, on the eve of Britain's withdrawal. The Tunbs, only 15 miles from the Iranian island of Qeshm and located on the Iranian side of the median line,[9] were historically part of the Ras al-Khaimah emirate, while Abu Musa, located on the Arab side of the median line 35 miles from the UAE coast, was part of the Sharjah emirate.[10]

Iran and Sharjah signed a Memorandum of Understanding in 1971 which gave Iran full jurisdiction over the range of hills on the northern side of Abu Musa, where it could maintain a military presence, while allowing Sharjah to control the rest of the island, including its small population.[11] In 1992, that arrangement proved unsustainable as Iranian fears for the security of the island led to the expulsion of all non-Sharjah nationals, including teachers, engineers in charge of water facilities, and health workers providing essential services for the UAE government.[12] Iran never denounced the 1971 agreement governing administration or made any additional claim to the island. Nonetheless, the UAE contends that the Iranian government is expansionist and seeks to annex the island. The crisis reached a peak in August 1992, when Iranian officials prevented one hundred residents, primarily Egyptian Arabic teachers and their families, from landing on the island. Subsequent talks held in Abu Dhabi in late September 1992 fell apart when the UAE delegation insisted on placing the Tunbs on the agenda for discussion.[13] The GCC, in the Abu Dhabi Declaration issued on December 23, 1992, rejected the acquisition of territory by force and emphasized UAE sovereignty over Abu Musa and the Tunb Islands.[14] The 1971 agreement between Iran and Sharjah also stipulated that any revenues accruing from oil would be shared equally.[15]

Although Iran and the UAE have commercial ties, the conflict over Abu Musa makes bilateral relations unstable. In February 1993, UAE President Sheikh Zayid bin-Sultan al-Nuhayyan vowed to regain control of the three disputed Gulf islands. Moreover, he stated that the "development of friendly ties between the two countries hinges on boosting confidence and measures that show Iran's adherence to international law and respect of the UAE sovereignty."[16] In 1994, both the GCC and the Arab League supported the UAE position on the islands, and toward the end of the year the UAE proposed that the matter of ownership be referred to the International Court of Justice (ICJ). So far, Iran has refused to agree to this step toward conflict resolution, and the increasingly bitter dispute continues. Teheran recognizes the significant strategic benefit from control of the islands as well as Iran's overall greater strength than the UAE. Especially with the possibility that oil fields may be discovered in the future, both sides are likely to press their claims vehemently. There are also countervailing pressures, such as the major trading relationship between Iran and Dubai, one of seven emirates in the UAE.

IRAN-QATAR

Like many disputes in the Gulf and Arabian peninsula, the one between Iran and Qatar is largely about how to divide natural resources. The Iran-Qatar dispute is about the maritime resources of the Gulf. Although the two countries signed an agreement on maritime boundaries in 1989, Iran claims 30 percent of Qatar's North Field natural gas reserves. The field is thought to possess significant reserves. Iran's claim has little historical basis; it is driven largely by the prospect of controlling a larger share of natural gas. Thus far, the dispute has been less intense than most others in the region.

SAUDI ARABIA–QATAR

Saudi Arabia and Qatar have a long-standing border dispute over a 10-square-mile strip of territory said to be rich in oil and gas deposits.[17] In September 1992, the dispute erupted into violence at a border outpost that has been claimed by both sides for over two decades.[18] Egypt brokered a border demarcation accord, signed in December 1992, to ease tensions and to end Qatar's boycott of the Gulf Cooperation Council; this accord set up a framework that was to lead to a final agreement within one year, but the deadline was not met.[19] Meanwhile, a series of shooting incidents between March and October 1994 resulted in several deaths, including one Qatari civilian.[20] Both nations have expressed their desire to resolve the dispute, and in mid-1996, they agreed to demarcate the border.[21] The Saudi kingdom remains at odds with Qatar over its maverick foreign policy; Qatar has permitted a significant U.S. presence on its territory and is trying to improve ties with Iran and Iraq while normalizing relations with Israel.[22]

BAHRAIN-QATAR

Bahrain and Qatar have been involved in a territorial dispute since their independence from Britain in the early 1970s. Like many others, the dispute over the potentially oil-rich Hawar islands and Fasht Al Dibal and Qit'at Jaradfah shoals, as well as a collection of reefs and seabanks, is driven primarily by economic interests. Britain officially accepted Bahrain's claim to the cluster of islands and reefs as early as the 1930s, but Qatar always has disputed Bahrain's sovereignty over the territory.[23] Saudi mediation in the late 1980s, and GCC efforts to keep the dispute from becoming explosive, have not resolved the tensions that continue to fester. Qatar brought the dispute before the International Court of Justice for the second time in November 1994 without the consent of Bahrain, which continues to control the disputed territory.[24] The ICJ has ruled that the case is within its jurisdiction and that it will proceed to hear the case on the basis of unilateral application by Qatar. The emir of Qatar, Sheikh Hamad Bin Khalifah al Thani, has explained, however, that "if the two parties reach acceptable results through the Saudi mediator, then the case will be withdrawn from the ICJ. We hope to reach a brotherly solution through the mediator that will satisfy the two parties. Otherwise, we will have to wait until the ICJ decides on this issue."[25] The rhetoric is sometimes friendly, but both states have a strong desire to take control of potentially resource-rich territory.

As of late 1996, the ICJ was still looking at the case, and relations between Bahrain and Qatar had taken a turn for the worse as each country charged the other with meddling in its internal affairs. Bahrain claimed that Qatar was aiding members of the repressed Bahraini opposition. Qatar protested that Bahrain supported efforts to restore the deposed Qatari emir—father of the current emir—through violence. Other members of the GCC have tried to mediate the dispute. The border question is still unresolved.[26]

SAUDI ARABIA–YEMEN

Saudi Arabia and Yemen also lack a fully agreed upon border and both covet the disputed areas partially because of expected oil deposits. In 1992, Saudi Arabia warned several international oil companies to stop searching for oil in disputed territories. The oil companies argued that they were operating on Yemeni, not Saudi, land.[27]

The dispute began in the early 1930s when Saudi Arabia defeated the Yemeni Imamate in a border war over the provinces of Asir, Najran, and Jizan. Since then, border skirmishes have erupted periodically; in addition, various Yemeni leaders have alleged over the years that Saudi Arabia has provided arms to factions within Yemen.[28] Several rounds of talks between the two governments have failed to produce an agreement. Saudi Arabia and Yemen signed a Memorandum of Understanding in February 1995 to re-demarcate their borders on the basis of the Taif agreement of 1934. Technical committees have met to discuss the issue, but little further progress has been made.[29]

KUWAIT–SAUDI ARABIA

Kuwait and Saudi Arabia have a long-standing territorial dispute over the islands of Qaruh and Umm al-Maradim, situated respectively 23 miles and 16 miles off the coast of the northern part of a "neutral zone" created in 1922 by Britain. The neutral zone was 2,500 square miles (6,500 sq. km) and administered by Britain as well as the precursors to the Kuwaiti and Saudi states; it was created as a first step in the effort to define what is now the Kuwaiti-Saudi border. During the 1960s, the two countries made a series of demarcation agreements that divided the zone between them; the agreements applied to the land boundaries and extended six marine miles into the seabed and subsoil.[30] The northern section of the neutral zone is part of Kuwait. Not covered in the agreements is the offshore territory, which remains to be partitioned and is the focus of current concerns. Ownership of the islands is intricately linked to this process of determining the maritime boundaries, which involves dividing the oil-rich Gulf waters between the two nations.

An exchange of letters between Iraq and Kuwait in 1923 and 1932 forms the basis of Kuwait's claim to the islands. Disagreements began as early as September 1949, when the Kuwaiti government granted the American Oil Company of California a concession to conduct oil exploration on the two disputed islands. Following protests from Saudi Arabia, the firm stopped its operations. In 1961, Kuwait offered Saudi Arabia a share of any oil proceeds which might accrue from the islands in return for Saudi acknowledgment of Kuwaiti sovereignty over them. Saudi Arabia refused.

Kuwaiti sovereignty over the islands remains contested by Riyadh,[31] but progress toward resolving the dispute appears possible. On July 18, 1995, Kuwaiti Foreign Minister Sheikh Sabbath al-Ahed al-Sabbath visited Saudi Arabia to discuss border demarcation.[32] Afterward he said that the talks had made progress toward demarcating the maritime boundary between the two nations and had led to "agreement on specific points," adding that experts from the two countries would follow up on those points in upcoming meetings.[33] Ownership of the islands is sure to be at the heart of future negotiations.

EGYPT-SUDAN

Since 1902, Egypt and Sudan have administered land south and north, respectively, of the internationally recognized boundary between them. Originally, they agreed to do this in order to facilitate tribal grazing, but now both states consider the land they control as sovereign territory. The Sudanese-controlled area in Egypt, known as the Halaib Triangle, could enlarge Sudan's claims to the Red Sea seabed. Sudan also lays claim to a smaller area, the Wadi Halfa salient, that is now mostly under the waters of Lake Nasser.[34] After an assassination attempt against Egyptian President Hosni Mubarak in June 1995, fighting erupted in the disputed areas as Egyptian officials pointed the finger at the Sudan. Reports that the region is oil-rich have also emboldened the rival claimants.[35]

Perhaps the greatest impediment to resolving the dispute is that almost a hundred years have elapsed since the land was

first divided in conflict with the international boundary. Genera-
tions have now grown up on each side with the assumption that
the land is part of their respective country, even if technically they
were aware that that is not the case. The two countries have no
real strategic, economic, or ideological interests in insisting on
their claims, unless perhaps oil is found on some portion of the
disputed area — then the dispute would be difficult to resolve.
Otherwise, Egyptian and Sudanese governments that see eye-
to-eye on other issues and have no need to use the territorial dispute as a staging ground for hostility should be able to move toward
an equitable resolution.

SYRIA-TURKEY

Syria rejected the 1939 cession by France of the Sanjak of Alexandretta (now Hatay Province) to Turkey. Over the years, this disputed area has been a source of friction between the two
states,[36] and Syria's U.N. delegation annually demands the return
of Hatay to Syrian control.[37] But Syria has taken little additional
action to press its claim, and this dispute does not appear likely to erupt into a larger conflict.

WATER: THE SOURCE OF FUTURE DISPUTES?

Much of the Middle East is an arid region in which states depend
upon shared water resources. Although it is difficult to
match precisely existing border disputes with the location of shared
aquifers, a water shortage could bring about a confrontation
between water rivals. With extensive irrigated agriculture, high water
demand in the oil industry, the expensive cost of desalination, demographic growth, urban expansion, and little conservation, the regional water situation could eventually reach crisis proportions.

Saudi Arabia and its neighbors share many drainage basins
and deep aquifers. Two drainage basins are shared by Saudi
Arabia, Jordan, and Iraq; one by Saudi Arabia, Iraq, and Kuwait;
three by Saudi Arabia and Yemen; and two more by Saudi Arabia, Oman, and the UAE. Shared deep aquifers extend from
Saudi Arabia into Kuwait; Iraq-Bahrain-Qatar-UAE-Oman; Yemen;
and Jordan-Syria. Given the paucity of regional water management and the abundance of territorial disputes, disputed lands
could quickly turn into rivalries over control of regional water
sources.[38] Like oil and natural gas, pumping water from one's own
territory often contributes to the depletion of water resources in

a neighboring state. Aquifers rarely respect international boundaries. In the near future, a country may complain about overpumping water in the same way that Iraq criticized Kuwait's overpumping of shared oil reserves.

Two regional water disputes not related to Arab-Israeli issues are also important. Syria and Iraq worry about Turkey's massive dam construction program in Eastern Anatolia, as well as Turkey's interference with the flow of the Tigris and Euphrates rivers.[39]

Finally, the Nile could be a source of dispute among countries that depend on its waters. As the longest river in the world, the Nile passes through nine African states before it dumps its waters into the Mediterranean. Egypt depends on the Nile for over 80 percent of its water, and uses about two thirds of the Nile's annual yield. Though the furthest downstream, Egypt has used its diplomatic muscle to guarantee the vast majority of the Nile waters. At times, Egypt's relationship with Ethiopia and Sudan has been tense because of Nile-related issues, and Egypt has warned both countries not to interfere with the flow of the river. Egypt and Sudan basically abide by a 1959 water-sharing agreement, though Egypt often borrows from the Sudanese allotment.[40] Rapid population growth and agricultural difficulties in many riparian states will keep control of the Nile waters in a prominent position on the regional agenda.

CHAPTER NINE
ECONOMIC, DEMOGRAPHIC, CULTURAL, AND POLITICAL ASYMMETRIES

The countries of the Middle East have a wide range of economic, demographic, and political/cultural traits. These characteristics influence how each country and group sees itself and its adversaries, determine the capabilities of aspiring regional powers, and cloud future efforts at conflict resolution and reconciliation.

ECONOMIC ASYMMETRIES: THE GAP BETWEEN RICH AND POOR

The Middle East contains some of the largest disparities between rich and poor countries in any region of the world. Oil wealth in the six GCC countries and Israel's Westernized economy place these seven states far ahead of their neighbors in terms of per capita income and growth potential. Until recently, the Arab Gulf states have been able to support costly education and health care programs for their populations even as they purchased large quantities of military hardware. Deficits in the early 1990s suggest that difficult trade-offs may be required in the future.

GNP per capita is a simple measure of relative economic wealth. According to World Bank figures for 1995, GNP per capita in the United Arab Emirates is $21,420; Qatar, Kuwait, and Israel all have GNP per capita incomes above $14,400. Saudi Arabia ($7,240), Bahrain ($7,500), and Oman ($5,200) occupy a relatively wealthy middle ground; others have incomes significantly less: Iran ($2,190 in 1992), Tunisia ($1,800), Jordan ($1,390), Syria ($1,170 in 1991), Egypt ($710), and Yemen ($280).[1]

This huge difference in per capita income has a direct impact on the relationship between rich and poor Arab countries.

It affects both labor migration and the flow of foreign assistance. Countries and groups dependent on foreign remittances from labor and/or on foreign assistance from wealthier countries are vulnerable to sudden changes in political relations. Palestinians in the West Bank and Gaza are acutely aware of this. For a long time, Israel provided a significant number of low-level jobs for Palestinians. In recent years, however, Israel, worried about personal security, has shifted to Thai, Romanian, and other foreign workers for agriculture, construction, and other menial tasks. This has created new problems for Israel: many foreign workers do not have adequate housing; immigration officials have not been able to stop thousands of workers from staying in Israel with expired visas; and the sudden influx of tens of thousands of non-Jews into Israel has posed identity questions for the Jewish state.

Similarly, during and after the Gulf War, many dependent countries experienced dramatic changes in their economies. Labor migration is an important way of redistributing wealth both within the Middle East and in parts of South, Southeast, and East Asia. In addition to Arab workers, millions of Indians, Pakistanis, Sri Lankans, Thais, and other Asians earn their living in the Gulf. Yet this dependency leaves some states vulnerable to sudden shifts in worker populations.

The war had a profound impact on the existing economic order in the Middle East. At the time of the crisis, poorer Arab countries lost billions of dollars in remittances when over one million Egyptians, Jordanians, Palestinians, and Yemenis left or were expelled from Iraq, Kuwait, and Saudi Arabia, in many cases because PLO and Yemeni leaders supported Saddam Hussein.

The Gulf countries were a leading source of employment and foreign exchange, providing a strong financial boost to the economies of labor-exporting states such as Jordan and Yemen.[2] With over five million foreign workers in 1990, 68 percent of the work force in the Gulf states was foreign.[3] The 1991 Gulf crisis dispersed much of the existing labor force. Rough estimates suggest that at least 400,000 foreign (mostly Arab) nationals lost work in Kuwait. Iraq, home to approximately one million Egyptians before the war, also witnessed a massive exodus of mostly Arab migrant workers. In September 1990, Saudi Arabia responded to Yemen's support for Iraq by toughening the rules for Yemeni workers; some 800,000 Yeminis returned home as a result. Non-Arab Asian workers, most heavily concentrated in the UAE and Saudi Arabia, were less affected. In fact, in later years, Asian workers stepped in to fill the void.[4]

Similarly, the long established foreign assistance system among Arab countries was dealt a blow by the Gulf War and the postwar economic problems of the Gulf states. For years, oil-rich states provided billions of dollars in aid to other Arab countries. As a result of the war, however, wealthy Arab supporters of the allied coalition cut or eliminated aid for countries they perceived as having been pro-Iraq, such as Jordan and Yemen.[5]

By the mid-1990s, even the wealthier Gulf states began to feel the economic ramifications of the war. Six years after the war, the region faces severe economic difficulties. The Arab Gulf states now have significant revenue shortfalls due to the costs of the war and (aside from the short-term rise in 1996) the low world price of oil. Since the legitimacy of the Gulf monarchies depends considerably on their ability to distribute resources and sustain extensive services, revenue shortages could endanger both internal stability and military capabilities, since these ultimately rest on their economic power.[6]

The economic problems of the richest countries in the Arab world provide telling lessons of failures of leadership. During the 1970s, known as the era of plenty, when the oil boom was at its peak, Arab leaders in the Gulf provided few incentives for private enterprise initiatives. Instead, the power and role of governments grew astronomically. Political goals were given priority over economic development objectives, and intra-Arab, Arab-Israeli, and Iran-Iraq issues dominated decision making.

The Gulf economies continue to depend on oil and natural gas for most of their revenue. In Saudi Arabia, oil accounts for about 75 percent of budget revenues, 35 percent of GDP, and almost all of the country's export earnings. In Iran, over 75 percent of export revenues are from oil. In Kuwait, oil accounts for nearly half of GDP and 90 percent of export and government revenues. Even the UAE, considered one of the strongest Gulf economies, depends on earnings from oil exports and is affected by the weak oil price on the world market.[7]

In most Gulf states, sectors of the economy not directly related to oil (e.g., the mercantile and service sectors or the construction industry) nevertheless are dependent on the oil industry. In both Saudi Arabia and Oman, for example, the agricultural sector is subsidized by the oil industry. Even in Gulf countries where the share of oil in the economy has fallen to below 50 percent, oil-related revenues from state petrochemical industries and other state industries built with oil money still play a significant role.[8] Although oil revenues are diminishing and diversification has progressed furthest in Bahrain, the oil sector remains important: petroleum production and processing accounts for about 80 percent of exports, 60 percent of government revenues, and 30 percent of GDP.[9]

The fluctuating price of oil in the world market affects the Gulf economies significantly. These countries suffer when prices are low and respond either by expanding production or by reducing production in an attempt to increase the price. However, the major oil exporters are often unable to embrace a common policy of freezing or reducing production to the levels necessary to succeed in raising prices. Past attempts to control or reduce output have been significant sources of tension among OPEC members and, indeed, contributed to Iraq's invasion of Kuwait in 1990.

Another important economic characteristic common among Gulf states is the dominant position of the central government. Governments own the national oil companies, fully controlling investment and production decisions. They collect oil revenues, redistribute the capital through the budget, and determine who will profit through spending and regulatory policies. Government policies and spending are critically important even for the private sector. Government spending, for example, is the engine of the construction industry, and even in sectors like banking and finance, government has a signficant role.[10] The role of governments in the Gulf economies complicates the economic reform necessary to increase government revenue. Privatization, reductions in government spending, and imposition of new taxes carry high political costs. For example, as noted in chapter 6, privatization is unpopular among Saudi citizens accustomed to generous government programs.

The combination of rapidly expanding populations, limited water resources, and acute financial problems could produce tensions among neighbors and increase the possibility of regional conflict, not only in the Gulf but in the Middle East region as a whole. According to the 1996 World Bank annual report, GDP growth rates in North Africa and the Middle East increased slightly in 1995, reversing earlier declines.[11] The 1995 growth rates were modest compared with the prosperous 1960s and 1970s, but better than those of the late 1980s and early 1990s, which the World Bank called a period of "crisis." The 1994 World Bank report described, "a deteriorating external economic environment— particularly the sharp drop in international oil prices—decreasing efficiency in the use of capital, low levels of private investment and poor export performance."[12]

Low or negative economic growth creates a potent and potentially dangerous mixture when coupled with population growth. Rich and poor countries throughout the Middle East face the daunting prospect of tens of millions of people needing employment and basic sustenance. Population issues both exacerbate economic concerns and pose security concerns; large numbers of discontented minorities (and, in some cases, out-of-power majority groups) could increase regional tensions and fuel a crisis irrespective of progress toward a comprehensive peace.

POPULATION ASYMMETRIES: POLITICAL, SOCIAL, AND SECURITY CONSEQUENCES

Continued and rapid population growth in the Middle East raises a host of issues for regional governments. The socioeconomic impact of population growth is important, especially in countries with large populations and low per capita incomes. The widespread availability of satellite television, even in the poorest areas, adds a potentially inflammatory component, as the poor are made aware on a daily basis of their relative deprivation. This can play into the hands of extremists seeking to exploit misery.

In mid-1995, the Middle East's fifteen countries plus the West Bank and Gaza, from Egypt to Iran and including Turkey, had approximately 274 million residents. Arabs form the largest ethnic group, followed by Turks (25 percent), Persians (12 percent), Kurds (7 percent), Jews (2 percent) and others (4 percent).[13] Since World War II, total population in the region has doubled, and some experts predict that it will double again in only twenty years.[14] Although certain assumptions must be made to arrive at this prediction, the possibility of minor variations in the time span required for this increase does not negate the clear trend toward a dramatically larger population. U.N. estimates are more conservative, but still predict that by 2025—less than thirty years from now—the population in the region will be 490-560 million.[15] The Population Reference Bureau estimates 494 million.[16]

A number of factors could alter long-range population forecasts if a regional consensus emerges that slower population growth is desirable and/or necessary, although they are unlikely to significantly slow population growth in the short or medium term. The timing and pace of decreases in the fertility rate, just beginning to drop, will affect future population growth. The U.N. estimate of a regional population of 490-560 million in 2025, for example, assumes the fertility rate will drop to nearly half of current levels.[17] If fertility declines more slowly, population levels will be higher.

The youthfulness of the Middle East's population is a second factor influencing future growth. In the developed world, only about 20 percent of the population is under age fifteen; in the Middle East, the proportion is much higher. In 1992, approximately 45 percent of the populations of Iran, Iraq, and Saudi Arabia were under fifteen; in the West Bank and Gaza, 50 percent.[18] As young women enter their childbearing years, further pressures on population will occur. Even if the fertility rate declines, a boom in the number of childbearers could offset downward population momentum. In addition, the youthfulness of a society is significantly related to political instability. Large numbers of young people without jobs or meaningful careers are susceptible to becoming political recruits for social movements that promise better opportunities through political change or upheaval. Some suggest that there is a strong causal link between the relative youth of a society and its propensity to engage in violence and revolutionary behavior.[19]

Social and educational issues related to women also affect population figures. Integrating women into society, intentionally or as a result of other social policies, is a proven method of reducing population growth.[20] Women's literacy and employment rates, as well as average age at marriage, are all related to fertility and population growth rates. Higher education, for example, is strongly correlated with greater use of birth control.

In many countries in the Middle East, women are still denied access to employment and educational opportunities that have contributed to lower fertility rates elsewhere, and there are wide disparities between men and women. In Egypt, for example, 34 percent of women and 63 percent of men are literate. In Iran, 43 percent of women and 64 percent of men are literate, and in Saudi Arabia, 48 percent of women and 73 percent of men. The Gulf countries, like most of the Middle East, have strikingly low rates of women in the labor force. On the Arabian peninsula, 5 percent of women are in the labor force; the world average is 50 percent.[21]

POLITICAL AND SOCIAL CONSEQUENCES

In many Middle Eastern countries, rapid population growth is causing enormous strains on social services. In areas such as education, housing, health services, labor, and agriculture, governments are unable adequately to meet the needs of the people. Some states simply maintain a limited number of services for an ever-expanding population; in these cases, residents experience more poverty, greater frustration, and a lower quality of life overall. The countries that have been able to avoid this trap are better able to meet the rising expectations of their inhabitants. Egypt and Iran are examples of countries struggling to satisfy the needs of their rapidly growing populations.

The young age of the population exacerbates the shortage of services. While the industrialized world has a 3:1 ratio of working adults to children, in the Middle East, the ratio is 1:1. In a sense, each working adult is responsible for supporting, either directly or through support of government programs, three times as many children as in the developed world.

Growing populations increase the urgency of controlling fresh-water for drinking and agriculture. To meet the food needs of expanding populations, the productivity of existing farmland must be increased, the amount of land used for farming must be increased, or food must be imported. In Cairo, urban growth "has been encroaching on the fertile agricultural lands along the Nile."[22] This creates a double-sided problem for Egypt: the growing population needs more food (and possibly more farmland) even as urbanization reduces the amount of available agricultural space. Similarly, as population increases, so do energy needs—a potentially troublesome issue for the non-oil-producing states in the region. In short, the growing regional population has begun to make greater demands on natural resources.

This combination of rapid population growth, pressure on natural resources, and overstretched government budgets has created an opening for Islamic fundamentalist organizations. Radical groups (that may or may not have a militant intent) have been able to fill the vacuum where governments or families have failed to provide sufficient social welfare services. These organizations build constituencies by providing social service work and outreach. The Muslim Brotherhood in Egypt and Hamas in the Gaza Strip both have built networks of schools, health clinics, mosques, and other institutions that provide much-needed services and generate support for their operations. Control of their own schools also allows them to inculcate values that may be at odds with the official government line.

Population size can be a key factor in determining the size and structure of the armed forces. Generating enough jobs for a rapidly expanding population is a difficult task; a large military provides one way of meeting that need. In states such as Egypt and Iran that face discontent stemming from a growing population and insufficient resources, large government forces may be used for policing and maintaining order. The line between police and soldiers is often less defined than in the United States. In a symbolic sense, countries struggling to provide enough government services may see extra soldiers as one way of increasing the appearance of government activity.

Middle East countries fall into two categories: those that have slowed high population growth rates and those whose population is still growing rapidly. Many countries once noted for rapid population growth have slowed their growth rates. In all the Arab Mediterranean countries, population growth rates have started to decline.[23] Egypt and Iran both have significant population-related problems, but are expected to have slower increases over the next thirty years. In other countries with high population growth rates, population is expected to increase in the next thirty years, anywhere from 94 percent (in Pakistan) to 175 percent (in the West Bank and Gaza). Afghanistan, Iraq, Jordan, Kuwait, Oman, Syria, and Yemen all fall into this category.[24]

Israel has avoided overpopulation problems.[25] Its advanced economy, high education and literacy levels, and a more Western approach on most women's issues have kept population growth relatively low. In fact, Israel would actually welcome a higher fertility rate. Ultra-orthodox (and some orthodox) Jewish families continue to have much higher fertility rates than the rest of the country, but secular Israeli Jews have followed a pattern similar to the United States and Western Europe.

Migration and refugee issues are often closely related to population issues. In the Middle East, they are often linked to military or political events. The wealthy Gulf states rely on large numbers of Asian workers, particularly in the aftermath of the Gulf War. Palestinian refugees, many living in underdeveloped camps, remain a stumbling block in Israeli-Palestinian negotiations. The influx into Israel of hundreds of thousands of Jews from the states of the former Soviet Union has had a profound impact on Israeli society, the 1992 elections, and to some extent the fears of its Arab neighbors. As already noted, labor migration within the Middle East has often served to redistribute wealth.

In general, the presence of foreign workers raises citizenship questions and often skews the age structure in both labor-exporting and labor-importing countries. It also fosters a superior-inferior relationship between the upper-class native population and the lower-class foreign workers.

DEMOGRAPHY AND SECURITY PROBLEMS

The characteristics of a given population also affect military and security considerations. A country's population size, literacy levels, and ethnic composition influence military power calculations and the choice of military doctrine best suited for the security posture of a particular country. In areas like the Gulf, the relative proportion of expatriates and indigenous population serving in the armed forces may decrease the real or perceived reliability of the armed forces. Countries with small populations such as Israel tend to rely more heavily on deterrent strategies, including alliances or preemptive strategies that call for a speedy end to conflict. In contrast, countries with larger populations such as Iran may be prepared to engage in longer conflicts with greater emphasis upon ground combat because of their ability to absorb higher casualties. It is difficult to imagine any war between Israel and the Arab states lasting for eight years, as did the Iran-Iraq war.

In addition to the more obvious links between population and security—strain on human and natural resources, size of the armed forces, and strength of opposition groups—population considerations also affect security in a more profound way. A number of countries believe that they face an existential demographic threat. To what extent do population issues foster military conflict? How deeply are population issues affected by conflict?

For years, Palestinian intellectuals made the argument that over time the demography of Israel and the occupied territories would eventually create a Palestinian majority because of higher birth rates in the Palestinian community. Under this scenario, Israel would be increasingly vulnerable. It could retain its uniquely Jewish institutions and deny equality to a growing Palestinian population. This, however, would put it at odds with its chief backers in the United States and Europe who would have to denounce its undemocratic behavior toward a large sector of its population; this could affect aid, trade, and ultimately political support. Alternatively, Israel could become a pluralistic society in which Jews would eventually become a minority. This approach would lead to a secular state in which the uniqueness of Israel would be diluted because of the Palestinian majority. The Palestinian majority could, through democratic means, turn Israel into a Palestinian/Arab state that happened to have a large Jewish minority. This scenario received a setback when the Soviet Union (and later, Russia, Ukraine, and other successor states) opened the gates for Jews to emigrate to Israel.

The demographic issue also has fueled concern among some Palestinians that the Gaza-Jericho approach is an attempt by Israel to retain control of the occupied territories while eliminating the possibility of citizenship for most Palestinians. By excluding the Palestinian population centers, Israel might even be able to annex the territories and maintain a democratic system for Israel proper. Some suggest that Israel's approach is similar to past South African efforts to move black South Africans into so-called independent homelands (Bantustans).

Lebanon provides a concrete example of how demographic issues affect security. In the mid-1970s, the threat to the existence of the Maronite community led first to Syrian and then to Israeli intervention. The Maronites, a Christian sect, felt that their position was precarious, living as they did (and still do today) surrounded by a Muslim community. Because population numbers in the past have often translated into political power, even conducting a census in Lebanon today is highly controversial; all parties fear demographic change. As part of the Taif agreement, the Christian minority lost their guaranteed upper hand in Lebanese politics; the agreement increased the number of Muslim parliamentarians to the same number as the Christian representatives; it also weakened the office of the Christian president while strengthening the office of the Muslim prime minister.

CULTURAL ASYMMETRIES: ETHNIC AND RELIGIOUS SCHISMS

Population is a concern not just for smaller countries fearing the numerical superiority of their adversaries (examples of which can be found throughout the Middle East). Population is also a concern within many countries struggling with majority and minority status issues. Population imbalances exist within almost every country in the region; these are often ethnic or religious in origin.

The presence of ethnic and religious minorities in Middle Eastern countries often arouses fear and suspicion among the ruling elite, opposition movements, and various segments of the population. Often adversaries—other countries—support elements seeking to exacerbate the differences. Historically, Israel considered forming an alliance with Iran and Turkey to combat Arab hostility. Kurdish organizations often gained and lost support based on the prevailing relations between Turkey, Syria, Iran, and Iraq. Iran meddled in Bahrain's affairs when it appeared that doing so would help the Shiites undermine the government. Discussed below are a number of ethnic and religious conflicts within the region.

ETHNIC CONFLICTS

Kurds. The Kurdish issue has been important to Turkey since the birth of the modern Kurdish state. The Treaty of Sevres in August 1920 prescribed the creation of a weak state from the ruins of the Ottoman empire; it stated that if, within a year, the Kurdish people desired a separate state, it should be created, provided the Council of the League of Nations approved.[26] By 1923, the treaty was irrelevant because the Turkish nationalists founded a modern and strong Turkish state, precluding the possibility of a separate Kurdish state.

Many Turkish leaders became convinced that the creation of a Kurdish state would weaken Turkey. The first major challenge to the fledgling Turkish state came from a Kurdish religious leader, who occupied a third of Kurdish Anatolia. This and two subsequent Kurdish revolts were ruthlessly suppressed by the government. For Turks, three major armed rebellions against the state have firmly established the Kurds as the primary challenge to their independent existence.[27]

In the unusual circumstances following the Gulf War, the Kurds in Iraq were given autonomy in northern Iraq by allied coalition leaders. Although the current Kurdish leadership is divided, all the leaders are sensitive to the fact that the Kurds in northern Iraq are vulnerable. None of the leaders are now pressing for independence; to the contrary, they constantly reiterate that a solution for Kurds need not threaten any existing state borders.

Turkey would prefer a unified, democratic Iraq, largely because the future of Kurds can best be addressed within the existing borders of an Iraq that is democratic and respects human rights. Neither Turkey nor any other power is confident, however, that a democratic regime will emerge as the successor to Saddam Hussein, nor do they have the political leverage to advance this agenda.

The Kurds spill across the frontiers of Turkey, Iran, Iraq, and Syria, complicating relationships among the four countries. The coalition commitment to the Kurds at the end of the Gulf War helped to internationalize the Kurdish question. The future of the Kurds—hostage to the future of Iraq and the successor of Saddam Hussein—has grave consequences for Turkey, Iran, and Iraq, and the relationship among these countries. For instance, if the Kurds of northern Iraq eventually establish an independent state because the Baghdad regime collapses, Turkey would face a serious dilemma concerning its own, increasingly restless Kurdish population. Similarly, Iran worries that the Kurdish enclave in northern Iraq will only whet the appetite of its own Kurds for independence or the right to join their brothers in Iraq. Clearly neither Turkey, Iran, Iraq, nor Syria wants to see an independent Kurdistan; but if they tried to crush a fledgling state with military force, they could face strong opposition in the West, especially if the Kurdish state was democratic. In these circumstances, a war over the independence of Kurdistan could escalate, creating grave problems for both regional and external powers, especially the United States.

Azeris. About twelve million Azeris live in northern Iran near the border with independent Azerbaijan.[28] Their proximity to Azerbaijan has been a mixed blessing. Conceivably, the external Azeri community could support Azeris within Iran against the central government. In reality, Azerbaijan is locked in a violent struggle with Armenia and has no resources to extend to other Azeris; fighting began in 1988 and lasted until a ceasefire in May 1994. Since 1988, more than 20,000 people have died in the dispute over Nagarno-Karabakh, an Armenian-populated enclave inside Azerbaijan. As of late 1996, the two sides had failed to agree on the terms of a peace treaty.[29] Iran, already home to the largest recent refugee population in the world, has received thousands of refugees from the fighting. Iranian Azeris cannot be impressed by Azerbaijan's poor military performance.[30] However, if Azerbaijan resolves its energy access problem and revenues from oil sales climb, this attitude could change.

The Baluch. Baluchistan is a region in southeast Iran and Pakistan. Except for a Baghdad-based movement called the Baluch Liberation Front in the 1970s, Baluchi nationalism has been quiescent. The Baluch are often involved in smuggling across Iranian borders with Afghanistan and Pakistan despite the presence of Iranian Revolutionary Guards. They are able to do so because the Iranian government is weak in the Baluch-inhabited provinces.[31] In early 1994, scattered attacks and violence rocked Iranian Baluchistan.[32] Iran has an estimated 1 to 1.3 million Baluch, and Pakistan an estimated 4.6 million, mostly in the southwest near the Iranian border.[33]

Throughout the Gulf, ethnic groups that spill across borders or show signs of discontent within a particular state are potential sources of instability, conflict, and violence. They become especially important when states are mutating and fragmenting and leaders see opportunities to achieve long-standing objectives. In this context, low-intensity violence can be extraordinarily effective and can trigger wider conflict.

RELIGIOUS CONFLICTS

Christian-Muslim. Christians form the largest religious minority in the Middle East. Egypt, Lebanon, and Syria have sizable Christian communities; the number of Israeli, Palestinian, and Jordanian Christians is smaller but nevertheless significant. The growth of fundamentalist Islam has highlighted discrimination and violence directed against Christians in the region. Incidents include the murder of Christian clergy, raids and vandalism against churches, and torture, ostracism, and imprisonment of converts and Church leaders. Noted cases of persecution and terrorism have taken place in Egypt, Iran, and Pakistan;[34] Lebanon was virtually destroyed by a civil war between Christian and Muslim militias. Anti-Christian activities have widespread support. In a much-publicized case in February 1995, after judges acquitted two Pakistani Christians of a trumped-up blasphemy charge, protesters rioted in Lahore, Pakistan.[35]

Jew-Muslim. A central motif of the Arab-Israeli conflict is the religious difference between the warring parties; both sides intermingle political and religious denunciations, and analysts and commentators frequently equate Israeli and Jew on the one hand, and Arab and Muslim on the other. The presence in Israel and the occupied territories of so many Christian, Jewish, and Islamic holy sites only adds to the tension. The massacre of forty Palestinians in Hebron on February 25, 1994, by an Israeli settler, Baruch Goldstein, was horrible in its own right. But the fact that these Muslim Palestinians were gunned down during prayer at the Cave of the Patriarchs, a West Bank mosque among other things, exacerbated the religious aspect of the conflict. Riots and other incidents in Jerusalem at places like the Dome of Rock and the Western Wall are other examples.

Those who combine their political militancy with religious fervor include Israeli settlers at Kiryat Arba (a large settlement next to Hebron) and members of Hamas and Islamic Jihad. Israel and many Arab states make an explicit link between the state and a particular religion (e.g., Israel, the homeland of the Jewish people; or Saudi Arabia, the Islamic state).

Shiite-Sunni. Of the many splits within the Muslim community, the most prominent is the division between Sunni and Shiite Muslims. The overthrow of the shah in Iran and his replacement with a theocratic Shiite regime fueled the Sunni-Shiite rivalry, and Iran today is the motherland for Shiites around the region.

Iraqi Shiites, numbering some ten or eleven million people, constitute a majority in Iraq. Like several other groups in Iraq, the Shiites are oppressed; their leaders have been arrested and executed by the hundreds. In March 1991, their uprising against Saddam Hussein was brutally crushed. The Iraqi government continues to target Shiites by draining and shelling marshlands in southern Iraq. The Shiites in Iraq have received little international support. Kuwait and Saudi Arabia are overtly hostile, and even Iran has done little. Most countries fear the fragmentation of Iraq and the possibility of an Iranian-dominated Shiite entity in southern Iraq.

Sunni-Shiite disagreements are prominent in several other states. In Lebanon, Shiites are probably the largest single ethnic or religious group in the country, numbering at least one million.[36] Already divided along Muslim-Christian lines, Lebanon has weathered numerous Sunni and Shiite warlords and militias. Hizbollah, a militant Shiite party backed by Iran, continues to battle Israel from southern Lebanon. Future Hizbollah military action against Israel is mostly dependent on Iranian-Syrian relations and Syrian negotiations with Israel on the terms of the peace agreements. An additional issue in Syria is the Alawi-Sunni relations. President Asad of the small Alawite (Islamic) minority keeps a watchful eye on the 74 percent Sunni Muslim majority. In Bahrain in 1994-95, the majority Shiite population rioted for months against the Sunni-led regime after three prominent Shiite religious leaders were arrested; interestingly, much of the security force that imposed order is composed of non-citizen Pakistanis.[37]

In Saudi Arabia, six percent of the population, living mostly in the Eastern Province along the Persian Gulf, is Shiite.[38] General discrimination and unfair employment practices against Shiites are entrenched in Saudi society. Incidents of unexplained sabotage of oil facilities in the early 1980s and periodic disturbances have been attributed to disgruntled Shiites. The Shiites are systematically harassed and denied full religious freedom. Some changes in Saudi policy led to marginal improvements for Shiites in 1993. Like elsewhere, some Saudi leaders are concerned that Iran might seek to use the Shiite minority to foment rebellion against the non-Shiite government.

POLITICAL ASYMMETRIES: THE PROBLEM OF LEGITIMACY

Challenges to state and regime legitimacy as well as pressures for more representative government and civil rights have long been serious problems in the Middle East, and the Arab-Israeli peace process highlights these concerns. The legitimacy of countries and regimes is frequently questioned by other regional parties, and adversaries use resolutions, speeches, propaganda, international declarations, summit communiqués, and official letters to play on existential fears. Such challenges to legitimacy feed upon existing disparities and exacerbate existing tensions. In the Middle East, the presence of multiple challenges to legitimacy helps explain why peaceful channels have not been found to deal with many regional asymmetries.

Recent Iranian and Egyptian history provide good examples of this phenomenon. During the 1960s and 1970s, the exiled Ayatollah Khomeini relentlessly attacked the shah of Iran, Mohammed Reza Shah Pahlavi, and the entire Pahlavi regime on the grounds that they were "illegitimate." To Khomeini, the shah was a Zionist agent, a "servant of the dollar," and a lackey of foreign powers. He charged that "Islam is fundamentally opposed to the whole notion of monarchy. . . . Monarchy is one of the most shameful and disgraceful reactionary manifestations."[39] In 1978, on the eve of the shah's overthrow, Khomeini marshaled countless arguments against the shah's continued rule, as Iran scholar Shaul Bakhash describes:

> He built up his case against the Shah carefully, often appealing to constitutional and legal arguments. The Shah's rule was not legitimate, he said, because his father had established the dynasty at the point of the bayonet. The Shah himself had been imposed on the country, and would not have survived without American backing. The Shah had personally ordered the killing of demonstrators, the repression of rights, the insults to Islam. . . . The Shah was therefore a "traitor and a rebel."[40]

In earlier years, Khomeini had criticized Reza Shah, the shah's father, calling him a usurper who ran a corrupt and illegitimate state.

In Egypt, Anwar Sadat was viewed as an infidel and a tyrant by the Islamic opposition.[41] Among Islamic opponents, Sadat's treaty with Israel and close ties to the United States and the West were striking symbols of his betrayal of Islam. Bernard Lewis explains that, "the crime of Sadat, the shah, and others like them was the abrogation of the holy law of Islam, and the paganization of Islamic society by the introduction and imposition of laws and usages imported from the outside world. . . . Rulers and regimes that have abandoned the sharia, though remaining nominally Muslim, have forfeited their legitimacy."[42]

Allegations that a regime is unfit pertain only to a particular regime. Challenges to a state's legitimate existence are more fundamental. Such challenges seek not just to undermine a particular regime, but charge that, regardless of the current leadership, the entire state apparatus is illegitimate and should be dismantled, replaced, or absorbed by another state.

In the Middle East, both levels of threat must be considered simultaneously. First, many leaders have been in power so long that it is difficult to distinguish between the state and the regime. King Hussein has been leading Jordan for some forty-five years. Asad, King Fahd, Qaddafi, Mubarak, and Saddam Hussein are other long-time leaders. Second, to many elites, the consequences of a threat to the regime and to the state are the same: at a minimum, they fall from power. At worst, they are killed.

What are the key regional legitimacy disputes? This section does not provide a comprehensive listing of legitimacy issues in the Middle East, but discusses some of the major ones: Arab coalition vs. Israel, Israel vs. Palestinians/Jordan, Iraq vs. Kuwait, Syria vs. Lebanon. In each case, the issue is the challenge by former of the latter's right to exist as an independent sovereign state.

Arab Coalition vs. Israel. From Israel's perspective, the refusal of most Arab and several non-Arab Muslim countries to accept until recently the legitimacy of the state of Israel lies at the heart of the Arab-Israeli conflict. For many years, Arab states refrained from even using the word "Israel," using instead such euphemisms as the "Zionist entity" or "Zionist state." At the post-1967-war Arab summit in Khartoum, the Arab states endorsed three pithy guidelines for relations with Israel: "no negotiations with Israel," "no peace with Israel," and "no recognition of Israel."[43] The 1968 Palestinian charter stated that the "Palestinian Arab people hereby affirm their unwavering determination to carry on the armed struggle and to press on towards popular revolution for the liberation of and return to their homeland."[44] After the 1973 war, one PLO official described the PLO mission as including, "the revolutionary Palestinian and Arab struggle to eliminate the Zionist entity and to establish the Palestinian democratic state."[45]

Some Islamic scholars have also argued that Islam precludes the permanent acceptance of the Jewish state of Israel in the midst of the Arab and Islamic world. Muhammad Husayn Fadlallah explains:

> There are two factors which make any peace with the Israeli Jews illegitimate. The first is that, under Islamic jurisprudence, usurpation is prohibited. We know that the Jews have usurped Palestine, territory and authority, and they have expropriated Palestinian land . . . We know that usurpation of territory is forbidden under the Shari'ah as is the usurpation of any Muslim property. . . . The second factor is that Islam rejects the idea of an infidel having authority over a Muslim. Jurisprudence ulema have deemed that illegitimate, and ruled that it is also illegitimate for a Muslim to give infidels authority over him. That is why we consider peace with Israel to be forbidden under the Shari'ah, and no Muslim can permit what is so forbidden.[46]

On April 24, 1996, the Palestine National Council (PNC), the old Palestinian parliament-in-exile, voted to amend the PLO charter; the resolution said that the Council "decides to amend the Palestinian National Covenant by canceling clauses which contradict the letters exchanged between the PLO and the Israeli Government." The 1993 Israeli-PLO letters essentially had called on the PLO to delete all references to the armed struggle for Palestine and a military solution to the conflict. Some Arab hardliners, notably those based in Damascus, rejected the changes. A few PNC members, including Hanan Ashrawi, voted against the changes because they did not want to appear to cave in to Israeli demands.[47]

In Israel, the changes met with mixed reaction. The Peres government praised the amendment, but many on the right questioned whether the changes were complete and binding. According to an Israeli press report, Israeli army intelligence, the General Security Services, and Civil Administration officials all agreed that the resolution amended the charter and revoked the clauses calling for Israel's destruction.[48]

Israel vs. Palestinians/Jordan. Israelis, especially on the right, have repeatedly challenged both the legitimacy of the Palestinian movement and the independence of Jordan. Those who advocate annexation of the West Bank and Gaza Strip dismiss the Palestinian right to self-determination. As an alternative, some claim that Jordan, which has a Palestinian majority, is "Palestine." Ariel Sharon, a minister in the current Israeli government, was the major advocate of the concept of Jordan as a Palestinian state: "The 'Palestinian problem' as a national-political problem is a propaganda lie. It is the result of systematic brainwashing by the PLO, with the help of cooperative leftists. For, since 1922, there has existed in the eastern Land of Israel, on three-quarters of the territory of the whole Land of Israel . . . the Arab Palestinian state, which is Jordan."[49] Sharon noted that some Israelis claim that the concept of "Palestinian People" is a recent political creation. He called for Israel to "expose the lie of 'the rights of Palestinians.' It must be explicitly and loudly proclaimed by the government and the Knesset that Jordan has been and is the Palestinian state in the Land of Israel."[50] In 1972, an Israeli minister without portfolio, Israeli Galili, said, "Gaza will not again be separated from Israel."[51]

Iraq vs. Kuwait. On August 8, 1990, Iraq annexed Kuwait, just a few days after invading the smaller state. According to Iraq, the invasion of Kuwait was not an illegal and unjust act of aggression, but the rectification of an earlier—colonial—error. Iraq regarded Kuwait as "an offspring of Iraq which had been dismembered by the British colonial scissors."[52] Iraq's Revolutionary Command Council "decided to return the part and branch, Kuwait, to the whole and root, Iraq, in a comprehensive, eternal and inseparable merger unity." Moreover, Iraq blamed British colonialism for unjustly dividing up the Arab world: "The spiteful pencil and scissors of imperialism began to draw up maps designed to ensure that every part of the Arab homeland . . . would remain weak and ineffective."[53]

After the invasion, Iraq began to systematically dismember all vestiges of Kuwaiti identity. Computer data bases listing vital social services and information about Kuwaiti citizens were destroyed; cultural entities such as museums and the zoo were pillaged and destroyed; and the Kuwaiti army's equipment was absorbed into Iraq's force structure. It was a violent and cruel annexation. After the Gulf War, as called for by the U.N. Security Council, Iraq annulled the annexation.

The entire episode can be seen as part of Iraq's long-running attempt to absorb all or part of Kuwait. The historical claim to Kuwait had previously been put forth by other Iraqi leaders, including King Ghazi and Taufiq al-Suwaidi in the late 1930s, Nuri al-Said at the time of the Hashemite Union in the late 1950s, and during the "first" Kuwait crisis.[54] Just a week after Kuwait's independence in 1961, Iraqi General Abdul Karim Qasim asserted that Kuwait had been part of the southern Iraqi province of Basra under Ottoman rule and that Iraq succeeded Turkish rule after World War I. Qasim was deposed in a 1963 coup; shortly thereafter, the claim was dropped and Iraq recognized Kuwait's independence.[55]

Syria vs. Lebanon. Syria has long maintained that Lebanon is a colonial creation that rightfully is part of greater Syria. As President Asad explained in 1976, "Throughout history, Syria and Lebanon have been one country and one people."[56] Syria has played the leading external role in bringing Lebanon's civil war to a close and providing direction to its postwar government.[57]

FEAR OF DEMOCRACY

Calls for democracy and civil rights raise political and cultural problems in the Middle East. Democratization is part of a contentious regional debate on the possible clash between Western values and indigenous Arab or Islamic identity. It is important to consider both the political systems of the various countries in the region and the concerns that calls for democracy, some tied to regime stability and state coherence, inevitably raise.

During the Gulf War, in a statement to Congress, U.S. Secretary of State James Baker discussed a "new world order," focusing on five challenges that needed to be addressed once Iraq had been defeated on the battlefield. Those five challenges were: greater security for the Persian Gulf; regional arms proliferation and control; economic reconstruction and recovery; peace and reconciliation in the Middle East; and reducing U.S. energy dependence on the Middle East. Not included, but also important, was the desire for more democratic institutions in the Middle East. In fact, Baker went out of his way to stress the need to "respect the sovereignty of the peoples of the Gulf and the Middle East." The focus on sovereignty rather than democracy was deliberate; it was believed that pushing too hard for democratization in the Arab Gulf at that time would have posed difficulties both for the United States and the friendly Gulf states.

This remains true six years later—pushing too hard and too publicly for fundamental changes in the way the Gulf states run themselves is likely to backfire. Rather the hope is that over time the educated elite in the Gulf will themselves press for reforms and begin to take more account of basic civil rights for citizens and the many non-citizens residing in their countries.

193

According to the Western approach of equating democracy with personal freedoms, few Middle East countries could be called democratic. Moreover, if these countries conformed to democracy's most basic principles, most of the regimes could not survive. Before reviewing which countries in the region are democratic or "free" and which are not, it is necessary to define these concepts. A bipartisan U.S. organization, Freedom House, compiles an annual *Survey of Freedom*, which classifies the state of freedom in sovereign countries and occupied territories around the world. The survey uses quantitative criteria to establish a classification system that goes beyond the simple dichotomies used during the Cold War (e.g., democratic vs. nondemocratic/authoritarian or free vs. totalitarian). Instead, the survey defines freedom as encompassing both political rights and civil liberties.[58] It defines these two concepts as follows:

> Political rights enable people to participate freely in the political process. By the political process, we mean the system by which the polity chooses the authoritative policy makers and attempts to make binding decisions affecting the national, regional or local community. In a free society this means the right of all adults to vote and compete for public office, and for elected representatives to have a decisive vote on public policies. A system is genuinely free or democratic to the extent that the people have a choice in determining the nature of the system and its leaders. Civil liberties are the freedoms to develop views, institutions and personal autonomy apart from the state.[59]

Using these definitions and a methodology that grades each country according to an elaborate set of criteria relating to the actual practice of political rights and civil liberties (as distinct from supposedly guaranteed constitutional or legal rights), the survey ranked countries and territories according to a three-tier scale: "free," "partially free," and "not free." Within each category, countries and territories were further ranked according to a more exacting scale that lists each country's performance numerically from one (best score) to seven (worst score). In 1995, Israel was the only country in the Middle East that could be classified as "free," but its occupied territories were identified as "not free."

The review suggests some interesting points about the nature of freedom, foreign relations, and stable allies. First, the majority of countries in the Middle East (79 percent) are classified as "not free."[60] Second, countries classified as not free include some of the United States' closest friends (UAE, Bahrain, Egypt, Saudi Arabia, Oman) as well as its most bitter enemies (Iran, Iraq). Third, Israel's most strident enemies are all on the not-free list (Iran, Iraq, Syria). Fourth, the neighbors with which Israel has the most cordial relations are classified as partially free (Jordan, Morocco, Turkey); with Egypt, classified as not free, Israel has what can be called a "cold peace." Fifth, until the territories under Israeli control are either handed over to another authority or are guaranteed the same freedoms that exist in Israel proper, Israel's claim to being a free country will have a hollow ring and will not be taken seriously by its adversaries.[61]

The distinction between freedom and democracy and efforts by Western powers to liberalize regimes in the Middle East has led to confusing signals. Two events in the Middle East, one in the late 1970s and one in 1992, provide evidence of the need for caution in supporting or endorsing efforts to bring about more democratic representation. In 1978, the shah of Iran, a close U.S. ally, was under pressure from the Carter administration to liberalize the country in view of numerous human rights abuses and widespread corruption. In part because of this pressure, opposition forces in Iran and overseas were emboldened to challenge the regime in increasingly strident ways. The subsequent revolution and ascendancy of Ayatollah Khomeini and the reign of the clerics might have been deflected or made less effective if the shah had felt more confident of U.S. support. While this would not have assured his survival, it might have limited the damaging fallout that followed.

The second example involves Algeria's elections in January 1992, when it was relatively clear that Islamic fundamentalists would win at the ballot box and then consider establishing an Islamic regime. The Western countries and most Arab states accepted the military's use of force to prevent Islamic extremists from gaining power; they believed it was a necessary evil to prevent the destabilization of North Africa. While the ballot box may be one of the cornerstones of democracy, it does not follow that the winners will continue to abide by the norms of democracy, including free elections, free speech, and an independent judiciary. Most observers believe that if extremists had assumed office in Algeria, their first task would have been to establish an Islamic state that would have been undemocratic. Indeed, many analysts believe that that the concept of an Islamic regime is not compatible with the basic tenets of freedom and democracy as practiced and advocated in the West.

For leaders such as Saddam Hussein and Hafez al-Asad, the Western concept of democracy must be anathema. Hafez al-Asad's regime in Damascus is a minority dictatorship; since the purpose of most dictatorships is to stay in power, a democratic challenge would threaten the very existence of the regime. Indeed, the Middle East is full of regimes that struggle to defend the interests of the rulers, even to the point of ignoring national interests when they conflict. General openness, a free press, greater foreign involvement, nongovernmental organizations, and democratic opposition movements are just a few examples of changes that threaten to undermine or unravel a dictatorship.

Asad, Saddam Hussein, and other Arab leaders watched in horror the fate of the dictators who ruled Eastern Europe, especially Ceausescu in Romania. Iranian leaders point to the fate of Mikhail Gorbachev in fear that a similar fate could befall them if they make concessions to Western concepts of democracy. After all, Gorbachev accepted the need to reform and was seen by the West as a hero; yet he could not stop the momentum toward freedom that engulfed his country and eventually deposed him.

The democratic threat is also related to the ongoing debate over so-called democratic peace theory. Many theorists and historians argue that democracies do not go to war against other democracies. This point has not been resolved in academic circles, but it has clearly caught on in political circles. Many Israeli and American analysts assume that the democratization of key Arab countries would greatly improve Israel's security situation. Yet it is far from clear that democratic elections in Egypt, Jordan, and Lebanon, for instance, would result in majority support for peace with Israel except at a price that democratic Israel may not be prepared to accept.

CHAPTER TEN

MILITARY IMBALANCE AND INSECURITY

The Middle East is one of the most militarized regions in the world. It spends more on defense as a proportion of GDP than any other region.[1] If Turkey is included as a Middle East power—as it should be—the region boasts some of the largest armies and air forces in the world. Many countries in the region have highly advanced military equipment. Most significant, the Middle East has the highest likelihood of nuclear, chemical, and biological weapons proliferation. Israel possesses a nuclear capability, and Iran and Iraq are aspiring nuclear powers; all three possess chemical weapons. Syria and Egypt have a chemical weapons capability. Libya is seeking chemical weapons. All six countries possess ballistic missiles capable of delivering chemical weapons. The absence of peace assures a continuing arms race and no arms control, a highly dangerous combination.

WEAPONS OF MASS DESTRUCTION

The survival of all regimes in the Middle East is threatened by the prospects of war waged with weapons of mass destruction, most specifically nuclear weapons. At the height of the Cold War, it was feared that a general nuclear war between the two superpowers would spill over into the region. At various times, and especially in October 1973, an Arab-Israeli war could have triggered the engagement of the nuclear forces of the Soviet Union and the United States, perhaps involving the entire Middle East in nuclear escalation. Since the end of the Cold War, such fears have ended—only to be replaced by the fear of a nuclear war originating in the region itself. The dangers of a nuclear Iraq or Iran are the grist for many troublesome scenarios, but the only operational nuclear power in the region today is Israel.

While it is difficult for Westerners to believe that Israel would ever use nuclear weapons, Arabs are less reluctant to speculate on this issue. The most apocalyptic fear of some Arab states and Iran is an outright nuclear attack by Israel. Like Israel,

197

several Arab states could be annihilated by just one nuclear bomb. States like Egypt, Jordan, and Lebanon, with their concentrated urban populations, are more vulnerable to a small nuclear attack than, for instance, Iran and Iraq. But the probable size of Israel's nuclear program means that no country in the region is too large or too decentralized to avert the devastating impact of a nuclear attack. Arabs' concerns that Israel would be willing to unleash a nuclear attack under some circumstances is based at least in part on the deep-seated antipathy that has characterized the Arab-Israeli confrontation and their continuing perception that Israelis often dehumanized them.

Arab leaders are also concerned that Israel could engage in nuclear blackmail, i.e., use its weapons to attempt to bring about Arab political capitulation or surrender. In a crisis situation, Arab leaders might be forced to submit to Israel's will in the face of Israel's unchallenged nuclear program. Most of Israel's neighbors agree privately that Israel is unlikely to use its nuclear arsenal to *directly* intimidate them in the absence of all-out war; they also admit privately that they are more fearful of a nuclear Iraq or Iran. Yet they worry that in times of extreme tension a hardline Israeli government might be tempted to use nuclear blackmail to achieve certain political or military objectives. As long as Israel has a nuclear monopoly, the temptation to intimidate neighbors creates an unacceptable asymmetry in the regional balance of power.

This theme, in various guises, underlies Arab governments' pressure on Israel to sign the Nuclear Nonproliferation Treaty. Egypt, the first Arab country to make peace with Israel, led the charge to put the Israeli nuclear program on the agenda of the NPT extension and renewal conference in New York in 1995. Egypt has complex reasons for making such an issue of the Israeli nuclear program, but the central reasons are related to asymmetry. Egypt would find it unacceptable for Israel to retain its nuclear monopoly indefinitely, since this would give Israel permanent military superiority. Thus Egyptian officials saw the NPT conference as a rare opportunity to put pressure on Israel with regard to nuclear matters; the prospect of indefinite treaty extension meant that the opportunity might not come along again soon. Egyptian and other Arab leaders understand that Israel will not abandon its nuclear forces overnight, but they insist on a timetable, a schedule whereby Israel commits to a nuclear free zone in the Middle East once certain political conditions have been met. It is accepted that these conditions must include a regional security regime that covers Iran, Iraq, and Libya—and possibly India and Pakistan—and that this will not happen until there have been further breakthroughs in the peace process. But this is no reason, Arab representatives insist, for not taking initial steps to develop the framework for such a regime.

The Gulf War, by reducing the Iraqi military threat, may have changed the balance in the regional power structure. But for many Arab countries, the effect has been to give Israel more prominence as the dominant regional power. Israel's nuclear capability is seen as evidence of the gross asymmetries in military strength, skewing the balance of power. Arabs see this capability as evidence that Israel is determined to remain the predominant military power in the region. Arab leaders view their own acquisition of chemical weapons and ballistic missiles as legitimate in the face of the Israeli nuclear threat. Although chemical weapons may not correct the imbalance in capabilities, they provide a deterrent against Israeli nuclear blackmail. Since Arab nuclear capabilities are limited and unlikely to catch up to Israel's for many years, emphasis on chemical weapons as a counterbalance makes sense.

For Israelis, the Gulf War strengthened Israel's need for a nuclear deterrent. Israel, too, has deep worries about weapons of mass destruction. Its greatest security fear concerns nuclear threats from terrorists or from a radical state equipped with a nuclear weapons program. A nuclear weapon, or other WMDs, could destroy the state of Israel. In the past, the greatest threat was from Soviet weapons. Since the breakup of the Soviet Union, however, nuclear threats from Iran, Iraq, or another Arab or other radical faction loom large in Israeli thinking. The breakup of the Soviet Union has also led to fears that nuclear weapons are being sold on the black market, so-called loose nukes. In theory, this would allow an enemy of Israel, whether a country or a terrorist organization, to circumvent the costly and time-consuming process of actually developing and producing nuclear weapons.

The small size of the country and the highly concentrated Jewish population in Tel Aviv and surrounding suburbs mean that a single nuclear weapon could, if not totally destroy Israel, at least shatter its very foundations and make its future existence problematic. The vast majority of Israeli industry and the Israeli population are located in the coastal region and Jerusalem. While the Islamic holy sites in Jerusalem might safeguard it from a direct nuclear attack from a Muslim country, Tel Aviv has no such religious protection.

For this reason, Israel's leaders are preoccupied with the possibility that Iran may acquire nuclear weapons. They note how close

Saddam Hussein was to achieving nuclear status and that he did so in spite of signing the NPT. The Gulf War provided Israel with ambiguous lessons concerning deterrence and the use of WMDs. Iraq fired Scud missiles against Israeli cities, but refrained from using chemical warheads. It remains unclear whether fear of Israeli or American nuclear retaliation deterred Iraq from using chemicals. Whatever the truth, Israelis do not believe deterrence can be assured, especially against fanatical regimes who believe that by threatening the survival of Israel they are serving God's will.

CONVENTIONAL WAR SCENARIOS

In the Arab-Israeli context, all sides have had valid reasons for fearing each other's conventional military power. A widespread and continuing fear among Israelis is that their country will one day be destroyed by hostile Arab armies that physically overrun Israel and drive the Jewish population into the sea. This fear began during the 1948 war.[2] Although Israel eventually won that war, the costs were very high: the more than 6,000 killed represented 1 percent of the total population. Thus, when combined Arab armies appeared poised to attack Israel in June 1967, the fear of being destroyed was intense and real. However, Israel's remarkably swift victory over its three most powerful neighbors began a new era of Israeli conventional military superiority which, though tested in 1973, remains in place in the mid-1990s. Yet deep down Israelis still fear that at some time in the future an Arab coalition armed with new advanced-technology weapons could once more pose a decisive conventional threat. The worst-case scenario envisioned by Israelis is an end to the peace with Egypt and Jordan and the prospect of having to fight not only its old neighbors once more, but also the highly advanced air force of Saudi Arabia and a re-armed Iraq.

For many years, Israel has been outnumbered in every category of conventional weaponry when the surrounding Arab states are considered together. In calculating the numerical superiority of Arab forces, Israeli analysts make a host of assumptions about the hostile nature of Arab states and their ability to achieve military and political unity. In the past it was easier to assume united Arab hostility; Sadat's trip to Jerusalem in 1977 was the beginning of the end of the standard method for assessing the Arab conventional threat. Today, with Egypt, Jordan, and several other Arab states in various stages of peace with Israel, the threat has been reduced, though observers disagree greatly on the degree to which it has lessened.[3]

Nonetheless, the conventional Israeli view is that the Arab threat remains relevant even if mollified somewhat by political changes in Arab-Israeli relations. Although fear of destruction by Arab armies has lessened, another major war with the Arabs would carry the risk of high casualties on all sides. The assumption remains that the Arab countries, because of their numerical superiority and autocratic regimes, are better geared to take high casualties than Israel.

Arab countries are differentially threatened by Israel. A large country such as Egypt is more capable of withstanding Israeli conventional and nonconventional attacks than small countries like Jordan or Lebanon, whose very existence could be threatened by Israel's military prowess in the event of another war. Since the 1948 war, neither country has been in a position to repel an Israeli invasion. Israel retains both a qualitative and a quantitative edge over Jordanian and Lebanese forces. In 1982, and to a lesser extent in 1978, Israel invaded Lebanon with a large conventional force. Although Israeli forces later became targets for counter attacks, due to domestic Lebanese divisions, terrorism, and guerrilla warfare, the initial invasion faced little significant resistance. Like any occupier, Israel paid a price in terms of casualties, resources, and international and domestic opposition, but it succeeded in demonstrating that it could invade a weaker Arab state with relative ease.

Although Syria has much larger armed forces than either Lebanon or Jordan, it also has good reason to fear Israel's conventional superiority. As long as Israel's army occupies the Golan Heights, it has an open downhill invasion route to Damascus. While any future conflict between Israel and Syria could be bloody and costly in terms of casualties, few doubt that without support from other Arab countries, Syria would lose a new war and Israel could easily occupy Damascus. This would threaten the existence of the Asad regime.

In the Arab-Israeli conflict, both sides still talk about plans by the other party to achieve hegemony and victory. Israelis, mostly on the right, argue that the PLO and other Palestinian groups that no longer openly advocate the destruction of Israel are still planning to destroy the state incrementally. In this view, the Declaration of Principles was a calculated move by Arafat to win control of Gaza and Jericho as a first step to reconquering Palestine.

201

Many Arabs describe a similar scenario in reverse. Israel, after taking more than it was allotted in the 1947 U.N. partition plan, has continually sought to expand. This theory was most fiercely argued in 1978, when Israeli forces entered Lebanon. At that time, Israel also occupied the Sinai, West Bank, Gaza Strip, and Golan Heights. The return of the Sinai to Egypt clearly creates a problem for defenders of the thesis that Israel is still seeking to expand its territory.

THE GULF WAR: IMPACT ON REGIONAL SECURITY PERCEPTIONS

The Gulf War had an important impact on thinking about modern warfare, the global demand for advanced arms and related technologies, and the relationship between weapons of mass destruction and conventional weapons.[4] The war revealed how vulnerable the infrastructure of modern societies is to precision bombardment. High technology has improved both the precision of strike aircraft and cruise missiles and their capacity to survive enemy counterattacks. Although the Gulf War demonstrated the potential effectiveness of high-tech arms, fiscal realities restrain many states and may force some to consider a short-cut, the less expensive option of developing certain types of weapons of mass destruction, especially chemical and biological weapons.

As missile and aircraft ranges become longer and longer, as power can be projected over wider and wider regions, these capabilities, together with the possibility that weapons of mass destruction may be developed, suggest that assessments of the military balance among the various regional enemies in the Middle East must encompass a larger area. Israel's strategic reach for both offense and defense now has to include concern about Iran and Iraq and, in theory, Pakistan, since these all have missiles and capabilities that could reach Israel. Similarly, as Israel's reach extends, these countries must worry about their vulnerability to Israeli power projection capabilities.

This phenomenon has important implications for regional security regimes in the Middle East and elsewhere. Participation in security regimes has always been a difficult issue in the context of European arms control, and it is even more difficult in the Middle East. Thus, even if Israel reaches a military agreement with Syria, Jordan, Egypt, Lebanon, and the Palestinians, it would not let its guard down so long as the GCC countries, Iran, and Iraq are outside the process. Since they have to be part of the process, and since there is a close relationship among Pakistan, the GCC countries, Iran, and Iraq, it is likely that Pakistan's capabilities will be included in Israel's calculus. Pakistan worries about Israel for similar reasons.

In many respects, Desert Storm was a highly misleading military encounter because it was so one-sided. One clear lesson, however, is that modern conventional munitions bear no resemblance to those used in most previous conventional confrontations. The combination of long range and high accuracy achieved by aircraft and missiles together with new real time reconnaissance capabilities portends to revolutionize warfare in the future.

Accurate, lethal weapons and better reconnaissance by themselves constitute a revolution. To the new conventional capabilities of modern weapons, however, must be added the dramatically changing target structures in the Middle East. If one compares a map of infrastructure in the Middle East in, for example, 1970 and 1990, and then projects forward to 2010, there has been and will continue to be an enormous change in the physical appearance of the region. This is most evident in the phenomenal increase in oil-producing capacity, pipelines, power generation, water desalination, and improved roads, ports, and airfields. These changes put increasing reliance on high-technology systems to assure the wealth and day-to-day operation of most countries. One lesson of the Gulf War was that small numbers of munitions, accurately delivered against utility systems (such as the Iraqi electrical grid), can have a devastating impact in a very short period of time. Thus it is possible that a future adversary, equipped with the type of technology the United States had as a monopoly in 1990-91, would be able to cripple the entire economic-industrial infrastructure of almost any country in the Middle East in a matter of hours.

In the coming decade, the ability of Middle East states to upgrade their military forces with some of the technologies used by the allies in 1991 will improve. If Iran and Iraq are able to purchase arms and technologies on the open market with few restrictions, they will be able to procure the types of forces that could pose a major threat to the economic well-being of their neighbors. In particular, they, or other regional powers such as Saudi Arabia or Israel, will be able to target high-value economic installations that have fixed coordinates and inflict great damage. However, it will be far more difficult to destroy high-value military targets that are either security protected or mobile. It is doubtful, for instance, that regional powers will be able to duplicate the sort of military operation conducted by the allies during the Gulf War. While the strike component of regional powers may improve dramatically if they get access to high technology, the reconnaissance component will, in all likelihood, remain beyond their means. During the Gulf War, the United States relied on an extraordinary array of advanced sensors and early warning systems including AWACS (airborne warning and control system aircraft), JSTARS (Joint Surveillance Target Attack Radar System), and a satellite-based communications system that could relay real-time information to the battlefield. Israel, with its own satellite-launching capability, is likely to come nearest to achieving this level of sophistication. A new Iraqi regime might have the funds to purchase space systems from China or Russia.

THE PROBLEM OF ARMS SALES

A further danger concerns continued arms sales to the Middle East. Although in many cases arms sales are justified, they can carry risks and huge economic costs. One concern for the United States and its friends, for example, is that a major recipient of advanced U.S. weaponry could undergo a coup or revolution and have a regime hostile to the United States assume power. This is what happened in 1978 in Iran, when anti-Western forces led by Ayatollah Khomeini overthrew the pro–U.S. shah regime. Another concern for the United States is that current adversaries such as the existing regimes in Iran and Iraq could get access to advanced arms and technology from other sources that are only too eager to sell.

What are the probabilities and consequences of these two conditions? In the first case, the major recipients of U.S. arms in the Middle East are Egypt, Israel, Kuwait, Saudi Arabia, and Turkey. Of these countries, only Israel can be considered a full-fledged democracy, and even in this case, a future Israeli government, particularly a radical-right coalition, could have very different policies toward the United States; conflict over the use of American arms and the use of force is conceivable. In the case of the other four countries, the dangers are much greater. Both Egypt and Turkey face strong internal opposition from radical forces; in conditions of near civil war, U.S. arms could be used for activities opposed by the U.S. government and in possible violation of U.S. laws. Saudi Arabia and Kuwait are ruled by undemocratic leaders, even though they are making gradual progress toward more openness and more personal freedom. If these regimes were toppled in a coup d'etat or civil uprising, advanced American arms could be used in a manner hostile to U.S. interests.

The major industrial powers promote arms sales because they want to support domestic industry. This means the only restraint on further arms sales is financial, which penalizes the small and poor countries who receive no economic assistance. The United States, Russia, and China must establish some basic ground rules for activity in the Gulf, including an understanding about arms sales and proliferation. The United States, while worried about continued conventional arms sales to Iran and other radical countries, is far more concerned about nuclear and missile proliferation. Therefore, it should offer that if Russia and China desist from nuclear cooperation with Iraq and Iran and adhere to Missile Technology Control Regime (MTCR) rules, Washington will be prepared to reach a modus vivendi on many conventional arms sales to Iran and Iraq. This is far from an ideal arrangement, but it is practical and realistic at this time.

DOMESTIC DEFENSE INDUSTRIES

A ttention to the question of military asymmetries in the Middle East is usually focused on weapons of mass destruction and on conventional capabilities. Such differences are facilitated by the wide variation in the military technological expertise of domestic defense industries in the Middle East.

The strength of various domestic defense industries has remained relatively constant over the last few years. The Israeli defense industry is still far ahead in the region in terms of technology and quality weaponry.[5] Israel's advanced defense industry has added to its qualitative edge, as has its good military relations with the United States. Israeli firms manufacture a wide array of products, including military computers, aircraft components, electronic radar systems, missiles, tanks, and ammunition. Israeli products are considered "very competitive on the world market," especially in aircraft upgrades, electronic and avionics equipment, and unmanned aerial vehicle (UAV) systems. Israel also offers an array of military services, such as conventional weapons testing.[6]

Among the Arab states, Egypt has the strongest domestic defense industry.[7] Yahya M. Sadowski notes that Egypt is "the only Arab state in which military industrialization has made considerable progress."[8] Yet Egypt is hard-pressed to find export markets for its military products. Moreover, most Arab states rely almost completely on outside suppliers. Egypt has produced, developed, and/or assembled a wide array of arms and military equipment, including combat and trainer aircraft, helicopters, tanks, armored vehicles, artillery, infantry weapons, guided missiles, and naval vessels. The most celebrated, and controversial, Egyptian product has been the M-1 Abrams tank; Egypt is licensed by the United States to produce up to 524 such tanks by 1998.[9] Many see the project as bloated and expensive, especially in comparison to purchasing the tanks from the U.S. manufacturer.

In the next few years, the Egyptian defense industry is unlikely to advance to a more autonomous status. There are too many financial, political, and technological gaps still remaining. The industry is still hampered by the larger production lines, and hence lower production costs per unit, of the major arms exporters. This and other obstacles should leave Egypt as the preeminent but restricted Arab defense industry leader.

Iran would like to move in the direction of Israel, or at least Egypt, in terms of the breadth and depth of its military-industrial complex. Currently Iran is a selective arms manufacturer and lacks the research and development or production facilities to sustain a comprehensive program. Early efforts in the 1970s to develop such infrastructure were sidetracked by the Islamic revolution. The state is heavily involved in most aspects of Iranian defense companies. In recent years, much of Iran's support and technology, including support for its missile program, has come from defense relationships with China, North Korea, and the Soviet Union (and now the former Soviet states).[10]

Major areas of research and/or production include surface-to-surface missiles, main battle tanks (MBT), foreign aircraft repairs, and ground forces equipment. Much of Iran's cooperation with other states has revolved around Scud missile technology. Indigenous Iranian missiles include the Oghab, Nazeat, and Shahin-2, but as one military analyst notes:

> Despite the high priority assigned to it [developing missiles], the results have not been impressive. . . . It is difficult to resist the conclusion that Iran's poor results are due to deficiencies of organization and management (rather than backwardness in technology). . . . [11]

Such results raise questions about Iran's ability to construct an effective weapons program in any field. The MBT program is shrouded in secrecy, though a prototype named Zulfiqar was unveiled in April 1994; few concrete details about the tank are available.[12]

206

The absence of military relations with Western countries left Iran little choice but to attempt the indigenous repair of Western-built technology such as F-4 and F-5 aircraft. The Iranians have had some success and this has contributed to a more forward-looking aerospace industry. Iran has developed local capabilities to manufacture equipment for ground forces, such as small arms, armored personnel carriers, ammunition, and artillery pieces. Overall, the Iranian program has relied on the transfer of technology, reverse engineering, and cooperation with former East bloc states in order to continue to build up the industry.

THE PROSPECTS FOR ARMS CONTROL

If a Middle East balance of power will be inherently unstable without a strong U.S. military presence, the alternative must be arms limitation agreements and more cooperative attitudes toward weapons procurement and force deployment.[13] In practice, this will depend upon the prevailing political climate, as demonstrated by the Israeli case. For years, Israel has asserted that it will use whatever means necessary to sustain its nuclear monopoly in the region. But it is no longer clear that Israel can do this unilaterally. In 1981, it destroyed Iraq's major nuclear facilities only to find ten years later that Iraq was once more on the verge of nuclear status. If Israel cannot forever monitor its own security independently, it will have to rely more and more on the United States and the international community to help prevent further nuclear proliferation. Such reliance may eventually require that Israel make compromises on its policy of technological superiority and endorse international arms control agreements. Thus the dilemma facing any future Israeli government will be how to retain a qualitative edge while at the same time making some concessions in its most sophisticated technology. This suggests that sooner or later Israel will have to put limits on its own nuclear capabilities. What those limits should be and under what circumstances Israel should negotiate them, particularly in the context of the ongoing peace process, will be a matter of intense debate in the coming years.

The effectiveness of arms control regimes in the Middle East, particularly the nuclear nonproliferation regime, will be strengthened if the parties are engaged in the peace process. The nonproliferation regime would be least effective if the peace process fails. Thus one of the best ways to strengthen the nuclear nonproliferation regime in the Middle East is to strengthen the peace process.

If Egypt and Israel were the only parties to the Arab-Israeli conflict, they might by now have begun discussions on regimes to restrict weapons of mass destruction and their delivery systems, including advanced conventional arms. However, due to Egypt's wider involvement in the Arab world and the absence of substantive peace talks, it is premature to expect substantial progress on such issues at this time. This is not to diminish the role of international efforts to negotiate a chemical weapons or nuclear weapons ban. But in the final analysis, the regional parties are unlikely to accept global weapons restrictions until regional peace has been achieved.

At the end of the Gulf War, the United States and others promoted a flurry of activity to see if the allied victory could be used as a platform for addressing the dangerous consequences of an open-ended Middle East arms race. Some lessons can be learned from those efforts. First, the most successful efforts have been against Iraq. Yet the circumstances under which Iraq was subjected to such draconian restraints were unique and are unlikely to be repeated. Thus while the excellent work by Ambassador Rolf Ekeus and his staff at UNSCOM—the post-Gulf War U.N. body in charge of dismantling Iraq's weapons of mass destruction programs and monitoring Iraq to prevent their reemergence— deserves praise, UNSCOM's job is not yet over.[14] There is no chance that the U.N. Security Council will impose such an intrusive regime on any other Middle East country unless it commits an egregious violation of international law as Saddam Hussein did in 1990.

The only other relatively successful effort is the work of the Arms Control and Regional Security (ACRS) working group. Yet ACRS has not made any progress on implementing limitations or constraints on regional military forces and has ceased to meet on a regular basis. The major regional players, especially Egypt and Israel, remain sharply divided on how to deal with the most controversial issues, including Israel's nuclear weapons programs. Without further breakthroughs in the peace process, especially an agreement between Syria and Israel, there is little possibility of negotiated arms control agreements, though continued progress on limited confidence-building measures is possible. Multilateral conventional arms sales restraint is a non-starter so long as other strategic, political, and economic factors take precedence over the desire for arms control.

The arms race in the Middle East is the most deadly manifestation of continuing conflict. Absent peace, the arms race will continue and increase the costs and dangers of new war and there will be no meaningful arms control. In short, until Iran and Iraq significantly change their behavior and join the peace process—and this will mean accepting Israel's right to exist—Israel will not abandon or negotiate away its military superiority including its nuclear monopoly, no matter how good relations are with its adjacent Arab neighbors. But Israel's continued unchecked nuclear monopoly and its "qualitative edge" in conventional weapons is unacceptable to its closest Arab partners, especially Egypt. These Arabs argue that until and unless Israel is prepared to consider putting limits on its military forces, international pressure to persuade the Gulf countries to accept constraints on their own forces will not work even if both Iran and Iraq are politically rehabilitated and join discussions on regional security.

PART III
CONCLUSION

CHAPTER ELEVEN

A RACE AGAINST TIME

T he Arab-Israeli peace process has passed a point of no return. There can be no going back to the status quo before the monumental Israeli-Palestinian breakthrough in September 1993. The advances set in motion by that agreement have locked the Middle East into a new reality. Yet acknowledging this new reality is not the same as stating that there is an inexorable drive toward peace underway. There is no guarantee of further peace treaties between Israel, the Arab states, and the Palestinians; a comprehensive Middle East settlement is even less certain. Optimists can point to the progress made and the considerable benefits that come from conflict resolution. Pessimists, on the other hand, draw attention to recurring Israeli-PLO crises and the litany of unresolved political problems throughout the region, including persistent ethnic and religious hatreds. They point to a looming, apocalyptic vision of renewed warfare and demographic and socioeconomic chaos.

A realistic appraisal of the Middle East must recognize that two conditions will determine its future. First, the Arab-Israeli conflict and other unresolved regional crises have an impact on each other. An Arab-Israeli peace would influence, but neither preclude nor guarantee, comprehensive regional peace. While many Arab-Israeli issues affect regional tensions, the enormity of the problems outlined in chapters 8-10 suggests that the status of Arab-Israeli relations is just one of several elements determining regional dynamics. If there is a final Arab-Israeli peace, resolution of the Israel-Palestinian problem would deprive regional radicals at both the state and sub-state levels of a major scapegoat. Arab nationalists and Islamic activists both have used Israel's presence and behavior in the Middle East as a rallying cry for their causes. The United States has expended great effort to balance support for Israel with its ties to moderate Arab states. This was especially difficult before the 1991 Arab-Israeli conference at Madrid. Today in the Persian Gulf, where the United States plays a central role in regional security, better Arab-Israeli relations would improve U.S. relations with Arab Gulf populations and weaken the appeal of radicals. More generally, Arab-Israeli peace would signal to a global audience that the region is advancing rather than stagnating or declining.

Similarly, regional sources of tension—such as demographic pressure, ethnic and religious disputes, and enduring, non-Arab-Israeli territorial conflicts—influence but do not preclude Arab-Israeli peace. When Iran provides support to Hamas, Hizbollah, Islamic Jihad, or other front-line groups fighting Israel, the impact of regional problems is felt in the Arab-Israeli arena. In contrast, the positive relationship that has evolved between the United States and the GCC states since the Gulf War undoubtedly has helped improve GCC relations with Israel. In neither case, however, are regional influences decisive: the front-line Arab states and Israel have been able to make progress toward peace (as well as to regress) regardless of regional issues.

Second, the region has reached a critical moment in its history and could evolve in either of the two very different directions predicted by the optimists and the pessimists. Indeed, one of the ironies of this study is that while most regional leaders understand the perils of procrastination on political and economic change, they also recognize that an environment more conducive to harmony and rapid structural change cannot be created overnight. In this sense the region is in a race against its own conflicting schedules.

If a new round of Middle East crises are to be prevented and a more solid foundation for permanent peace established, what must be done? Though this book is not about detailed policy prescriptions, further progress will not happen unless vigorous and effective policies are pursued. The preceding chapters have outlined the long list of political, economic, and military problems that must be addressed. In this chapter, we single out three fundamental preconditions necessary for a comprehensive regional settlement: a continuing and assertive U.S. role in the Arab-Israeli peace process and Persian Gulf security; a final Israeli-Palestinian peace agreement; and continued structural economic reform by the key regional players.

THE ROLE OF THE UNITED STATES

At this moment in history, the U.S. role in the Middle East is paramount. The United States is the only remaining superpower and thus has global status and influence. It has a unique, close relationship with Israel, giving it special and indispensable leverage in the conduct of Arab-Israeli peace negotiations. It maintains a formidable military presence in the Persian Gulf, providing an essential security umbrella for the most important oil-producing allies. No other country has this capacity.

Yet the very reasons that make the United States essential to the peace process and Gulf security also make its role in the Middle East controversial. Strong differences of opinion exist, both in and outside the region, as to how the United States should use its power and whether this period of dominance has peaked or is likely to remain constant or grow over the coming decade.

The regimes controlling the most radical states of the Middle East—Iran, Iraq, Libya, and Sudan—regard the United States as the single greatest threat to their existence. The rhetoric these regimes use against the United States comes from a realistic appraisal that their future is in jeopardy as long as the United States challenges them at every level (in the case of Iraq even including U.S. calls for the overthrow of the regime). These countries conclude that they must be constantly vigilant and use the tools of anti-Americanism and terrorism to sustain their fragile domestic base. In contrast, some regimes that formerly posed a radical challenge, particularly Syria, may now be more inclined to believe that dealing with the United States is the preferred way to remain a relevant player in the post-Cold War era.

Countries such as Israel, Egypt, Turkey, Jordan, and the GCC countries have strong security links with the United States and, in varying ways, regard the United States as their protector of last resort. They recognize that peace diplomacy will make little progress without a dedicated and high-profile U.S. involvement, and that a U.S. military role will be decisive in the event of a new Middle East war. These countries have different views, however, about how much and what type of leverage the United States should apply to achieve its diplomatic and military goals. The Arab countries generally argue that the United States does not use enough clout to change Israeli policy. Many Israelis, on the other hand, believe that Arab countries are re-arming with U.S. weapons while letting the United States do the work of pressuring Israel into making significant concessions.

The U.S. hegemonic shadow should not be regarded as permanent. After a brief hiatus, external power rivalry is looming once more as an important ingredient in Middle East politics. Russia is no longer a pliant and passive supporter of U.S. diplomacy as was the case during and in the immediate aftermath of the Gulf War. Russia's policies toward the region have taken on a more assertive and independent tone. Russia has good relations with Iran, including an arms supply relationship, and has been eager to end sanctions on Iraq, in part to retrieve outstanding debts. Since the election of Netanyahu, Russian officials at times have been critical of Israel and have made significant gestures to improve relations with Egypt. None of these actions has been truly detrimental to U.S. interests, but they reflect Russia's own agenda in its "near abroad" (the Soviet successor states) and in the Middle East.

Likewise, China is emerging as a player in the Middle East both as an arms supplier (currently to Pakistan and Iran) and as a purchaser of energy. If China's economy continues to grow, it will become increasingly dependent on foreign energy, including oil and natural gas from the Middle East and Caspian Basin. This will draw China more directly into Middle East diplomatic activity. Furthermore, sometime in the next twenty years, China's growing navy may begin patrolling the Indian Ocean as well as the South China Seas.[1]

Some European states are asserting a more independent role and taking different positions, some of them quite adversarial, from the United States on Arab-Israeli and Gulf issues. France, under the leadership of President Jacques Chirac, refused to support U.S. military action against Iraq in August 1996. In October 1996, Chirac visited Syria, Israel, the Palestinian Authority, and Egypt and at each stop announced a much harder line against the Netanyahu government than was forthcoming from the Clinton administration. Germany has been less critical of Israel, but the German and European Union policy of seeking "critical dialogue" with Iran's mullahs has been treated with dismay by Washington. The failure of the European powers to support U.S. economic pressure against Iran led the U.S. Congress to pass the Iran-Libya Sanctions Act, which was signed into law in August 1996. This law has provisions to penalize foreign companies operating in the United States who engage in certain types of business with Iranian and Libyan oil and gas industries; the European Union has strongly opposed these secondary sanctions on the grounds that they infringe on European countries' sovereignty.

Despite these challenges, the United States still has a window of opportunity to exploit its predominant position in the Middle East. In the case of the peace process, this means continued high-level diplomatic engagement, including participating in the detailed negotiations necessary for further political breakthroughs. U.S. Secretary of State Madeleine K. Albright's visit to the region in September 1997—her first—is an important sign of U.S. diplomatic involvement. With respect to Gulf security, the United States must not only exercise continued military vigilance, but also undertake more assertive actions to remove the Saddam Hussein regime from power in Baghdad and to pressure Iran to fundamentally change its behavior on issues such as terrorism, the development of weapons of mass destruction, and opposition to the Oslo agreements between Israel and the PLO.

Whatever different views the Middle East countries have of the U.S. role, all agree that the United States is the critical regional catalyst. If the United States downgraded its role or withdrew from the region altogether, the consequences would be far-reaching and the regional balance of power radically upset.

A FINAL ISRAELI-PALESTINIAN PEACE AGREEMENT

The second essential requirement for a comprehensive Middle East settlement is a final resolution of the Israeli-Palestinian conflict. While other agreements, such as an Israeli-Syrian treaty, are highly desirable, the Palestinian issue is the Rosetta stone of the peace process.

The year 1997 marks the fiftieth anniversary of the United Nations vote to partition Palestine between the Jews and the Arabs. On November 29, 1947, a majority of U.N. members supported a two-state solution to what had even then already been a long and bloody conflict. After years of rejection, war, and confrontation, the Oslo process has now created a pathway toward a revised version of the two-state solution. Oslo's ultimate success depends upon the acceptance, on the one hand, of an independent, demilitarized Palestinian state and, on the other hand, of Israel as a permanent, sovereign state with an unchallenged right to exist.

An independent, demilitarized Palestinian state in Gaza and the greater part of the West Bank is the only acceptable resolution to the Arab-Israeli conflict. Historians may continue to argue about blame, just causes, and motivations, but a pragmatist in 1997 must come to recognize not only that the Oslo process has opened the door to compromise, but that a Palestinian state is the only sustainable end result. Israeli-Palestinian final status discussions about the exact borders, the military restrictions, the status of East Jerusalem, and other issues will be intense and difficult to resolve, but a negotiated solution will be much more likely if the overall context is the transition to a Palestinian state. Many on the Israeli left have already reconciled themselves to the fact

217

that an independent state is the minimum outcome Palestinians will accept as part of the peace process. But it is just as important for the Israeli right to come to this conclusion. Greater Palestinian autonomy is an interim solution that could only remain in place indefinitely through the use of force and repression. The aspirations of a majority of West Bank and Gaza Palestinians will not be satisfied with anything less than an internationally recognized independent state. It would be myopic to believe that improved Palestinian prosperity—itself a necessary condition for progress—will dampen the desire for political emancipation. Evidence from history suggests otherwise.

At the same time, Palestinians and other Arabs will have to accept a two-state solution as the final outcome to the conflict. Acceptance of a Palestinian state is logically coupled with recognition and acceptance of Israel within its borders (as finalized under future agreements). It is not enough that King Hussein, Yasser Arafat, and Hosni Mubarak already accept Israel's right to exist along the lines of a final settlement. It is just as important that political opposition movements and Arabs on the street, be they in Amman, Cairo, Nablus, or Palestinian refugee camps, come to the same realization. This will require a fundamental change in the attitudes of the Arab intelligentsia, including journalists, who, unlike Arab businessmen, still retain a romantic and dangerous nostalgia for the past.

Resolution of the Israeli-Palestinian conflict will put greater pressure on Syria, Lebanon, and eventually the rest of the Arab world to sign peace treaties with Israel; this could, in turn, lead to further accommodations throughout the region.

REGIONAL ECONOMIC REFORM

The third requirement for a comprehensive regional settlement is fundamental economic reform. In a 1995 study on the prospects for Middle East prosperity, the World Bank called for four significant measures in addition to maintaining macroeconomic stability: "promoting non-oil exports, making the private sector more efficient, producing more skilled and flexible workers, and reducing poverty through faster growth."[2] This prescription will require tough political decisions by national leaders. The infusion of private capital is particularly important, but it will not be forthcoming unless certain conditions are present, especially political stability, good management, an educated population, and good infrastructure. While the World Bank downplayed the possibility of a peace dividend from reduced military budgets or massive international aid infusions as a reward for peace agreements, it did suggest that a successful peace process could lower the "perceived risk for the region." Lower risk means higher investment, lower interest rates for international borrowing, and stable revenue projections for "key growth sectors [such] as tourism."[3] Private money is skittish and will go elsewhere if the region remains unstable.

Egypt, Jordan, Syria, and other Arab countries will have to implement tougher measures to assure the modernization of their economies and the elimination of corruption and mismanagement. Privatization is a phrase heard frequently throughout the Middle East these days, but unless it is paralleled by competition, it may be an excuse for the enrichment of a select few through monopoly control. When the ownership of public assets is transferred from the government to individuals without any parallel benefits to the people and without competition, it merely creates a new oligarchy of super-rich. One positive sign is that Egypt's leaders now understand the paramount importance of economic reform and competitive privatization and have taken steps to implement a farreaching reform program.

Certain sectors of the region's economies could benefit significantly from peace. For tourists interested in sightseeing, less confrontation and easy transport between Israel, Egypt, the West Bank, and Jordan (and some day perhaps Syria and Lebanon) makes the region an attractive package. For tourists simply looking for a warm and safe destination, a peaceful Middle East could be ideal.

Infrastructure development is another area of potential benefit to all parties. Many roads, railroads, ports, airports, pipelines, and waterways in the Middle East were built or developed over the last fifty years with the Arab-Israeli conflict as the key determinant of routes. To a large degree, Israel was cut off from surrounding states. New routes that follow topographic rather than political contours could provide significant economic benefits. A number of proposals have been made to join electricity grids so that each state can better regulate supply and demand and make more efficient use of existing electricity supplies. In general, trans-national rather than regional projects are likely to emerge; examples include possible tourist, transport, and infrastructure projects in the Aqaba-Eilat-Taba area and the Amman-Jericho-Jerusalem corridor. Distances are short among the front-line states; as the crow flies, Cairo-Jerusalem-Amman-

Damascus-Beirut is comparable to the Boston-Washington corridor in the northeastern United States.

On the Arabian peninsula and in Iraq and Iran, economic reform is essential for improved economic performance. While the future of Iraq remains hostage to Saddam Hussein and U.N. sanctions, the leaders of the GCC countries and Iran know that their mounting social and political problems will worsen without economic reform. Fortunately most countries in the Gulf are blessed with abundant energy resources and possess the basic ingredients for prosperity. Their challenges are, as is so often the case, political.

CONCLUSION

Despite the long list of unresolved Middle East problems, the situation in the region today is less hopeless than in the 1980s and earlier. Most Arab leaders now accept Israel's right to exist, and even Israel's Likud coalition government recognizes the need to deal with the Palestinians on a more equal basis. Supporters of a peaceful settlement currently exercise the most political influence in the region. Admittedly, this could unravel if expectations are thwarted and violence once again refocuses regional priorities.

U.S. diplomacy and military power are vital to continued progress on the peace process and to the security of the wider Middle East region. However, the Arab countries must abandon expectations that the United States will use this power to weaken Israel. Although Israel can rely on continued support from the United States, the belief that it can forge its own relations and prosperity with the rest of the world and be indifferent to its immediate neighborhood is a dangerous illusion. Likewise, although the energy resources of the region will always be in demand, it is unrealistic to believe that the oil-rich Arab states will remain oases of affluence and stability while surrounded by poverty, demographic pressure, and bitter unresolved conflicts.

The road to Middle East stability will continue to be dangerous and risky, with periodic upsurges of violence. In the last resort, the regional countries must cooperate and make the necessary compromises for further progress. If they do not cooperate and, by default or preference, continue to put off the tough choices and perpetuate the hatreds of the past, they will have no one to blame but themselves for the inevitable disasters that will follow.

NOTES

Introduction

[1]   Emphasis added. See James Rogers, *Dictionary of Clichés* (New York: Facts on File, 1985), p. 201.

Chapter 1. Can the Arab-Israeli Peace Process Succeed?

[1]   Egypt's military strategy during the war already assumed more modest goals than the destruction of Israel. In that sense, Egypt saw the war as part of the move to the bargaining table even before the war began. Some observers would date the begining of the current peace process to the cease-fire agreement that ended the War of Attrition in 1970.

[2]   Yahya M. Sadowski, *Scuds or Butter? The Political Economy of Arms Control in the Middle East* (Washington, DC: The Brookings Institution, 1993), p. 17.

[3]   *Facts on File,* November 2, 1990, p. 812.

[4]   Sadowski, *Scuds or Butter?* p. 33.

[5]   Data from U.S. Arms Control and Disarmament Agency, *World Military Expenditures and Arms Transfers 1993-1994* (Washington, DC: U.S. Government Printing Office (GPO), February 1995), pp. 141-42; U.S. Arms Control and Disarmament Agency, *World Military Expenditures and Arms Transfers 1990* (Washington, DC: GPO, November 1991), p. 134.

[6]   Judith Miller, "After the War: The P.L.O.-Arafat Sees No Damage to P.L.O. in War Stand," *New York Times,* March 15, 1991, p. A12.

[7]   "Address Before a Joint Session of the Congress on the Cessation of the Persian Gulf Conflict," March 6, 1991, in *Public Papers of the Presidents of the United States: George Bush, 1991,* vol. 1 (Washington, DC: GPO, 1992), p. 220.

[8]   For two viewpoints on the development of the Oslo agreement, see David Makovsky, *Making Peace With the PLO: The Rabin Government's Road to the Oslo Accord* (Boulder: Westview Press in cooperation with the Washington Institute for Near East Policy, 1996); and Graham Usher, *Palestine in Crisis: The Struggle for Peace and Political Independence After Oslo* (London: Pluto Press in association with the Transnational Institute and the Middle East Research and Information Project, 1995).

[9]   Yasser Arafat, "We Share Your Values For Freedom, Justice," *Washington Post,* September 14, 1993, p. A10; and Yitzhak Rabin,"We Have No Desire For Revenge . . . No Hatred," *Washington Post,* September 14, 1993, p. A10.

Notes

10   Shimon Peres with Arye Naor, *The New Middle East* (New York: Henry Holt and Company, 1993), p. 62.

11   Ibid., p. 94.

12   Ibid., p. 66.

13   Yossi Beilin, "The Past, Present and Future of the Oslo Process: View from the Labor Party," *Peacewatch*, no. 112, December 11, 1996.

14   Beilin spoke on August 2, 1993. Yossi Beilin, "Welcome to the Peace Plan," *Midstream* 39, no. 8 (November 1993), p. 4.

15   Dani Rubinstein, Ha'aretz, June 23, 1995, p. B3, in Foreign Broadcast Information Service, *Daily Report–Near East and South Asia* (FBIS-NES), June 28, 1995, pp. 7–9.

16   Zaki Abu-al-Halawah, *Al-Quds*, June 18, 1995, p. 7, in FBIS-NES, June 21, 1995, p. 12.

17   Amy Henderson, *Jordan Times,* January 25, 1995, pp. 1, 7, in FBIS-NES, January 30, 1995, p. 46.

18   Peter Waldman, "Jordan's King Hussein Finds Peace With Israel Means Strife at Home," *Wall Street Journal,* March 24, 1995, p. A1.

19   Michael C. Hudson, "After the Cold War: Prospects for Democratization in the Arab World," *Middle East Journal* 45, no. 3 (Summer 1991), pp. 409, 418, 419.

20   Saad Eddin Ibrahim, "Crises, Elites, and Democratization in the Arab World," *Middle East Journal* 47, no. 2 (Spring 1993), p. 297.

21   Islamists are sometimes referred to as Islamic fundamentalists. They are conservative in their view of Islam and the need for greater adherence to Islam among the Arab people, but their often anti-Israel and anti-Western views are seen as radical.

22   Waldman, "Jordan's King Hussein Finds Peace."

23   Douglas Jehl, "Jerusalem is Milestone for Arab Leaders," *New York Times*, November 7, 1995, pp. A1, A12.

24   "Israel's Diplomatic Relations," updated May 1996, from Israeli Ministry of Foreign Affairs web site, http://www.israel.org.

25   For a more elaborate expose of this optimistic thesis, see Geoffrey Kemp, "Cooperative Security in the Middle East," in Janne Nolan (ed.), *Global Engagement: Cooperation and the Twenty First Century* (Washington, DC: Brookings Institution, 1994), pp. 391–419.

26   To a large degree, top Likud officials are aware of the economic risk of a controversial or seemingly uncompromising approach to the peace process. Private communication by Geoffrey Kemp with Likud officials, Israel, July 1996.

27   Though attacks began in 1968, Egypt did not formally launch the war until 1969. See Daniel C. Diller (ed.), *The Middle East* (Washington: Congressional Quarterly, Inc., 1994), pp. 30–31.

28   John Rossant and Stanley Reed, "Maybe the Mideast Just Can't Afford to Keep Fighting," *Business Week*, no. 3239, November 11, 1991, p. 39.

29   John Rossant and Neil Sandler, "Why Israeli Business is so Fed Up," *Business Week*, June 29, 1992, p. 55.

30   Alan Cooperman and David Makovsky, "New Middle East, Old Middle East," *U.S. News & World Report*, November 13, 1995, p. 62.

31   "EC Linking Trade, Peace Progress," *Ha'aretz*, March 11, 1992, p. A3, in FBIS-NES, March 12, 1992, pp. 26–27.

32   See "The Palestinian Economy: No Divorce," *Economist*, February 10, 1996, p. 44.

33   Jim Lederman notes greater potential in four areas: electricity grids, fuel pipelines, road transport, and telecommunications. See Jim Lederman, "The Investments that Cement Arab-Israeli Peace," *Middle East Quarterly* (March 1996), pp. 33–42.

34   Sadowski, Scuds or Butter?: An abbreviated version, "Sandstorm with a Silver Lining: Prospects for Arms Control in the Arab World," was published by the *Brookings Review* (Summer 1992).

35   Sadowski also pointed to a new anti-militarist sentiment that he detected in certain Arab countries, particularly among the elites. Along with the desire to cut defense spending, this suggests that Arab states may be beginning to recognize the opportunity cost of continued military spending and looking for cheaper ways to provide security. In examining alternatives, interest in arms control proposals or regional security arrangements may be growing. Of particular interest is a Jordanian proposal to trade debt forgiveness for reductions in military expenditures. Jordan has made unilateral force reductions and is actually promoting the arms-debt swap idea. Sadowski's empirical work reveals new insights in Arab elite thinking and suggests that economic factors, from macro issues concerning the new structure of the world economy to more specific questions relating to the economic impact of high military spending at home, now influence debates in both Arab countries and Israel and point to the need for—or at least benefits of—conflict resolution.

36   Shawn Tully, "The Best Case For Mideast Peace," *Fortune* 123, no. 10, May 20, 1991, p. 129.

37   Gideon Fishelson (ed.), *Economic Cooperation in the Middle East* (Boulder: Westview Press, 1989), pp. 10–11.

38   Tully, "The Best Case," p. 132.

39   Ethan Bronner, "These Mideast Talks Forsake Politics in Favor of Economics," *Boston Globe*, October 31, 1994, p. 16; Ethan Bronner, "Mideast Summit Spurred Trade-In Business Cards," *Boston Globe*, November 2, 1994, p. 17.

40   *RTM Television Network* (Rabat), November 1, 1994, in FBIS-NES, November 2, 1994, pp. 8-10 (text of the conference declaration).

41   Israeli Ministry of Foreign Affairs and Ministry of Finance, *Development Options for Regional Cooperation* (Government of Israel Advertising Department, October 1994), p. II–3.

42   *Jordan Television,* October 31, 1995, in FBIS-NES, November 1, 1995, p. 12.

43   "Public Ventures, Private Doubts," *Economist,* November 4, 1995, p. 48.

44   David Gardner and Julian Ozanne, "US Voices Optimism Over Development Bank," *Financial Times*, November 1, 1995, p. 6.

45   For a text of the summit declaration, see *Jordan Television,* October 31, 1995, in FBIS-NES, November 1, 1995, pp. 11–13.

46   Julian Ozanne, "Israel Signs First Gulf Arab Deal," *Financial Times*, November 1, 1995, p. 5; and "Israel and Qatar Sign Understanding on Gas Deal," *Israel Line*, October 31, 1995, http://www.israel.org.

47   David Makovsky, *Jerusalem Post*, October 26, 1995, p. 12, in FBIS-NES, October 27, 1995, pp. 35–36.

48   Salih Salih, "Who is Gaining and Who is Footing the Bill?" *Al-Ba'th*, October 31, 1995, p. 3, in FBIS-NES, November 2, 1995, p. 51; see also *Syrian Arab Republic Radio*, November 2, 1995, in FBIS-NES, November 3, 1995, pp. 44-45; and "Amman Economic Summit and Its Shortcomings," *Al-Quds Al-'Arabi* (London), October 30, 1995, p. 11, in FBIS-NES, November 1, 1995, pp. 14–15.

49   *Voice of Lebanon,* November 1, 1995, in FBIS-NES, November 1, 1995, p. 73.

50   "Public Ventures," *Economist,* p. 48; and Cooperman and Makovsky, "New Middle East," p. 62.

51   For example, see the comments of Israel's central bank governor, Yaacov Frenkel in "Israel's Economy Sticks Out," *Wall Street Journal*, September 14, 1995, p. A14. Also see Eliyahu Kanovsky, "Assessing the Mideast Peace

Economic Dividend," the BESA Center for Strategic Studies at Bar-Ilan University (Israel), Security and Policy Studies no. 15 (March 1994); and Elias Tuma, "Economic Cooperation and Middle East Regional Stability," in Steven L. Speigel and David J. Pervin (eds.), *Practical Peacemaking in the Middle East: Volume II, The Environment, Water, Refugees, and Economic Cooperation and Development* (New York: Garland Publishing, Inc., 1995), pp. 287–301.

[52]   Atif Kubursi, "The Economics of Peace: The Arab Response," in "Regional Economic Development in the Middle East: Opportunities and Risks," special report of the Center for Policy Analysis on Palestine (Washington, DC, December 1995), p. 41. The paper was actually delivered on October 6, 1995.

[53]   Ibid., p. 39.

[54]   Address to the Business Council for International Understanding, New York, September 26, 1995, in "Trends in the Middle East Provide Opportunities for U.S. Businesses," *U.S. Department of State Dispatch 6*, no. 41, October 9, 1995, pp. 727–29.

Chapter 2: Unresolved Bilateral Issues

[1]   For a comprehensive classification system for territorial disputes, see J. R. V. Prescott, *Political Frontiers and Boundaries* (London: Allen & Unwin, 1987), especially pages 98–135.

[2]   See Appendix G in William B. Quandt, *Peace Process: American Diplomacy and the Arab-Israeli Conflict Since 1967* (Los Angeles: University of California Press, 1993), p. 468.

[3]   At a minimum, moderate Israelis would like to see modificantions in areas such as metropolitan Jerusalem, the Latrun salient, along the narrow waist of pre-1967 Israel, and in the Jordan Valley.

[4]   The West Bank aquifer is composed of the Eastern Aquifer, the Northeast Aquifer, and the Western Aquifer. The original metric figure for the West Bank mountain aquifer is 670 mn m³/year.

[5]   Julian Ozanne and David Gardner, "Middle East Peace Would Be A Mirage Without Water Deal," *Financial Times*, August 8, 1995, p. 3.

[6]   For detailed discussions of the Israeli-Syrian border throughout the twentieth century, see Aryeh Shalev, *Israel and Syria: Peace and Security on the Golan* (Tel Aviv: Jaffee Center for Strategic Studies, 1994), JCSS Study no. 24, pp. 18–43.

[7]   Ozanne and Gardner, "Middle East Peace Would Be A Mirage."

[8]   Shalev, *Israel and Syria*, pp. 156-157; and Yahia Bakour and John Kolars, "The Arab Mashrek: Hydrologic History, Problems and Perspectives," in Peter Rogers and Peter Lydon (eds.), *Water in the Arab World: Per-*

spectives and Prognoses (Cambridge: Harvard University Press, 1994), p. 131. The original metric figures are as follows: Dan River (250-272 mn m³/year), Banias River (121-125 mn m³/year), Hasbani River (122-125 mn m³/year), and run-off from precipitation and springs on the Golan Heights (105 mn m³/year).The Yarmuk River provides an additional 100 mn m³/year.

9   Shalev, *Israel and Syria*, p. 163.

10   Ahmad Beydoun, "The South Lebanon Border Zone: A Local Perspective," *Journal of Palestine Studies* 21, no. 3 (Spring 1992), pp. 35-53. A former Israeli minister noted that the "quasi-casual line became the de facto border between us and Lebanon." Yossi Beilin, "The Harmful Security Zone," *Yedi'ot Aharonot (24 Sha'ot* supplement), July 17, 1996, p. 5, in FBIS-NES, July 18, 1996, p. 33.

11   Beilin, "The Harmful Security Zone." Former Prime Minister Peres told an interviewer that "we have no territorial aims in Lebanon. We wholly accept the international border between Israel and Lebanon." Interview by Charles Enderlin, *France-2 Television Network*, April 19, 1996, http://wnc. fedworld.gov.

12   Foundation for Middle East Peace, "Jerusalem at a Glance," *Report on Israeli Settlement in the Occupied Territories* (February 1994), p. 1.

13   For instance, see Walid Khalidi, "Toward Peace in the Holy Land," *Foreign Affairs* (Spring 1988), pp. 771–789.

14   See session one, "The Historical, Cultural, Religious and National Significance of Jerusalem," in *Jerusalem: Perspectives Towards A Political Settlement* (Tel Aviv: New Outlook/United States Institute for Peace, July 1993), pp. 6–25.

15   For instance, "Jerusalem, as we have said, is our soul, heart, the future of our coming generation, and our history, which we will not relinquish." *Voice of Palestine* (Jericho), July 13, 1996, in FBIS-NES, July 15, 1996, p. 11.

16   Glenn Frankel, "Historic Arab Mansion Becomes Jerusalem Issue," *Washington Post*, July 14, 1996, p. A23.

17   See Dore Gold, *Jerusalem* (Tel Aviv: Jaffee Center for Strategic Studies, 1995), Final Status Issues: Israeli-Palestinian, study no. 7. Gold endorses a Jerusalem security zone in which Israel controls a wide belt of land surrounding Jerusalem.

18   Mark A. Heller and Sari Nusseibeh, *No Trumpets, No Drums: A Two-State Settlement of the Israeli-Palestinian Conflict* (New York: Hill and Wang, 1991), p. 114.

19   See Joseph Alpher, "Israel: The Challenges of Peace," *Foreign Policy* (Winter 1995-1996), especially pp. 139-40; Ian Lustick, "Reinventing Jerusalem," *Foreign Policy* (Winter 1993-1994), pp. 41-59; session two, "Alternative

Models for a Solution," in *Jerusalem: Perspectives Towards*, pp. 26-56; Adnan
Abu Odeh, "Two Capitals in an Undivided Jerusalem," *Foreign Affairs* 71,
no. 2 (Spring 1992), pp. 183–88.

[20]   Naomi Chazan, with commentary by Fouad Moughrabi and Rashid I.
Khalidi, *Negotiating the Non-Negotiable: Jerusalem in the Framework of an Israeli-Palestinian Settlement* (Cambridge, MA: American Academy of Arts and Sciences, March 1991), occasional paper no. 7, especially pp. 16–24.

[21]   Heller and Nusseibeh, *No Trumpets, No Drums*, p. 124.

[22]   Beilin, "The Past, Present and Future."

[23]   UNWRA and Israeli figures are from Shlomo Gazit, *The Palestinian Refugee Problem* (Tel Aviv: Jaffee Center for Strategic Studies, 1995), Final Status Issues: Israeli-Palestinian, study no. 2, pp. 2–3 and 35.

[24]   Rashid Khalidi, "Toward a Solution," in *Palestinian Refugees: Their Problem and Future* (Washington, DC: The Center for Policy Analysis on Palestine, October 1994), a special report, p. 24. Despite significant differences of opinion, Khalidi and Gazit both suggest relatively moderate solutions for the refugee problem. See also Jeffrey Boutwell and Everett Mendelsohn, principal authors of the Report of a Study Group of the Middle East Program Committee on International Security Studies, *Israeli-Palestinian Security: Issues in the Permanent Status Negotiations* (Cambridge, MA: American Academy of Arts and Sciences, 1995), pp. 71–75.

[25]   Gazit, *The Palestinian Refugee Problem*.

[26]   "Guidelines of the Government of Israel," June 1996, Israeli Ministry of Foreign Affairs, http://www.israel.org.

[27]   Beilin, "The Past, Present and Future."

[28]   Foundation for Middle East Peace, *Report on Israeli Settlement in the Occupied Territories*, vol. 3, no. 6 (November 1993) and vol. 6, no. 2 (March 1996).

[29]   For example, Joseph Alpher writes that in a scenario involving territorial compromise, "Settlers wishing to remain [in the Palestinian entity] would be subject to Palestinian authority." Joseph Alpher, *Settlements and Borders* (Tel Aviv: Jaffee Center for Strategic Studies, 1994), Final Status Issues: Israeli-Palestinian, study no. 3, p. 40.

[30]   Beilin, "The Past, Present and Future."

[31]   For example, see Aluf Ben, *Ha'aretz* (Israel), July 25, 1996, p. A3, in FBIS-NES, July 25, 1996, pp. 28–29.

[32]   For a compilation of these ideas, see Alpher, *Settlements and Borders*.

[33]   Yigal Allon, "Israel: The Case for Defensible Borders," *Foreign Affairs* 55 (October 1976), pp. 38–53. It should be noted that the Allon plan has a number of variations.

[34]   Alpher, *Settlements and Borders*, pp. 36–41 and 45.

[35]   Beilin, "The Past, Present and Future."

[36]   Some on the Israeli right might accept a Palestinian state only in Gaza.

[37]   Beilin, "The Past, Present and Future."

Chapter 3: Israel, the Palestinians, and the Peace Process

[1]   A classic example was the case of Rabbi Moshe Levinger, a longtime militant and founding settler at Qiryat Arba outside Hebron. After his convoy was stoned in downtown Hebron in 1988, Levinger responded by firing indiscriminately into Arab shops, killing Kayed Hassan Salah, a forty-two-year-old shoestore owner not involved in the stoning. After initially being charged with manslaughter, Levinger was allowed to plead guilty in 1990 to a charge of causing death by negligence and was sentenced to only five months in jail. He served just over three months of his sentence. Michael Sheridan, "Five Months in Jail for Settler Who Killed Arab," *Independent,* May 3, 1990, p. 14; and "Rabbi Who Killed Arab Freed from Jail Early," *Washington Times*, August 15, 1990, p. A2. For more recent examples, see Tova Tzimuqi, "The Attorney General's Contingency Plan for Dealing With a Settler Uprising," *Yediot Aharonot* (Leshabbat supplement), June 23, 1995, in FBIS-NES, June 28, 1995, pp. 43–45. See also a new and compelling study by Ilana Kass and Bard O'Neill, *The Deadly Embrace: The Impact of Israeli and Palestinian Rejectionism on the Peace Process* (Lanham, MD: University Press of America, 1997).

[2]   "IMF: Israeli Economy Shows Highest Growth Rate for 1994," *Israel Line*, July 12, 1995, http://www.israel.org.

[3]   This is acknowledged by top Likud finance officials. Private communication with Geoffrey Kemp, Tel Aviv and Jerusalem, July 21–22, 1996.

[4]   Ora Koren, "Gulf Businessmen Serve Warning: Representations Will be Closed if Political Deadlock Persists," *Globes*, July 23, 1996, http://www.globes.co.il; Haggai Golan, "Netanyahu Discovers America," *Globes,* July 17, 1996, http://www.globes.co.il; and Orna Raviv, "GM Hewlett Packard: Multinational Co's May Halt Ventures in Israel," *Globes*, July 17, 1996, http://www.globes.co.il.

[5]   In a comparison with a variety of other countries, Israel still stands out. For example, South Korea saw a slightly higher increase (47 percent) but many others were lower over the same time period: Egypt (9 percent), Italy (2 per-

cent), Saudi Arabia (4 percent), Turkey (13 percent), and the United States (32 percent). See *Direction of Trade Statistics* (Washington, DC: International Monetary Fund, 1996).

6   See Amy Dockser Marcus, "Israeli Businesses Leapfrog Neighbors to Seek Richer Rewards Deeper in Asia," *Wall Street Journal,* November 2, 1995, p. A15; and Allon Groth, "Israel's Search for New Markets," *MEI,* November 3, 1995, pp. 16–17.

7   Marcus, "Israeli Businesses Leapfrog."

8   The United States is second. *Direction of Trade Statistics,* pp. 250–51.

9   "Israel and EU Initial Agreement on Cooperation and Commerce," *Israel Line,* September 29, 1995, http://www.israel.org.

10   Hugh Carnegy, "EC Links Trade Deal to Israeli Peace Progress," *Financial Times,* July 11, 1991; and Jonathan Levy, "Israel Wonders Where It Will Fit Into Single-Market EC," *Journal of Commerce,* September 30, 1991. The Israeli daily *Ha'aretz* reported that "Israeli sources believe that if the current trade agreements are not adjusted, Israel stands to lose its relative advantage in the EC." "EC Linking Trade, Peace Progress," *Ha'aretz,* March 11, 1992, p. A3, in FBIS-NES, March 12, 1992, p. 26.

11   Jackson Diehl, "Israeli Quest for 'Normalcy' Reshaping Society," *Washington Post,* June 8, 1992, pp. A1, A14–15.

12   Marjorie Olster, "Investors Wary of Israel's Future," *Washington Post,* June 2, 1996, p. H2.

13   Julian Ozanne, "State of Attraction," *Financial Times,* October 24, 1995, p. 16.

14   David Weinberg, "The Arab Boycott of Israel: 1991 Update" (New York: Anti-Defamation League, 1991), pp. 4-8.

15   David Rosenberg, "The Boom Goes Bust," *Jerusalem Report,* August 8, 1996, p. 44.

16   The fee hikes and cuts are 3.2 percent of the 1997 Israeli budget (excluding debt servicing). Daniel Sternoff, "Strike Brings Israel to Halt," *Reuters,* July 17, 1996.

17   Some details on the status of Israel's economy and Netanyahu's economic approach came from private communication with Likud finance officials by Geoffrey Kemp, Tel Aviv and Jerusalem, July 21–22, 1996.

18   For Israeli economic news, see http://www.globes.co.il. See also Mitti Basok, "Frenkel Expected to Raise Interest Rates Following Huge Money Supply Increase," *Ha'aretz,* August 18, 1997, http://www.haaretz.co.il/eng.

19   One could relate this discussion to the attempts to assign blame after the assassination of Rabin. Without commenting on most of that debate, it should be noted that right-wingers of all types are trained and indoctrinated in the Israeli army, at Yeshivas (religious schools), and/or through political movements.

20   For more on Israel and normalcy, see Myron J. Aronoff, "The Origins of Israeli Political Culture," in Ehud Sprinzak and Larry Diamond (eds.), *Israeli Democracy Under Stress* (Boulder: Lynne Rienner Publishers, 1993), pp. 47–63, especially 57–58.

21   Benjamin Netanyahu, *Fighting Terrorism: How Democracies Can Defeat Domestic and International Terrorists* (New York: Farrar Straus Giroux, 1995).

22   *Israel Television*, July 13, 1992, in FBIS-NES, July 14, 1992, p. 24.

23   Ian Lustick, *For the Land and the Lord* (New York: Council on Foreign Relations, 1988), p. 105.

24   For some examples, see Jack Miles, "Promised Land?," *New York Times*, December 6, 1995, p. A23.

25   Lustick, *For the Land and the Lord*, p. 106.

26   Though the term "Greater Israel" lacks the long history and biblical connection associated with the Land of Israel, it is useful in describing those who support retaining control of the occupied territories. In this book, we describe supporters of greater Israel in a generic sense, referring to any one of the different visions of the Land of Israel explained in this chapter.

27   Meir Kahane, *Uncomfortable Questions For Comfortable Jews* (Secaucus, New Jersey: Lyle Stuart, 1987), p. 159, as quoted in Charles S. Liebman, "Religion and Democracy in Israel," in Sprinzak and Diamond (eds.), *Israeli Democracy Under Stress*, pp. 289–90.

28   For more on the Israeli right, see Ehud Sprinzak, *The Ascendance of Israel's Radical Right* (New York: Oxford University Press, 1991).

29   See Harvey Sicherman, *Palestinian Self-Government (Autonomy): Its Past and Its Future* (Washington, DC: Washington Institute for Near East Policy, 1991), policy paper no. 27.

30   Michael Widlanski, editor and project coordinator, *Can Israel Survive a Palestinian State?* (Jerusalem: Institute for Advanced Strategic and Political Studies, 1990), p. 94.

31   Foundation for Middle East Peace, "Rabin's Final Defense of Oslo II," *Report on Israeli Settlement in the Occupied Territories* 5, no. 6 (November 1995), http://www.clark.net/pub/jeff.

32   *Qol Yisra'el,* June 15, 1992, in FBIS-NES, June 16, 1992, p. 16; *IDF Radio,* June 8, 1992, in FBIS-NES, June 9, 1992, p. 34; and *Israel Television Network,* July 13, 1992, in FBIS-NES, July 14, 1992, p. 25.

33   Private communication with Geoffrey Kemp, Israel, July 1996.

34   Some advocates of withdrawal from the Golan raised the possibility of stronger U.S.-Israeli defense ties to compensate for Israel's loss. For a review of Israeli-U.S. strategic relations, see Shai Feldman, *The Future of U.S.-Israel Strategic Cooperation* (Washington, DC: Washington Institute for Near East Policy, 1996).

35   Yossi Klein Halevi, "Soldiers of Zion," *New York Times,* November 15, 1995, p. A23.

36   Michael Walzer, "Reasons to Mourn," *New Yorker,* November 20, 1995, p.8.

37   For a well-known Palestinian perspective reflecting acceptance of a two-state solution, see Walid Khalidi, "Toward Peace in the Holy Land," *Foreign Affairs* 66, no. 4 (Spring 1988), pp. 771–89.

38   For an in-depth analysis of how Arafat came to agree to Oslo I and how the Oslo process has affected the Palestinian communtiy, see Usher, *Palestine in Crisis.*

39   Private communication with Geoffrey Kemp and Palestinian leaders, Gaza, July 1996.

40   There are some 50,000 armed officers and secret police, according to Ilene R. Prusher, "Palestinians Wonder Why Some Seem More Equal than Others," *Christian Science Monitor,* April 30, 1997, p. 6. In early 1996, there were 30,000 in the police force, according to Barton Gellman, "With Passport, Palestinians Seek Passage to Nationhood," *Washington Post,* February 25, 1996, p. A24.

41   *Amnesty International Report 1996* (London: Amnesty International Publications, 1996), pp. 184-88. Also see Joel Greenberg, "West Bank Protest Against Torture of Prisoners by Palestinian Police," *New York Times,* August 2, 1996, http://www.nytimes.com.

42   Sara Roy, paper on the Gaza Economy, Middle East Studies Association annual meeting, Washington, DC, December 8, 1995.

43   Dennis Ross, remarks at American-Israel Public Affairs Committee and the National Jewish Community Relations Advisory Council conference, *Federal News Service,* December 12, 1995.

44   Much of the following economic material is from Sara Roy, paper on the Gaza Economy.

45   Private communication between Geoffrey Kemp and Palestinian official, Gaza, July 23, 1996.

46   Private communication between Geoffrey Kemp and Palestinian leaders, Gaza, July 1996. See also Daniel Sternoff, "Palestinians Take Battered Economy to Cairo Summit," *Reuters*, November 11, 1996.

47   Interview of Arafat by Khayrallah Khayrallah, *Al-Hayah* (London), February 6, 1996, pp. 1, 6, in FBIS-NES, February 6, 1996, pp. 1–3.

48   Shimon Peres, remarks at American-Israel Public Affairs Committee and the National Jewish Community Relations Advisory Council conference, *Federal News Service*, December 12, 1995.

49   Sara Roy, paper on the Gaza Economy.

50   Jihad al-'Idan, *Voice of the Islamic Republic of Iran*, September 25, 1995, in FBIS-NES, September 26, 1995, p. 7.

51   On splits in Hamas, see Ehud Ya'ari, "Inside Hamas: Political Disputes, Internal Crisis," *Peacewatch*, no. 89, March 19, 1996.

52   *Al-Ra'y* (Amman), March 24, 1995, p. 20, in FBIS-NES, March 24, 1995, p. 6.

53   Christopher Walker, "Radicals Challenge Arafat's Peace Deal," *London Times*, September 26, 1995, p. 12, in FBIS-NES, September 26, 1995, p. 8.

54   Hamas Communique No. 125, "No to Discrimination and Division. . . . Yes to the Release of the Detainees," *Filastin al-Muslimah* (London), August 1995, p. 7, in FBIS-NES, August 8, 1995, p. 13.

55   *Voice of the Oppressed*, September 30, 1995, in FBIS-NES, October 2, 1995, p. 8.

56   Nora Boustany, "Palestinian Militants Declares Self-Rule Accord 'Effectively Dead'," *Washington Post*, February 5, 1995, p. A33.

57   *IRIB Television First Program Network* (Teheran), November 2, 1995, in FBIS-NES, November 3, 1995, p. 9.

58   'Atif al-Jawlani, *Al-Mujtama'* (Kuwait), October 31, 1995, pp. 32-33, in FBIS-NES, December 7, 1995, p. 11.

59   Joel Greenberg, "Palestinian 'Martyrs,' All Too Willing," *New York Times*, January 25, 1995, p. A8.

60   Clovis Maksoud, "Peace Process or Puppet Show?" *Foreign Policy*, no. 100 (Fall 1995), p. 120. For a response to Maksoud, see Jeremy Pressman, "Letters: Middle East," *Foreign Policy*, no. 101 (Winter 1995-96), pp. 181–82.

61   Irwin Block, "Palestinian Leader Fears Peace Process is Dead," *Gazette* (Montreal), June 26, 1995, p. B8.

62   Edward W. Said, "The Mirage of Peace," *Nation*, October 16, 1995, p. 420.

63   The importance of Jerusalem goes beyond symbolism and holy sites for West Bank Palestinians. It is the center of the Arab West Bank in terms of trade and commerce, services, political activities, libraries, and medical care. Israel has made it difficult for Palestinians to worship, work, visit, or get medical care in Jerusalem, ostensibly for security reasons. To a large degree, the difficulty in traversing Jerusalem also separates the northern West Bank from the southern West Bank for Palestinians. Giving greater Palestinian access to the city might lessen the Palestinian pressure for sovereignty and allow a functional division of the city.

64   *Voice of Palestine*, September 25, 1995, in FBIS-NES, September 26, 1995, p. 6.

65   For example, see Edward Said, "Cry Palestine," *New Statesman and Society*, November 10, 1995, pp. 24–27.

66   Peter F. Sisler, "Palestinian Says Arafat Blocks Democracy," *United Press International,* July 7, 1995.

67   Said, "The Mirage of Peace," p. 413.

68   Joel Greenberg, "4 Palestinian Officials Call for Halt to Israeli talks," *New York Times*, January 10, 1995, p. A3.

69   *Al-Dustur* (Amman), September 26, 1995, p. 1, in FBIS-NES, September 26, 1995, p. 5.

70   Said, "Cry Palestine," p. 24.

71   Maksoud, "Peace Process or Puppet Show?" p. 124.

72   Said, "The Mirage of Peace," p. 420.

73   "Palestinian Activist Concerned About Press Freedom," *Reuters*, January 2, 1996.

74   Ibid.

75   Private Communication with Jeremy Pressman, Israel, June 1997.

Chapter 4: Egypt, Jordan, and the Peace Process

[1]   James Leonard, "Threat Perceptions in the Middle East," in United Nations Institute for Disarmament Research, *National Threat Perceptions in the Middle East* (New York: United Nations, September 1995), research paper no. 37, p. 2. See also Shai Feldman, *Nuclear Weapons and Arms Control in the Middle East* (Cambridge, Massachusetts: MIT Press, 1997).

[2]   Fouad Ajami, "The Sorrows of Egypt," *Foreign Affairs* (September/October 1995), pp. 72–88.

[3]   Douglas Jehl, "Egyptians Get a New Premier And Hopes for the Economy," *New York Times,* January 5, 1996, p. A8.

[4]   For a review of Egypt's positive economic changes, see David Butter, "Reforms Ready Economy for Real Growth," *MEED,* April 19, 1996, pp. 25–28; and David Butter, "Privatisation Genie Let Out of the Bottle," *MEED,* March 8, 1996, pp. 2–4.

[5]   Projected population for 2025 is based upon official country projections, or upon series issued by the United Nations, the U.S. Census Bureau, World Bank, or Population Reference Bureau (PRB) projections. See PRB, World Population Data Sheet (Washington, DC: 1995).

[6]   Diller (ed.), *The Middle East,* p. 194.

[7]   "Egypt: Economic Policy," EIU Country Reports, November 3, 1995.

[8]   "Egypt: Economic Structure," EIU Country Reports, November 3, 1995.

[9]   "Egypt—Economic Update: Basic Data and Macro Economic Indicators," undated Government of Egypt handout to Geoffrey Kemp in Egypt, July 1996.

[10]   Abdel Monem Said Aly, "From Geopolitics to Geo-Economics: Egyptian National Security Perceptions," in United Nations Institute for Disarmament Research, *National Threat Perceptions*, pp. 24–25.

[11]   "Egypt: Economic Policy."

[12]   Private communication with Geoffrey Kemp, Cairo, July 1996.

[13]   Amy Docker Marcus, "Rising Sphinx: Egypt Quickly Turns an Investment Famine into Times of Plenty," *Wall Street Journal,* April 4, 1997, p. 1.

[14]   For more on the government battle with political Islam, see Ajami, "The Sorrows of Egypt," especially pp. 75–79.

[15]   This is the official estimate, and it includes all non-Muslims. *The World Factbook 1994* (Washington, DC: CIA, 1994), p. 117.

16   Throughout the Islamic campaign there has been a disagreement as to whether the Mubarak regime was ever truly threatened, a debate which we choose not to enter into here because today nearly all sides agree that the government is on relatively solid footing.

17   David Butter, "Heavy Hand Squeezes the Opposition," *MEED*, April 19, 1996, p. 26.

18   "Egypt: Transport and Tourism."

19   The defectors returned to Iraq in February 1996 and were killed a few days later.

20   Douglas Jehl, "Jordan's Now Succeeding in Mending Gulf Ties Frayed by Iraq," *New York Times*, February 8, 1996, p. A15.

21   Abby Harrison, "The Haves and Have-Nots of the Middle East Revisited," *SAIS Review* 11, no. 2 (Summer-Fall 1991), p. 153.

22   Ariel Sharon, "Jordan is the Palestinian State," *Jerusalem Post*, April 4, 1991.

23   Ariel Sharon, "Autonomy Means Statehood," *Jerusalem Post*, August 13, 1992.

24   Arthur Day, "Hussein's Constraints, Jordan's Dilemma," *SAIS Review* 7, no. 1 (Winter-Spring 1987), p. 89.

25   Elaine Sciolino and Douglas Jehl, "Syria's Game: Both Ends Against the Middle," *New York Times*, June 15, 1996, pp. 1 and 4.

26   James Whittington, "Fear Over Taking Road to Isolation," *Financial Times*, August 22, 1995, p. 4.

27   Based on private conversations, Amman, Jordan, March 1995.

28   The text of the Israeli-Jordanian treaty is in *SIPRI Yearbook 1995: Armaments, Disarmament and International Security* (New York: Oxford University Press, 1995), pp. 197–203 (appendix 5A).

29   One analyst argues that the Israeli-Jordanian treaty is a pax Americana, rather than a step toward genuine peace. See Stephen Zunes, "The Israeli-Jordanian Agreement: Peace or Pax Americana?," *Middle East Policy* 3, no. 4 (April 1995), pp. 57-68.

30   John Lancaster, "Palestinian Strides Resound Through Mideast," *Washington Post*, February 26, 1996, p. A14.

Chapter 5: Syria, Lebanon, and the Peace Process

[1]   Julian Ozanne, "Israel to Present New Initiative to Break Deadlock in Talks with Syria," *Financial Times,* December 7, 1995, p. 5; and Serge Schmemann, "Israel and Syria Set Peace Talks for Washington," *New York Times,* December 17, 1995, pp. A1 and A14. For a fascinating Syrian perspective on the results of the talks, see interview with Walid al-Moualem, "Fresh Light on the Syrian-Israeli Peace Negotiations," *Journal of Palestine Studies* 26, no. 2 (Winter 1997), pp. 81–94.

[2]   See Barbara Crossette, "U.N. Report Suggests Israeli Attack Was Not a Mistake," *New York Times,* May 8, 1996, p. A3; and Serge Schmemann, "Peres's View: Modest Boon," *New York Times,* April 27, 1996, p. 1.

[3]   Daniel Pipes explains that Greater Syria includes Syria, Lebanon, Israel, Jordan, the Gaza Strip, and Alexandretta; this is what Syrian leaders "dream of reclaiming." M. Zuhair Diab calls Greater Syria a British colonial term and suggests instead the term natural Syria, the natural boundaries in accordance with the General Syrian Congress of 1920. Diab argues that while natural Syria is part of Syria's history and national ethos, Syria has no grandiose dreams of bringing parts of natural Syria back together. See Pipes, *Greater Syria: The History of an Ambition* (New York: Oxford University Press, 1990); Diab, "Have Syria and Israel Opted for Peace?," *Middle East Policy,* no. 2 (1994), pp. 77–90; and Diab, "Syrian Security Requirements in a Peace Settlement with Israel," *Israel Affairs* (Summer 1995), pp. 71–88.

[4]   Syrian Arab Republic Radio, May 28, 1994, as quoted in Daniel Pipes, "Understanding Asad," *Middle East Quarterly* 1, no. 4 (December 1994), p. 56.

[5]   Shalev, *Israel and Syria,* p. 111; and Diab, "Syrian Security Requirements," p. 72.

[6]   Hisham Dajani, "The Golan: Still A Long Way from Resolution," *Middle East International,* no. 466, March 4, 1994, p. 19.

[7]   The Gaza Strip was dealt with in the context of Palestinian needs; Egypt never claimed that Gaza was part of Egypt. Taba, a small disputed area on the Egyptian-Israeli border, was turned over to Egypt after the International Court of Justice ruled in Egypt's favor.

[8]   See Daniel Pipes, *Syria Beyond the Peace Process* (Washington, DC: Washington Institute for Near East Policy, 1996), policy paper no. 40.

[9]   *Syrian Arab Television Network,* September 10, 1994, in FBIS-NES, September 12, 1994, pp. 41–48.

[10]   *Israel Television Channel 1 Network,* June 10, 1995, in FBIS-NES, June 12, 1995, p. 35.

[11]   *IDF Radio,* June 11, 1995, in FBIS-NES, June 12, 1995, p. 35.

[12]   Former Israeli Foreign Minister Ehud Barak told the *Washington Post* that Israel wants diplomatic relations, an open border, trade, tourist exchanges, "a free flow of goods, services and people," communication and transportation links, joint water projects, and integration of the two countries' electricity grids. See Thomas W. Lippman, "Israel's Vision Of Syrian Pact Is Ambitious," *Washington Post*, January 24, 1996, p. A26.

[13]   Remarks by Anthony Lake at the Washington Institute for Near East Policy, May 17, 1994, transcript provided by Federal News Service. See also Steven Greenhouse, "Israeli-Syrian Round Ends Without Breakthrough," *New York Times*, May 19, 1994, p. A6.

[14]   For a critique of the Pipes view and a different view of the Syrian regime and the peace process, see Raymond A. Hinnebusch, "Syria: The Politics of Peace and Regime Survival," *Middle East Policy* 3, no. 4 (April 1995), pp. 74–87.

[15]   John Lancaster, "Netanyahu to Seek Limited Accords in Talks With Syria," *Washington Post*, June 5, 1996, p. A25.

[16]   On the Syrian military buildup, see Pipes, *Syria Beyond the Peace*, pp. 41–45.

[17]   Clyde Haberman, "Peace Pact With Syria Needed to Prevent War, Rabin Says," *New York Times*, June 25, 1994, p. 4.

[18]   Muhammad Muslih, "The Golan: Israel, Syria, and Strategic Calculations," *Middle East Journal* 47, no. 4 (Autumn 1993), p. 625.

[19]   *Syrian Arab Republic Radio*, August 3, 1994, in FBIS-NES, August 3, 1994, p. 59.

[20]   *The World Factbook 1995* (Washington, DC: Central Intelligence Agency, 1995), p. 408.

[21]   Fred H. Lawson, "Domestic Transformation and Foreign Steadfastness in Contemporary Syria," *Middle East Journal* 48, no. 1 (Winter 1994), p. 51.

[22]   "Syria," EIU Country Reports, October 2, 1996; Lawson, "Domestic Transformation," p. 64; and Patrick Clawson, "Syrian Prospects After the Cold War," in a Report from a Public Workshop, "Syria and the Future of the Mideast Peace Process," United States Institute for Peace, December 7, 1993, p. 7. See also 1996 *Direction of Trade Statistics,* p. 416.

[23]   Phyllis Berman Johnson, "Blackmail," *Forbes*, July 31, 1995, p. 84.

[24]   Stanley Reed, with Neal Sandler and Amy Borrus, "Why Assad May Be Ready to Come in From the Cold," *Business Week*, no. 3385, August 15, 1994, p. 45. See also Andrew Rathmell, "Syria's Insecurity," *Jane's Intelligence Review* (September 1994), p. 414.

25   Johnson, "Blackmail," p. 85; and "Syria: Political Stability in Syria," EIU Country Reports, March 16, 1995.

26   "Syria: Brief Overview," EIU Country Reports, January 16, 1995; "Syria: Political Stability in Syria"; "Syria: No Go," EIU Country Reports, August 1, 1995; and "Syria: Inertia," EIU Country Reports, December 1, 1995.

27   "Syria: No Go."

28   For more details, see Peter Waldman, "Mideast Prize: Syria Tightens Its Grip On Lebanon, May Get Indefinite Control of It," Wall Street Journal, July 19, 1995, pp. A1 and A5.

29   Pipes, Syria Beyond the Peace Process, pp. 59-64; Rathmell, "Syria's Insecurity," p. 416; Thana al-Imam, Radio Monte Carlo, January 30, 1996, in FBIS-NES, January 30, 1996, p. 39; Hugh Pope, "The Looming Crisis Over the Tigris-Euphrates Waters," Middle East International, June 9, 1995, p. 17; and Jonathan C. Randal, "Euphrates Dam Aids Turkish Rebels," Washington Post, May 15, 1992, p. A27.

30   John Barham, "Dam Developers Wear Down Bureaucrats' Hostility to BOT," Financial Times, December 7, 1995, p. 4.

31   "Neighbor States Call for Undivided Iraq," United Press International, September 8, 1995.

32   For a discussion of Israel's objectives, see Ze'ev Schiff and Ehud Ya'ari, Israel's Lebanon War (New York: Simon and Schuster, 1984).

33   "Putting Back the Pieces," Economist, February 24, 1996, survey p. 10.

34   "Putting Back the Pieces," survey p. 4. It is difficult to find accurate population figures for Lebanon; these numbers may have significant errors resulting from inclusion of overseas Lebanese or exclusion of Palestinian refugees.

35   Asad speech to members of newly elected Syrian provincial councils, July 10, 1976, as reported on Radio Damascus (and FBIS). See Itamar Rabinovich, The War for Lebanon, 1970-1983 (Ithaca, NY: Cornell University Press, 1984), pp. 187-88. See our discussion of natural Syria and greater Syria earlier in this chapter.

36   "Israel's Buffer in Southern Lebanon," New York Times, December 22, 1992, p. A3. See also Ahmad Beydoun, "The South Lebanon Border Zone: A Local Perspective," Journal of Palestine Studies 21, no. 3 (Spring 1992), pp. 35–53.

37   Otto Johnson (ed.), Information Please: 1995 Almanac (Boston: Houghton Mifflin Company, 1994), pp. 208, 220.

38   "Putting Back the Pieces," survey p. 12.

Chapter 6: The Arab Gulf Countries

[1] "Worldwide Look at Reserves and Production," *Oil and Gas Journal 92*, no. 52, December 26, 1994. The International Petroleum Encyclopedia also offers a figure of 66 percent as cited by the Department of Defense, Office of International Security Affairs, "United States Security Strategy for the Middle East," (Washington, DC: 1995). However, *World Oil* cites a figure approaching 54 percent in "Estimated Proven World Reserves, 1994 versus 1993," *World Oil* (August 1995), p. 30.

[2] See *Beyond the White House Lawn: Current Perspectives on the Arab-Israeli Peace Process* (New York: Anti-Defamation League, 1994), p. 39.

[3] See chapter 1, including note 46.

[4] "Multilateral Talks on Environment Held in Oman," *Israel Line*, June 28, 1996, http://www.israel.org.

[5] Anti-Defamation League (ADL), "From Pariah to Partner: Israel's Integration into the Community of Nations (II)," ADL International Notes (pamphlet series), January 1996.

[6] For instance, see charts in *World Energy Outlook* (Paris: International Energy Agency/Organization for Economic Cooperation and Development, 1996), pp. 26 and 31.

[7] "Estimated Proven World Reserves, 1994 versus 1993."

[8] The U.S. figure is from the *Monthly Energy Review*, National Energy Information Center, Energy Information Administration (Washington, DC). See also U.S. Bureau of the Census, *Statistical Abstract of the United States 1995* (Washington, DC: GPO, September 1995), p. 598. Other figures are from Nadim Kawash, *AFP*, June 14, 1995, in FBIS-NES, June 14, 1995, p. 31.

[9] *Middle East Economic Monitor* 4, no. 9 (September 1994), pp. 3–4; "Saudi Arabia: Privatisation Progress Report, EIU Country Reports, December 1, 1996.

[10] Eliahu Kanovsky, lecture at the National Defense Institute conference on "Energy Security in the 21st Century," November 10, 1994.

[11] Clay Chandler, "Bentson Urges Saudis to Make Spending Cuts," *Washington Post*, October 6, 1994, p. D14.

[12] "Saudi Arabia: Economic Structure," EIU Country Reports, October 10, 1996.

[13] "Saudi Arabia: Structural Review," The Economist Intelligence Unit Risk Service, October 22, 1996.

[14] *The World Factbook 1995*, p. 370.

¹⁵   See chapter 7 for more details. *Strategic Survey, 1995-96* (London: International Institute for Strategic Studies, 1996), p. 163.

¹⁶   Middle East Watch estimated that 2-7 percent of the Saudi population is Shiite while the CIA's *Atlas of the Middle East* noted a higher figure of 8 percent. See Andrew Whitley, "Minorities and the Stateless in Persian Gulf Politics," *Survival* 35, no. 4 (Winter 1993–94), p. 50.

¹⁷   For more on Iraqi and Saudi Shiites, see Whitley, "Minorities and the Stateless," pp. 36-39, 41-42, 50.

¹⁸   *Ulema* (or *ulama*) is a body of learned persons (such as Imams, judges, teachers in religious faculties of universities) competent to decide upon religious matters. See Cyril Glasse, *The Concise Encyclopedia of Islam* (San Francisco: Harper and Row, Inc., 1989), p. 407.

¹⁹   In the population of 1.58 million, 39 percent are nationals, 35 percent other Arab, 9 percent South Asian, and 4 percent Iranian (with the rest not identified). International Institute for Strategic Studies (IISS), *The Military Balance 1996-1997* (London: Brassey's, 1996), p. 137.

²⁰   For more on Oman, see Joseph A. Kechichian, *Oman and the World: The Emergence of an Independent Foreign Policy* (Santa Monica, CA: RAND, 1995).

²¹   For more on Oman's history, see Malcolm C. Peck, "Eastern Arabian States: Kuwait, Bahrain, Qatar, United Arab Emirates, and Oman," in David E. Long and Bernard Reich (eds.), *The Government and Politics of the Middle East and North Africa* (Boulder: Westview Press, 1995), pp. 142–43.

²²   For a more favorable view of the Omani consultative council, see Abdullah Huma al-Haj, "The Politics of Participation in the Gulf Cooperation Council States: The Omani Consultative Council," *Middle East Journal* 50, no. 4 (Autumn 1996), pp. 559–71.

²³   IISS, *The Military Balance 1994-1995* (London: Brassey's, 1994), p. 135.

²⁴   John Lancaster, "Running on Fumes," *Washington Post*, December 19, 1995, p. A25.

²⁵   The International Institute for Strategic Studies says that of a total population of 2,415,000, about 76 percent are expatriates. A *Financial Times* article used the 70 percent figure for a total population of 2.5-3 million. See IISS, *The Military Balance 1994-1995*, p. 140; and Robin Allen, "Imported Labour May Not Be Cheap for Gulf States," *Financial Times*, October 13, 1995, p. 5.

²⁶   IISS, *The Military Balance 1994-1995*, p. 140.

²⁷   Allen, "Imported Labour."

28   Whitley, "Minorities and the Stateless," p. 44.

29   Allen, "Imported Labour."

30   IISS, *The Military Balance 1994-1995*, p. 140.

Chapter 7: The Rejectionist States

1   "Iraq Threatens to Gas Israel," *Facts on File*, April 6, 1990, p. 237C2.

2   "Iran to Dismantle Privately Owned Satellite Dishes," *Washington Post*, April 18, 1995, p. B5.

3   *The World Factbook 1995*.

4   "Iran: Economic Structure," EIU Country Reports, November 23, 1995; "Iran: Economy," The EIU Country Profiles, November 1, 1996. See also Cherif Cordahi, "Middle East-Economy: Declining Growth Rates Hint at Future Crises," *Inter Press Service*, Cairo, September 26, 1994. Most Iranian annual figures are calculated from March 21. A 1993 date, for instance, usually signifies data for March 21, 1993 to March 20, 1994, and might also be listed as a 1993/1994 figure. The Iranian government also has a tendency to manipulate some economic numbers such as the Iranian inflation rate.

5   Jahangir Amuzegar, "Iran's Economy and the US Sanctions," *The Middle East Journal* 51, no. 2 (Spring 1997), p. 190.

6   Liz Kirkwood, "A Rising Tide in the Gulf," *Institutional Investor Inc.* (July 1993), p. 93.

7   "Iran: Economy."

8   "Iran: Economic Structure."

9   Ibid.

10   "Iran: Economy."

11   "Iran: Economic Policy and Economy," EIU Country Report, November 17, 1996.

12   Elaine Sciolino, "Iran's Difficulties Lead Some in U.S. To Doubt Threat," *New York Times*, July 5, 1994, p. A1.

13   "Iran: Economic Structure"; "Iran:Quarterly Indicators of Economic Activity," EIU Country Reports, November 17, 1996.

14   "Iran: Economic Structure"; "Iran: Outlook," EIU Country Reports; "Iran: Economy."

15   Amuzegar, "Iran's Economy and the US Sanctions," p. 191.

[16]   Hobart Rowen, "Over the Barrel," *Washington Post,* October 13, 1994, p. A19.

[17]   Philip Shenon, "OPEC Seeking to Raise Prices by Output Freeze," *New York Times,* November 22, 1994.

[18]   "Iraq-UN Oil Deal Signed But Problems Remain," *Reuters,* May 20, 1996; and "Iraq Signs Oil Deal to Bolster Economy," *Reuters,* May 21, 1996.

[19]   "Saddam Hailed as Iraqi Oil Flows Again," *San Diego Union-Tribune,* December 11, 1996, p. A16 (see http: //www.union-tribune.com); Christopher Lockwood, "Iraqis Rejoice as UN Deal Ends Oil Trade Embargo," *Electronic Telegraph* (internet version of the *Daily Telegraph* at http://www.telegraph.co.uk), November 27, 1996, no. 553.

[20]   UNDP, *Human Development Report 1994* (New York: Oxford University Press, 1994), p. 42.

[21]   *The World Factbook 1995.*

[22]   For a provocative challenge to the conventional wisdom on Iraqi territorial integrity, see Daniel Byman, "Let Iraq Collapse," *The National Interest,* no. 45 (Fall 1996), pp. 48-60.

[23]   *The World Factbook 1994,* p. 191.

[24]   Robert Litwak, *Security in the Persian Gulf 2: Sources of Inter-State Conflict* (Montclair, New Jersey: Allanheld, Osmun and Co. Publishers, Inc., 1981), p. 25.

[25]   Historically, there have been other incidents, including a 1974 Iraqi-Syrian controversy over Syria's al-Thawra dam. Peter H. Gleick, "Water and Conflict," *International Security* 18, no. 1 (Summer 1993), pp. 88–89.

[26]   Eric Pianin, "Clinton Approves Sanctions For Investors in Iran, Libya," *Washington Post,* August 6, 1996, p. A8.

[27]   Douglas Jehl, "Arab Lands Warn Israel of Danger to Improved Ties," *New York Times,* June 24, 1996, p. A1; John Lancaster, "Arabs Warn Netanyahu On Land Return," *Washington Post,* June 24, 1996, p. A1. For the text of the final communique, see *Arab Republic of Egypt Radio Network,* June 23, 1996, http://wnc.fedworld.gov.

[28]   *Patterns of Global Terrorism 1995* (Washington, DC: U.S. Department of State, April 1996), publication no. 10321, p. 27. For more on Libya and Sudan, see also pp. 23–24 and 26.

Chapter 8: Other Middle East Territorial Disputes

[1]   Ahmad Mardini, "Gulf: Regional States Determined to Resolve Border Disputes," *Inter Press Service,* July 21, 1995.

[2]   There are some settled and other minor disputes. On July 10, 1995, Oman and Saudi Arabia initialed the final maps and documents demarcating their common border, stretching over 400 miles; the border demarcation agreement was signed on March 24, 1990, in the Saudi City of Hafr al-Batin. See Mardini, "Gulf: Regional States Determined." In June 1995, Oman also settled its twenty-year border dispute with Yemen, conceding 1,900 square miles of territory to Yemen. Saudi Arabia's borders with the UAE have yet to be defined, but the two nations are close to an agreement regarding minor technicalities in their border demarcation. See *Reuters World Service,* July 8, 1995. Saudi Arabia has a long-standing, though muted, dynastic dispute with Jordan over the Hejaz region, which was taken by King Abdel Aziz (Ibn Saud) during the 1920s after he defeated the Hashemites. Saudi Arabia restored diplomatic relations with Jordan in November 1994, after having severed them on September 22, 1990, because Jordan appeared sympathetic to Saddam Hussein. Relations remain cool, however, as the Hashemite Kingdom has not renounced its claim to the Hejaz. See "Saudi Arabia—Territorial Disputes Will Continue," *Arab Press Service Diplomatic Strategic Balance in the Middle East,* May 1, 1995.

[3]   Geoffrey Kemp, *The Control of the Middle East Arms Race* (Washington, DC: Carnegie Endowment, 1991), p. 38.

[4]   Ali Mohammed Khalifa, *The United Arab Emirates: Unity in Fragmentation* (Boulder: Westview Press, 1979), p. 155.

[5]   Edward J. Perkins and George F. Ward Jr., "Iraq's Non-Compliance With UN Security Council Resolutions," *Department of State Dispatch,* August 3, 1992, p. 604.

[6]   Miriam Amie, "UNIKOM Expects Long-term Kuwait Mission," *United Press International,* April 18, 1994.

[7]   Ewan Anderson and Jasem Karam, in "The Iraqi-Kuwaiti Boundary," *Jane's Intelligence Review* (March 1995), pp. 120-21, clarify that the Ratga oilfield is south of any previously recognized border, placing it in Kuwait proper. They also explain that it differs in structure, oil type, and production conditions from Rumaila, from which it is separated by a major fault. On the Umm Qasr question, the authors are somewhat vague in their assessment of Iraqi losses. They evasively argue that the land boundary did not place Iraq's naval base in Kuwait while stating that "the entire *commercial* port, with all the major installations, together with the town of Umm Qasr, remains in Iraq. The loss amounts to two small wooden jetties . . . together with *some military accommodation.*" (emphasis added)

[8]   Perkins and Ward, Jr., "Iraq's Non-Compliance," pp. 604–605.

9   Alasdair Drysdale and Gerald H. Blake, *The Middle East and North Africa: A Political* Geography (New York: Oxford University Press, 1985), p. 126.

10   Drysdale and Blake, *The Middle East and North Africa,* p. 126.

11   Richard Schofield (ed.), *Territorial Foundations of the Gulf States* (New York: St. Martin's Press, 1994), p. 39.

12   Shahram Chubin, *Iran's National Security Policy: Capabilities, Intentions and Impact* (Washington, DC: Carnegie Endowment for International Peace, 1994), pp. 101–102.

13   Schofield, *Territorial Foundations of the Gulf States*, p. 72fn.

14   Geoffrey Kemp, *Forever Enemies: American Policy and the Islamic Republic of Iran* (Washington, DC: Carnegie Endowment, 1994), p. 120.

15   John B. Allcock et al., *Border and Territorial Disputes*, third edition (London: Longman Group, 1992), p. 382.

16   Kemp, *Forever Enemies*, pp. 47-48.

17   "Commentary Approves Qatar's Approach to Regional Problem Solving," *British Broadcasting Corporation*, July 12, 1995. Source: Voice of the Islamic Republic of Iran Network 1, Teheran, July 10, 1995.

18   "Saudi Arabia, Qatar Discuss Improvement of Ties," *Xinhua General Overseas News Service,* May 19, 1993.

19   "Saudi Defense Minister, Qatari Emir Hold Talks," *Reuter Library Report*, May 18, 1993.

20   *Mideast Mirror*, June 27, 1995.

21   "GCC Ministerial Council Session," *Moneyclips*, June 5, 1996.

22   *Times Newspapers Limited*, June 28, 1995.

23   Andrew Rathmell, "Threats to the Gulf—Part 1," *Jane's Intelligence Review* 7, no. 3 (March 1995), p. 132.

24   *Mideast Mirror*, June 27, 1995.

25   "Emir of Qatar Comments on Border Disputes, Relations With Iraq and Israel," *British Broadcasting Corporation*, July 11, 1995, from QBS Radio (Doha), July 9, 1995.

26   "Qatar and Bahrain Squabble On," *Middle East International,* no. 540, December 20, 1996, pp. 12-13; "Bahrain and Qatar Reject GCC Mediation," *MEED* 41, no. 4, January 24, 1997, p. 13; and "GCC Attempts Bahrain-Qatar Reconciliation," *MEED* 41, no. 3, January 17, 1997, p. 18.

27   Youssef M. Ibrahim, "Saudis Using Oil in Yemeni Dispute," *New York Times*, June 7, 1992.

28   "Yemeni Minister Arrives in Riyadh with Message for King Fahd," *Agence France Presse*, April 30, 1994; "Yemen, Saudi Arabia Postpone New Border Talks," *Reuters World Service*, April 26, 1994; and James Wyllie, "Perpetual Tensions—Saudi Arabia and Yemen," *Jane's Intelligence Review* 7, no. 3 (March 1995), pp. 118–19.

29   *Agence France Presse*, July 8, 1995.

30   Allcock et al., *Border and Territorial Disputes*, p. 397.

31   Ibid.

32   "Kuwait, Saudi Arabia Discuss Drawing Border," *Agence France Presse*, July 18, 1995.

33   "GCC Affairs—Saudi-Kuwait Border Talks," *Arab Press Service Diplomat Recorder*, July 22, 1995. For a similar, more recent statement, see *Saudi Arabian Kingdom Radio Network*, January 22, 1996, in FBIS-NES, January 24, 1996, p. 22.

34   Drysdale and Blake, *The Middle East and North Africa*, p. 91.

35   John Lancaster, "Egyptian, Sudanese Forces Exchange Fire at Border," *Washington Post*, June 29, 1995, p. A35.

36   Allcock et al, *Border and Territorial Disputes*, pp. 402-406.

37   Pipes, *Syria Beyond the Peace Process*, p. 54.

38   Jamil Al Alawi and Mohammed Abdulrazzak, "Water in the Arabian Peninsula: Problems and Perspectives," in Rogers and Lydon (eds.), *Water in the Arab World*, 181.

39   For more details on Turkey's disputes with Syria and Iraq over water supplies, see Geoffrey Kemp and Robert E. Harkavy, *Strategic Geography and the Changing Middle East* (Washington, DC: Carnegie Endowment for International Peace in cooperation with Brookings Institution Press, 1997), chapter 3.

40   "Water in the Middle East: As Thick as Blood," *Economist*, December 23, 1995/January 5, 1996, pp. 53-55; "Nile Conference: Into the 21st Century," *Africa Research Bulletin*, July 16/August 15, 1990, pp. 10038-10039; and "The Nile: The Politics of Water," *Middle East* (August 1990), pp. 44–45.

Chapter 9: Asymmetries

[1]   Figures for Iran and Syria are from *The Europa World Year Book 1994* (London: Europa Publications Limited, 1994), vol. I, p. 1490, and vol. II, p. 2842. Other figures are from *The World Bank Atlas 1996* (Washington, DC: World Bank, 1995), pp. 18-19. We have not included Iraq, since reliable estimates have been difficult to obtain since the Gulf War ended in 1991.

[2]   J. Addleton, "The Impact of the Gulf War on Migration and Remittances in Asia and the Middle East," *International Migration* 39, no. 4 (December 1991), p. 509.

[3]   Abdel R. Omran and Farzaneh Roudi, "The Middle East Population Puzzle," *Population Bulletin* 48, no. 1 (July 1993), p. 24.

[4]   The information in this paragraph is drawn from Addleton, "The Impact of the Gulf War," pp. 509-25. Other estimates suggest that the total exodus of foreign workers in the region from August through November 1990 was two million, including 250,000 Jordanians and Palestinians working in Kuwait and 750,000-800,000 Yeminis working in Saudi Arabia. See Sharon Stanton Russell, "International Migration and Political Turmoil in the Middle East," *Population and Development Review* 18, no. 4 (December 1992), p. 721.

[5]   "A New Arab Order," *Economist*, September 28, 1991, p. 5 of survey section.

[6]   James Bruce, "Land of Crisis and Upheaval," *Jane's Defense Weekly*, July 30, 1994, pp. 23–35.

[7]   *World Factbook 1994*, pp. 221, 345-46, 413. See also "Iran: Economy."

[8]   F. Gregory Gause III, *Oil Monarchies: Domestic and Security Challenges in the Arab Gulf States* (New York: Council on Foreign Relations, 1994), pp. 45-46.

[9]   *World Factbook 1994*, p. 32.

[10]   The discussion of characteristics of Gulf economies is based on Gause III, *Oil Monarchies*, pp. 44-58.

[11]   *World Bank Annual Report 1996* (Washington, DC: World Bank Group, 1996), p. 120.

[12]   Cherif Cordahi, "Middle East Economy: Declining Growth Rates Hint at Future Crises," *Inter Press Service*, Cairo, September 26, 1994.

[13]   Other groups include Armenians, Baluch, and others native to the region, as well as Africans, Asians from outside the Middle East, and Europeans. See Omran and Roudi, "The Middle East Population Puzzle," p. 17.

14   See, for example, Thomas Naff, "Hazards to Middle East Stability in the 1990s: Economics, Population, and Water," in Phebe Marr and William Lewis (eds.), *Riding the Tiger: The Middle East Challenge after the Cold War* (Boulder: Westview Press, 1993), p. 145.

15   Omran and Roudi, "The Middle East Population Puzzle," p. 34.

16   Population Reference Bureau (PRB), *World Population Data Sheet* (Washington, DC: 1995).

17   Omran and Roudi, "The Middle East Population Puzzle," p. 34.

18   All Persian Gulf demographic figures are from "Demographic Data," *Middle East Report* (March-April 1993), p. 8.

19   See, for instance, Neil W. Chamberlain, *Beyond Malthus: Population and Power* (New York: Basic Books, 1970), pp. 49–54.

20   Omran and Roudi, "The Middle East Population Puzzle," p. 35. See also Michael Elliot and Christopher Dickey, "Body Politics: Population Wars," *Newsweek*, September 12, 1994, pp. 22–26.

21   Philip Fargues, "From Demographic Explosion to Social Rapture," *Middle East Report* (September-October 1994), no. 190, p. 9.

22   Nazy Roudi, "Population Policies Vary in Middle East," *Population Today* (April 1993), p. 3.

23   Fargues, "From Demographic Explosion," p. 7.

24   PRB, *World Population Data Sheet.*

25   Not including the Gaza Strip, where demographic issues are at the top of the agenda.

26   For the political clauses of the Treaty of Sevres, see J.C. Hurewitz, *Diplomacy in the Near and Middle East: A Documentary Report, 1914-1956* (Princeton: D. Van Nostrand Company, Inc., 1956), vol. II, pp. 81–87.

27   Philip Robins, "The Overlord State: Turkish Policy and the Kurdish State," *International Affairs* 69, no. 4 (1993), pp. 657-76.

28   Some say the figure is closer to 14.3 million (1990). Ted Robert Gurr, *Minorities at Risk* (Washington, DC: United States Institute of Peace, 1993), p. 332. The CIA claims there are 15.2 million Azeris in Iran; see *World Factbook 1993*, p. 185.

29   "Armenia-Azerbaijan Dispute Threatens Summit Accord," *Agence France Press*, December 3, 1996.

30   Whitley, "Minorities and the Stateless," p. 35.

³¹   Ibid.

³²   "Martial Law Declared in Sistan Va Baluchistan," *Middle East Intelligence Report,* February 10, 1994.

³³   Gurr, *Minorities at Risk,* p. 332; and *The World Factbook 1993,* p. 185.

³⁴   Michael Horowitz, "New Intolerance Between Crescent and Cross," *Wall Street Journal,* July 5, 1995, p. A8.

³⁵   "Why is Islam Turning Violent in Pakistan," *Economist,* March 4, 1995, pp. 35–36.

³⁶   Lebanon, Walden Country Reports, 1993.

³⁷   John Lancaster, "The Two Worlds of Bahrain," *Washington Post,* June 13, 1995, p. A15.

³⁸   For Iraqi and Saudi Shiites, see Whitley, "Minorities and the Stateless," pp. 36-39, 41–42.

³⁹   William Shawcross, *The Shah's Last Ride* (New York: Simon and Schuster, 1988), pp. 113–16.

⁴⁰   Shaul Bakhash, *The Reign of the Ayatollahs: Iran and the Islamic Revolution* (New York: Basic Books, Inc., 1986), pp. 23, 29, and 45–46.

⁴¹   Mohammed Heikal, *Autumn of Fury: The Assassination of Sadat* (New York: Random House, 1983), especially pp. 264-70.

⁴²   Bernard Lewis, *The Shaping of the Modern Middle East* (New York: Oxford University Press, 1994), p. 119.

⁴³   Statements made at Arab summit on September 1, 1967, in Khartoum, Sudan. Cited in *New York Times,* September 1, 2, 3, 7, 8, 10, 13, 26, 1967, and in Fred J. Khouri, *The Arab-Israeli Dilemma,* third edition (New York: Syracuse University Press, 1985), p. 313. Khouri argues that Arab moderates also left their mark on the summit declaration. Arab states should work for the "maintenance of the rights of the people of Palestine in their nation." It also called for "unified efforts at international and diplomatic levels to eliminate the consequences of [Israeli] aggression and to assure the withdrawal of the aggressor forces. . . . from Arab lands."

⁴⁴   PLO on Israel, Article 9 of the Palestinian National Charter as outlined in the Palestinian National Covenant, 1968. Cited in Charles L. Geddes (ed.), *A Documentary History of the Arab-Israeli Conflict* (New York: Praeger Publishers, 1991), pp. 321–28.

⁴⁵   Khalid al-Hasan, "The Future of the Palestinian Struggle after the Ramadan War," *al-Jumhuriyya,* June 17, 1974, in Walter Laqueur and Barry Rubin, *The Israeli-Arab Reader* (New York: Facts on File Publications, 1984);

and in Barry Rubin, *Revolution Until Victory? The Politics and History of the PLO* (Cambridge: Harvard University Press, 1994), p. 46.

[46]   Fadlallah was described as an "Islamic scholar." See *Filasatin al-Muslimah* (London), September 1995, pp. 32-34, in FBIS-NES, September 13, 1995, p. 1.

[47]   Serge Schmemann, "P.L.O. Ends Call for Destruction of Jewish State," *New York Times*, April 25, 1996, pp. A1 and A10.

[48]   *Qol Yisra'el* (Israel), May 9, 1996, in FBIS-NES, May 9, 1996, p. 21.

[49]   Ariel Sharon, "Jordan is the Palestinian State," *Jerusalem Post*, April 4, 1991.

[50]   Ibid.

[51]   "Full Service in Gaza is Favored by Dayan," *New York Times*, April 26, 1972, p. 5.

[52]   "Iraq on Kuwait," press release by the press office of the Embassy of the Republic of Iraq, London, September 12, 1990, in E. Lauterpacht, C.J. Greenwood, Mark Weller, and Daniel Bethlehem (eds.), *The Kuwait Crisis: Basic Documents* (Cambridge: Grotius Publications, Ltd., 1991), p. 74.

[53]   "Iraqi Revolution Command Council Statement on Merger with Kuwait," BBC:SWB: ME/0839, pp. A1-A3, August 10, 1990, as cited in Richard Schofield, *Kuwait and Iraq: Historical Claims and Territorial Disputes*, second edition (London: Royal Institute of International Affairs, 1993), p. 143.

[54]   Schofield, *Kuwait and Iraq*, p. 144.

[55]   *Keesing's Record of World Events*, News Digest for August 1990, p. 37632.

[56]   Asad's speech on Lebanon to members of the newly elected Syrian provincial councils on July 10, 1976, was monitored from Radio Damascus by the U.S. Foreign Broadcast Information Service. See Itamar Rabinovich, *The War for Lebanon, 1970-1983* (Ithaca: Cornell University Press, 1984), pp. 187–88.

[57]   In chapter 5, endnote 3, see the rival views of Daniel Pipes and Zuhair Diab on Syrian expansionism.

[58]   Adrian Karatnycky, "Democracy and Despotism: Bipolarism Renewed?" *Freedom Review* 27, no. 1 (January-February 1996), pp. 5–11.

[59]   "Survey Methodology," *Freedom Review* 27, no. 1 (January-February 1996), pp. 11–12. Neither Freedom House's definition of freedom nor the more general support for Western democracy in the Middle East and South Asia assumes the objective superiority of these concepts of government over other systems. While we, like most in the West, happen to believe this, other points

of view must be taken seriously. These include the beliefs of fundamentalist religious groups (Christian, Jewish, Muslim, and Hindu) that stress the inherent flaws of secular societies, and Marxist and authoritarian ideologies that
stress the importance of the state or the majority over the rights of individuals.
The important point here is that arguments about the merits of particular
political systems and ethics reflect fundamental asymmetries in the region.

60   Included are Israel (free); Jordan and Kuwait (partly free) and Bahrain,
Egypt, Iran, Iraq, Lebanon, Oman, Qatar, Saudi Arabia, Syria, UAE, and
Yemen (not free).

61   An interesting question is what kind of freedom scores democracies
like the United States and Britain would have received in different periods
of history. For instance, during World War II, the civil liberties of numerous
citizens and non-citizens were suspended in both counties. Until the 1960s,
systematic violation of the civil rights of black people in the United States
would surely have produced poor scores on such rankings.

Chapter 10: Military Imbalance and Insecurity

1   *The Military Balance 1995/96*, p. 126.

2   "Revisionist" Israeli historians have challenged a number of the founding myths of the Israeli state, including the course of the 1948 war. For a view
suggesting Israel was not as much of an underdog as traditionally alleged, see
Simha Flapan, *The Birth Of Israel: Myths and Realities* (New York: Pantheon Books,
1987). For a rebuttal to the work of Flapan and others, see Efraim Karsh, "Rewrit-
ing Israel's History," *Middle East Quarterly* 3, no. 2, pp. 19–29.

3   For one example of continued Israeli fears of united Arab aggression,
see Efraim Inbar, "Israel's National-Security Challenges," *International Defense
Review* 27, no. 7 (1994), pp. 25–27.

4   For more details see Patrick J. Garrity, *Why the Gulf War Still Matters:
Foreign Perspectives on the War and the Future of International Security* (Center for National Security Studies, Los Alamos National Laboratory, July
1993), report no. 16.

5   In Israel, private companies, including Elbit, Tadiran, and El-Op, have
been more profitable than the somewhat troubled government and quasi-
government firms such as TAAS-Israel (Israel Military Industries), the Rafael
Armament Development Authority, and Israel Aircraft Industries (IAI). R.A.
Kaminer, "Shake-up In Israel's Defense Industry," *International Defense
Review* 26, no. 4 (1993), pp. 302-304. See also an article based on a dis-
cussion with David Ivry, director general of the Israeli defense ministry, by
Ruth Kaminer, "Sweeping Changes in Israel's Defense Structure," *International
Defense Review* 27, no. 3 (1994), pp. 27–28.

6   "The Peace Business," *International Defense Review* 26, no. 12 (1993), p. 967.

7   For a full treatment of the Egyptian Defense Industry, see Yezid Sayigh, *Arab Military Industry: Capability, Performance and Impact* (London: Brassey's, 1992), pp. 45-102; and Andrew Rathmell, "Egypt's Military-Industrial Complex," *Jane's Intelligence Review* 6, no. 10 (October 1994), pp. 455-460.

8   Sadowski, *Scuds or Butter?* p. 28.

9   Mohammad Ziarati, "Egypt's Military Modernisation Objectives," *MEI*, September 23, 1994, p. 21.

10   For a review of the Iranian defense industry, see Anoushiravan Ehteshami, "Iran Boosts Domestic Arms Industry," *International Defense Review* 21, no. 4 (1994), pp. 72–73.

11   Shahram Chubin, *Iran's National Security Policy: Capabilities, Intentions and Impact* (Washington, DC: Carnegie Endowment for International Peace, 1994), p. 46.

12   "Tehran Claims Latest MBT is in Production," *Jane's Defence Weekly*, January 7, 1995, p. 4.

13   For a number of views on arms control and regional security, see Shai Feldman (ed.), *Confidence Building and Verification: Prospects in the Middle East* (Tel Aviv: Jaffee Center for Strategic Studies, 1994), JCSS Study no. 25; and Shai Feldman and Ariel Levite (eds.), *Arms Control and the New Middle East Security Environment* (Tel Aviv: Jaffee Center for Strategic Studies, 1994).

14   Ambassador Ekeus resigned in the summer of 1997 to become Sweden's Ambassador to the United States. He was replaced by Ambassador Richard Butler, an Australian career diplomat.

Chapter 11: A Race Against Time

1   For more on the emerging strategic relationships in the Middle East, see Kemp and Harkavy, *Strategic Geography and the Changing Middle East.*

2   *Claiming the Future: Choosing Prosperity in the Middle East and North Africa* (Washington, DC: World Bank, 1995), p. 4.

3   Ibid., p. 50.

INDEX

133-34, 135, 136-37; regional relations, 134; relations with Iran, 133, 134, 136, 149; relations with Iraq, 158; relations with Jordan, 97; relations with Kuwait, 138; relations with Oman, 140-41; security issues, 132, 133; Shiite population, 136, 240n

Savir, Uri, 28

Scud missiles, 26

Security issues: Arab-Israeli territorial disputes, 35, 37-39, 40, 42-43, 68-69, 72, 106-7; boundaries of strategic regions, 202-3; democratization and, 196; demographic factors, 181-84; economic development and, 27-28; Gulf Cooperation Council countries, 131-32; Gulf War outcomes, 202-4; international arms sales, 204-5; Iran, 147, 148, 149-50; Israeli military policy, 68-72; Israeli perceptions of Syria, 105; Israeli settlement activities, 48; Jordan, 97, 98-99; Kuwait, 137-38; Oman, 139-41; Palestinian refugees, 47; Saudi Arabia, 132, 135-36; significance of, for peace process, 22-23, 33; Syria-Turkey relations, 119-20; United Arab Emirates, 141

Shamir, Yitzhak, 12, 48, 97

Sharon, Ariel, 24, 51, 96-97

Shiite Muslims, 116; in Iran, 149; in Iraq, 155-56; in Saudi Arabia, 136, 240n; Sunni Muslims and, 188

Shiqaqi, Fathi, 79

Sinai peninsula, 67, 86

Soviet Union, 3; in advancement of peace process, 10, 11; Iraqi relations, 120-21; military aid to Middle East, 10, 11; Syrian-Israeli relations and, 104; Syrian relations, 120-21

Spero, Joan, 34

Sudan, 16, 159, 173; border disputes with Egypt, 171-72; terrorist activities, 159

Sunni Muslims, 116, 149; in Iraq, 155; in Lebanon, 122; Shiite Muslims and, 188

Syria, 1; border disputes with Turkey, 172; commitment to Palestinian cause, 106, 107; economy, 116-18, 175; foreign relations, 104, 108; in Gulf War, 11; historical borders, 40, 236n; Lebanon and, 109-10, 118-19, 123, 124-25, 193; military power, 24, 25, 201; relations with Iraq, 120-21, 158, 242n; relations with Israel. See Syrian-Israeli relations; relations with Jordan, 97, 99; relations with Turkey, 119-20, 157; religious divisions in, 116; significance of, for peace process, 103, 105; Soviet relations, 10, 120-21; status in Arab world, 106-7; United States and, 104-5

Syrian-Israeli relations, 12; benefits of peace, 121-22; determinants of, 103, 115-16; Golan Heights dispute, 40-42, 69, 72, 105-7; implications of normalization for Syria, 110, 111, 112; Iranian perception, 146-47; Israeli goals, 110-11; Israeli motivation, 113-14; Israeli offensive in Lebanon and, 104; Israeli-Palestinian relations and, 106, 107; Israeli perceptions, 105; Lebanon and, 34, 103, 109-10, 114-15, 118-19, 124-25; military issues, 108, 114-15; objections to peace process, 32; political environment in Israel and, 56-57; political environment in Syria and, 108-9, 110; possibilities for advancing, 107-8; recent developments, 103-4; Soviet Union and, 104; Syrian economy and, 117, 118; Syrian religious/ethnic issues, 116; Syria's goals, 105; territorial disputes, 36, 56; U.S. influence, 112-13; U.S. policy, 111-12

Tajikistan, 150

Techiya, 67

Tel Aviv, 1, 2, 56

Territorial disputes, 243n; borders of Palestine, 50-51; as colonial legacy, 163; Egypt-Sudan, 171-72; Eretz Yisrael concept, 64-66, 67; forms of, 35-36; Gulf Cooperation Council efforts to resolve, 163; Iran-Iraq, 163-65; Iran-Qatar, 168; Iran-United Arab Emirates, 167-68; Iraq-Kuwait, 165-67; Israeli-Jordan Peace Treaty provisions, 98; Israeli settlement activities, 48-50; Jerusalem, 43-46; Jordanian boundary issues, 95-96; Kuwaiti-Saudi Arabia, 170-71; Lebanon-Israel, 125-26, 226n; obstacles to peace, 36-39; Palestinian right of return issues, 46-48; policy disagreement within Israel, 68-71; Qatar-Bahrain, 169-70; Saudi Arabia-Qatar, 169; Syria-Turkey, 120, 172; water-related, 172-73; Yemen-Saudi Arabia, 170

Terrorism: effects on Israeli citizens, 58; Iranian support, 147; in Lebanon, 67; Libya-sponsored, 159; by Palestinian extremists, 78-80; peace process and, 56; practitioners, 26-27; prevention, 27; and prospects for peace, 26-27; Sudan-sponsored, 159; suicide bombings of 1994-96, 56, 57; Syrian, in Jordan, 97

Third Way, 56

Tourism industry, 93

Truman, Harry, 15

Tunisia, 14, 21, 130, 131, 175

Turkey, 14, 16; border disputes with Syria, 172; Kurdish minority, 185-86; Kurdish minority in, 119; Muslim fundamentalists in, 2; relations with Iraq, 157; relations with Israel, 120; relations with Syria, 119-20, 157

U.N. Resolutions: *194*, 47; *242*, 13, 105; *338*, 13; *425*, 106

United Arab Emirates, 31, 175; border disputes with Iran, 167-68; foreign population, 142; future prospects, 143-44; Gulf Cooperation Council and, 143, 144; military resources, 143; political power, 143; relations with Iran, 149-50; security issues, 141; state cohesion, 143

United States, 14; arms sales, 204-5; Gulf War outcomes, 11-12; importance of peace process for, 2-3; importance to peace process, 16, 214-17, 220; influence on Syrian-Israeli negotiations, 112-13; Iran-Iraq dual containment policy, 145-46, 148; Iraq policy, 153; Jordan and, 99; Libya policy, 159; mistrust of, 82, 215; policy on democratization in Middle East, 193, 195; policy on Syrian-Israeli relations, 111-12; relations with Gulf Cooperation Council countries, 130, 131-32; relations with Saudi Arabia, 133; Sudan policy, 159; Syria and, 104-5

Urbanization, 181

U.S. aid: distribution in Middle East, 88, 89; to Egypt, 92; to Jordan, 99, 100; rewards to Gulf War allies, 11, 86-87

Water resources: aquifer distribution, 172, 225n; Iran-Iraq bor-

ABOUT THE AUTHORS

Geoffrey Kemp is the Director of Regional Strategic Programs at the Nixon Center for Peace and Freedom. He served in the White House during the first Reagan administration and was Special Assistant to the President and Senior Director for Near East and South Asian Affairs on the National Security Council staff. Prior to assuming his current position, he was a Senior Associate at the Carnegie Endowment for International Peace, where he was Director of the Middle East Arms Control Project. In the 1970s, he worked in the Defense Department and for the U.S. Senate Committee on Foreign Relations. He was also on the faculty of the Fletcher School of Law and Diplomacy, Tufts University. Dr. Kemp is the author and editor of several books on U.S. policy in the Middle East and South Asia.

Jeremy Pressman was Project Associate for the Middle East Arms Control Project at the Carnegie Endowment for International Peace from 1991 to 1996. His articles and letters on Arab-Israeli relations and other Middle East issues have appeared in publications including the *Christian Science Monitor, Foreign Policy,* the *New York Times*, and the *Washington Post*. He is currently pursuing a doctoral degree in the Department of Political Science at the Massachusetts Institute of Technology.

THE CARNEGIE ENDOWMENT FOR INTERNATIONAL PEACE

The Carnegie Endowment for International Peace was established in 1910 in Washington, D.C., with a gift from Andrew Carnegie. As a tax-exempt operating (not grant-making) foundation, the Endowment conducts programs of research, discussion, publication, and education in international affairs and U.S. foreign policy. The Endowment publishes the quarterly magazine, *Foreign Policy*.

Carnegie's senior associates—whose backgrounds include government, journalism, law, academia, and public affairs—bring to their work substantial first-hand experience in foreign policy. Through writing, public and media appearances, study groups, and conferences, Carnegie associates seek to invigorate and extend both expert and public discussion on a wide range of international issues, including worldwide migration, nuclear nonproliferation, regional conflicts, multilateralism, democracy-building, and the use of force. The Endowment also engages in and encourages projects designed to foster innovative contributions in international affairs.

In 1993, the Carnegie Endowment committed its resources to the establishment of a public policy research center in Moscow designed to promote intellectual collaboration among scholars and specialists in the United States, Russia, and other post-Soviet states. Together with the Endowment's associates in Washington, the center's staff of Russian and American specialists conduct programs on a broad range of major policy issues ranging from economic reform to civil-military relations. The Carnegie Moscow Center holds seminars, workshops, and study groups at which international participants from academia, government, journalism, the private sector, and non-governmental institutions gather to exchange views. It also provides a forum for prominent international figures to present their views to informed Moscow audiences. Associates of the center also host seminars in Kiev on an equally broad set of topics.

The Endowment normally does not take institutional positions on public policy issues. It supports its activities principally from its own resources, supplemented by nongovernmental, philanthropic grants.

**Carnegie Endowment
for International Peace**
1779 Massachusetts Ave., N.W.
Washington, D.C. 20036
Tel: 202-483-7600
Fax: 202-483-1840
e-mail: carnegie@ceip.org
Web Page: www.ceip.org

Carnegie Moscow Center
Ul. Tverskaya 16/2
7th Floor
Moscow 103009
Tel: 7-095-935-8904
Fax: 7-095-935-8906
e-mail: info@carnegie.ru
Web Page: www.carnegie.ru